THAT
THIN, WILD
MERCURY
SOUND

THAT THIN, WILD MERCURY SOUND

DYLAN, NASHVILLE, AND THE MAKING OF
BLONDE ON BLONDE

DARYL SANDERS

CHICAGO
REVIEW
PRESS

An A Cappella Book

Copyright © 2019 by Daryl Sanders
All rights reserved
First hardcover edition published 2019
First paperback edition published 2020
Published by Chicago Review Press Incorporated
814 North Franklin Street
Chicago, Illinois 60610
ISBN 978-1-64160-273-0

The Library of Congress has catalogued the hardcover edition as follows:

Names: Sanders, Daryl, author.
Title: That thin, wild Mercury sound : Dylan, Nashville, and the making of
    Blonde on blonde / Daryl Sanders.
Description: First edition. | Chicago, Illinois : Chicago Review Press,
    [2018] | Includes bibliographical references.
Identifiers: LCCN 2018021680 (print) | LCCN 2018022916 (ebook) | ISBN
    9781613735480 (Pdf) | ISBN 9781613735497 (Mobipocket) | ISBN
    9781613735503 (Epub) | ISBN 9781613735473 (cloth)
Subjects: LCSH: Dylan, Bob, 1941-. Blonde on blonde.
Classification: LCC ML420.D98 (ebook) | LCC ML420.D98 S2 2018 (print) |
    DDC 782.42164092—dc23
LC record available at https://lccn.loc.gov/2018021680

Cover design: Marc Whitaker/MTWdesign.net
Cover photo: Copyright © Jerry Schatzberg. Used by permission of Iconic
Images.
Typesetting: Nord Compo

Printed in the United States of America
5 4 3 2 1

Permissions

Lyrics from the songs by Bob Dylan on the album *Blonde on Blonde* were used with permission:

Dedicated to all the men and women who helped
Nashville earn the nickname Music City

CONTENTS

PROLOGUE

WHEN BOB DYLAN ARRIVED at Columbia Records' Nashville studios on Valentine's Day in 1966 to continue work on the follow-up to *Highway 61 Revisited*, he was a man on a mission, a musical mission, searching for a particular sound he could hear in his head, a sound he would describe twelve years later as "that thin, that wild mercury sound—metallic and bright gold."[1]

Dylan had begun his search for that thin, wild mercury sound thirteen months and two albums earlier in the label's New York studios, with his initial forays being released on *Bringing It All Back Home*, the first of the trilogy of albums on which he famously "went electric." While only side one of that record actually included accompaniment by musicians using amplified instruments, it obviously was the side that inspired the album's title, for he truly was bringing it back home—back to the music of his youth, the music that first inspired him to write songs and take up an instrument.

Dylan was reaching back into that Bermuda triangle of rock and roll—blues, country, and R&B—where so many teens like himself got lost; back to a thrilling era when music that could indeed be described as *metallic and bright gold* challenged the status quo and broke down cultural barriers.

Dylan was aiming to break down some barriers of his own. The particular sonic quicksilver he was hearing in his head, a blend of guitar, keyboards, and harmonica, emerged more fully on his next album, *Highway 61 Revisited*, beginning with guitarist Al Kooper crashing the first session only to find Michael Bloomfield there. Although only twenty-two, Bloomfield had already made a name for himself as a blues guitarist of note. Undeterred and demonstrating the boldness that would lead him to become a prominent figure in the history of popular music, Kooper put away his guitar, slid behind the studio's Hammond B-3 organ, an instrument he had never before played, and delivered the signature organ riff for "Like a Rolling Stone." It was one of those lightning-in-a-bottle moments when something that wasn't planned led to an artistic breakthrough; in Dylan's case, the result was a recording that singlehandedly elevated popular music as an art form.

Although the rest of the album didn't quite match the artistic heights reached on "Like a Rolling Stone," some critics and music scholars consider *Highway 61 Revisited* Dylan's greatest achievement. The title is a reference to US Highway 61, which before the advent of the interstate highway system was the primary roadway connecting Dylan's home state of Minnesota to the South. Sometimes called the Blues Highway, Highway 61 generally follows the path of the Mississippi River, running through St. Louis, Memphis, and the Mississippi Delta before ending in New Orleans, a total of fourteen hundred miles from its beginning in Wyoming, Minnesota.

In many ways, Dylan's musical compass had always been pointing south. The radio stations in his hometown of Hibbing, Minnesota, and other towns nearby, only played the pop fare of the day; but that was in the heyday of AM radio, when after the sun went down, fifty-thousand-watt clear-channel radio stations dominated the airwaves. Late at night in his bedroom, often with his radio under the covers so the music wouldn't wake anyone, Dylan would search the dial for the broadcast behemoths south of the Mason-Dixon line that were pumping blues, country, R&B, and early rock and roll into the nighttime air.

"It set me free, set the whole world on fire," he recalled in the liner notes to the box set *Biograph*.[2]

Two of the clear channel stations Dylan listened to regularly were broadcasting out of Nashville: WSM and WLAC. Those stations represented his earliest introduction to the city, nightly reminders that Nashville was a source for the new and exciting sounds that were enlivening his mostly uneventful life in Hibbing.

WSM was where he discovered his first musical idol, Hank Williams. "The first time I heard Hank he was singing on the *Grand Ole Opry*, a Saturday night radio show broadcast out of Nashville," Dylan wrote in his 2004 memoir. "The sound of his voice went through me like an electric rod."[3]

The first records Dylan ever owned were a collection of Hank Williams 78s, and on them, he found the archetypes of "poetic" songwriting. He told radio host Les Crane in 1965, "I started writing songs after I heard Hank Williams."[4]

Williams was ground zero for him as far as song craft was concerned. "You can learn a lot about the structure of songwriting by listening to his records, and I listened to them a lot and had them internalized," he wrote in his memoir.[5]

Dylan's second musical idol was Little Richard, whom he almost certainly heard for the first time on Nashville's other clear channel powerhouse, WLAC. He regularly listened to the station with its trio of legendary deejays (Gene Nobles, John Richbourg aka John R., and Bill "Hoss" Allen). It was arguably the most influential R&B station in the eastern half of the United States during the 1950s and '60s. With its powerful reach, 'LAC promoted itself as "the nighttime station for half the nation" and on a clear night could be heard from Canada to the Caribbean.

When he was introduced to the Staple Singers in 1962, Dylan told Mavis Staples that he first heard their music on Randy Wood's show on WLAC.[6] Wood, who went on to launch the highly successful independent label Dot Records, got his start as owner of Randy's Record Shop in Gallatin, Tennessee. In 1947, he began sponsoring a forty-five-minute R&B show every night on WLAC, and by the early '50s, the *Randy's Record Shop* show was fueling the most successful mail-order record business in the South. The show was hosted by Gene Nobles, the first white disc jockey in America to regularly program black music. Nobles is credited with helping artists like Chuck Berry, Fats Domino, and Little Richard break out to a wider audience.

Late in 1955, WLAC was the station that broke Little Richard's first hit, "Tutti Frutti," a sanitized version of the song he had performed to packed nightclubs on Jefferson Street in the early '50s while living in Nashville. The original version was bawdier and included the hook line, "Tutti frutti, good booty." Dylan probably first heard "Tutti Frutti" on *Randy's Record Shop.*

"I don't think I'd have even started without listening to Little Richard," he told the audience at his induction into the Rock & Roll Hall of Fame in 1988.[7] After hearing Little Richard's music, he soon was doing imitations of his new musical hero on the family piano in the corner of their living room. Not long after that, he started his first band, the Golden Chords. As bandmate LeRoy Hoikkala recalled in an interview with *On the Tracks* magazine, "Bob loved Little Richard, so we did a lot of Little Richard stuff."[8] In his 1959 high school yearbook, Dylan's stated ambition was "to join Little Richard."

Around the same time, Dylan was first struck by another iconic artist associated with Nashville—Johnny Cash. "I knew of him before he ever heard of me," Dylan said in a statement he released after Cash's death in 2003. "In '55 or '56, 'I Walk the Line' played all summer on the radio, and it was different than anything else you had ever heard. The record sounded like a voice from the middle of the earth. It was so powerful and moving. It was profound, and so was the tone of it, every line; deep and rich, awesome and mysterious all at once."[9]

Cash already was recording for Columbia when they signed Dylan, and he immediately became aware of his label mate's music. In his 1997 autobiography he wrote, "I was deeply into folk music in the early 1960s . . . so I took note of Bob Dylan as soon as the *Bob Dylan* album came out in early '62 and listened almost constantly to *The Freewheelin' Bob Dylan* in '63. I had a portable record player I'd take on the road, and I'd put on *Freewheelin'* backstage, then go out and do my show, then listen again as soon as I came off. After awhile at that, I wrote Bob a letter telling him how much a fan I was. He wrote back almost immediately, saying he'd been following my music since 'I Walk the Line,' so we began a correspondence."

Cash recalled, "Mostly it was about music: what we ourselves were doing, what other people were doing, what I knew about so-and-so and he didn't and visa versa. He asked about country people; I asked him about the circles he moved in."[10]

Later in 1963, Dylan and Cash met briefly backstage at The Gaslight Cafe in Greenwich Village, but they didn't have a chance to spend any real time with one another until the following year at the Newport Folk Festival, where they became fast friends. After the performances one evening, Dylan, Cash, June Carter, Ramblin' Jack Elliot, Sandy Bull, and a few others went to Joan Baez's hotel room to hang out and swap songs. That was the night Dylan playfully jumped up and down on one of the hotel beds and joyfully proclaimed, "I met Johnny Cash, I met Johnny Cash."

It was also the night he played a pair of songs—"It Ain't Me, Babe" and "Mama, You Been on My Mind"—that Cash would cover on his next album. "It Ain't Me, Babe," which featured a duet with Carter, became a top five country single. Columbia promoted the record in ads as "A new song from Bob Dylan on a new single sung by Johnny Cash." At the end of that evening, Cash gave Dylan his Martin acoustic guitar; within the community of songwriters and musicians in Nashville it was a gesture that signified the utmost respect.

While it's well documented that producer Bob Johnston had been pushing Dylan to record in Nashville, Cash actually was the first person to suggest he go there. He told *Record Mirror*'s Norman Jopling in June of 1965 that Dylan "may come to Nashville and let me produce an album with him if the A&R men agree."[11] That was more than a month before Johnston and Dylan first met.

Cash was cutting his records at Columbia's Nashville studios backed by members of his band and some of the city's celebrated session musicians, so he was able to give Dylan firsthand information about the label's facilities there and the caliber of the musicianship.

A session in Nashville scheduled for late November 1965 was canceled at the last minute, possibly because the label bosses in New York, for reasons not entirely clear, were opposed to Dylan recording there. But when he didn't get what he was looking for during more than forty hours of sessions at Columbia's New York studios in the late fall and early winter, he decided to give Nashville a try despite the label's opposition.

Dylan knew what he was doing; he knew he might find what he was searching for there. He would later say the closest he ever came to capturing the sound he heard in his head was with the musicians who backed him in Nashville in 1966 during the making of *Blonde on Blonde*.[12]

The *Blonde on Blonde* sessions often have been portrayed as the unlikely musical marriage of New York hipster and southern good ole boys. While it's true the musicians were primarily native southerners, they also were around Dylan's age and had been inspired to pick up their instruments by the same music that inspired him, the music that had that thin, wild mercury sound. When it came to that, they were plenty hip.

In many ways, they were more intimate with that music than Dylan was. They were from the South, so they were closer to the source; it was an expression of their culture, it was in their blood. Plus, despite being only in their twenties, they were highly versatile, world-class studio musicians with thousands of recording sessions under their belts. They were ready and able to take Dylan wherever he wanted to go. And where he wanted to go, no rock artist had ever gone before.

PART I

NEW YORK CITY

1

"I'M BOB, TOO"

THE BEGINNINGS OF THE *BLONDE on Blonde* story can be traced all the way back to July 29, 1965, more than two months before the first session for the album. On that mild summer morning, Bob Dylan returned to the Columbia studios at the corner of Seventh Avenue and Fifty-Second Street in New York City to resume work on material for the album that would become *Highway 61 Revisited*.

Just four days earlier Dylan had made his now-legendary appearance at the Newport Folk Festival where he performed with an electric band, received a chorus of boos from the folk purists in attendance, and sparked a controversy that would follow him across the globe for the next ten months. While the experience had left Dylan visibly shaken, it did not diminish his resolve to continue his transition from folk singer to rocker, a move that he had begun on his hit LP *Bringing It All Back Home*.

Bringing It All Back Home was the highest-charting album of his career to that point, peaking at number six during a forty-three-week stay on the *Billboard* album chart. Although it had been released back in March, the LP was still maintaining altitude, sitting at number twelve when Dylan entered Studio A that morning.[1]

He already had the album opener in the can, the single "Like a Rolling Stone," which was blowing up on the radio and climbing the sales charts with its captivating blend of electric guitar, organ, and harmonica. The guitarist (Mike Bloomfield) and organist (Al Kooper) were back in the

3

studio with Dylan that day, ready to try to capture some more of that thin, wild mercury.

But there was one key person from the "Like a Rolling Stone" session who wasn't there—producer Tom Wilson. Wilson, who had also produced *Bringing It All Back Home*, was out, and another Columbia staff producer, Bob Johnston, was in. It was a surprising switch, considering Wilson not only had helmed Dylan's previous three albums, but was also one of the visionaries who had helped give birth to folk rock.

The question of why Wilson was replaced has never been definitively answered, but it almost certainly was triggered, at least in part, by an exchange he had with Dylan at the session on June 15 just after the master take of "Like a Rolling Stone" was recorded. During the playback, Dylan said, "Turn the organ up," to which Wilson replied, "Hey, man, that cat's not an organ player."

It's true that prior to that day Kooper was a session guitarist and hit songwriter who had never recorded even one note on an organ, but he had contributed the song's signature riff and Dylan knew it. As Kooper recalled that moment in his memoir, Dylan bristled at Wilson's response, and told him, "Hey, now, don't tell me who's an organ player and who's not. Just turn it up."[2]

While that seems to have been the final straw for Dylan, it certainly wasn't the first time he and Wilson had disagreed. Their split had been building for some time. The previous year, Dylan had wanted a different title for his album *Another Side of Bob Dylan*. "Tom Wilson, the producer, titled it that," he explained in the liner notes for *Biograph*, the 1985 box set of his material. "I begged and pleaded with him not to do it. You know, I thought it was overstating the obvious. I knew I was going to have to take a lot of heat for a title like that and it was my feeling that it wasn't a good idea coming after *The Times They Are A-Changin'*, it just wasn't right. It seemed like a negation of the past which in no way was true. I know that Tom didn't mean it that way, but that's what I figured that people would take it to mean, but Tom meant well and he had control, so he had it his way."

Dylan also wasn't pleased with a session in early December 1964 that Wilson booked without him—and without his knowledge. While he was performing a series of dates on the West Coast, Wilson overdubbed electric backing on four of his earlier acoustic recordings. Dylan rejected all four of the tracks, although the version of "House of the Rising Sun" produced at that session eventually would be released on the 1995 CD-ROM *Highway 61 Interactive*. Six months after that session, Wilson would have more success overdubbing electric instruments onto an acoustic track by Simon and Garfunkel, "Sounds of Silence," which was released as a single without the duo, who had recently broken up, even knowing about it. The song became a number-one hit, prompting the pair to reunite.

That was before the days of artists having creative control over their recordings, and Wilson was old-school in his thinking and approach. A cum laude graduate of Harvard, he came out of a jazz background, having owned his own independent jazz label as well as having worked for the United Artists and Savoy labels, producing artists like Cecil Taylor and Sun Ra before becoming Columbia's first black staff producer. Wilson acknowledged he thought "folk music was for dumb guys" and that Dylan "played like the dumb guys," so perhaps his high-handedness was to be expected.[3] But expected or not, it was no longer tolerable to the label's rising young star.

As Johnston recalled to author Greil Marcus, he first heard from Columbia vice president Bill Gallagher that Wilson was on his way out. "He called me in and said, 'We're going to get rid of Tom.'" Gallagher went on to tell him Dylan's manager Albert Grossman didn't like Wilson and was pushing for him to be replaced. Before Johnston left Gallagher's office he told the executive, "I want Dylan."

Although he had received the news in confidence, Johnston immediately went to see Wilson. "I said, 'Bill Gallagher just called me in and said they're going to get rid of you and that Grossman hates you.' And he said, 'Hell, I knew that anyway.'" Johnston told him he wanted to produce Dylan and planned to lobby for the opportunity, to which Wilson replied, "Man, be my guest, because I am out of here anyway."[4]

A decade later, Wilson told *Melody Maker* he and Dylan had had a major disagreement and Dylan had suggested to him, "Maybe we should try Phil Spector."[5]

When in 1969 *Rolling Stone*'s Jann Wenner asked about the change in producers, Dylan ducked the question. "Well, I can't remember, Jann," he said. "I can't remember . . . all I know is that I was out recording one day, and Tom had always been there—I had no reason to think he wasn't going to be there—and I looked up one day and Bob was there. (laughs)"[6]

Not long after he was replaced as Dylan's producer, Wilson left Columbia to become head of East Coast A&R for MGM/Verve, where he signed the Mothers of Invention and produced their highly regarded debut, *Freak Out*, one of rock's first double albums. He brought the Velvet Underground to Verve and worked with them on their first two albums. He also signed Kooper's new band, the Blues Project, and produced their studio debut for the label.

In multiple interviews over the years before his death in 1978, Wilson took credit for Dylan going electric. When Wenner asked if that was true, Dylan said, "Did he say that? Well, if he said it . . . (laughs) more power to him. (laughs) He did to a certain extent. That is true. He did. He had a sound in mind."[7]

There were some similarities in the backgrounds of the two producers who worked on *Highway 61 Revisited*—roughly the same age, both were musicians from Texas who had stopovers in Nashville as they made their way to New York City. But Wilson was a jazz guy and Johnston was a rock guy, and they had different ideas about record production.

In his book *Like a Rolling Stone: Bob Dylan at the Crossroads*, Marcus compares Wilson's work with Dylan through "Like a Rolling Stone" and Johnston's work with him after that: "Johnston's sound is nearly the opposite of Wilson's; the metal-on-metal screech of 'Maggie's Farm' is the farthest thing from 'It Takes a Lot to Laugh, It Takes a Train to Cry' or 'Ballad of a Thin Man.' Johnston's sound is not merely whole; song by song the sound is not the same, but it is always a thing in itself. There is a glow that seems to come from inside the music."[8]

Johnston was far more deferential to Dylan than Wilson—another key difference. "I'm an artist's producer," Johnston said, describing his approach to record production in an interview with Dylan biographer Bob Spitz. "I give my artists lots of freedom."[9]

"Most record producers look at an artist and conceptualize in their head a production that's usually quite a bit different from what the artist brought through the door, and the producer goes about trying to sell this idea to the artist." says Norbert Putnam, who worked several dates with Johnston as a session bassist in the late 1960s before successfully transitioning into record production himself with artists such as Joan Baez, Dan Fogelberg, and Jimmy Buffett. "Of course, the producer calls in a band and pretty much dictates how the band is to play, and the artist tries to fit his personality into that.

"But Bob [Johnston] was smart enough that when he had a unique artist, rather than trying to second-guess where he was going, he would let them lead, and I think that was genius," Putnam continues. "I think that was true with Dylan especially, because Dylan was breaking new ground."[10]

In the film *The Other Side of Nashville*, Johnny Cash, who later worked with Johnston on a number of albums, made a similar point, calling the producer "an artist's dream." "Bob Johnston likes to sit back and watch an artist produce himself, and then he puts it together," Cash explained. "Bob Johnston is smart enough to know when he gets an artist who believes in himself—to let him run with it."[11]

Songwriter-guitarist Mac Gayden, whose first solo album Johnston produced, described the producer as "a spirited type guy." "He was encouraging," Gayden says. "He had the ability to include the musicians and the artist all in one team, you know. He would bring a team vibe into the studio. He made the musicians feel spontaneous, so it was infectious. That was the strongest quality about his producing skill—he made us all feel spontaneous and creative. It takes some skill to do that, you can't just fake it.

"And there's a feeling when a producer is putting out that kind of creative vibration," he continues. "It's like being on a horse, and you feel like running and the horse feels like running and you just take off. It's the same feeling you have when you're in the studio and the producer lets you fly."[12]

Engineer Roy Halee, who would work with Johnston on recordings by Dylan, Simon and Garfunkel, and others, echoed that point in a 2008 interview with *Sound On Sound* magazine. "I thought he was a good producer, very exciting," Halee said. "He got a lot of emotion going in the studio, which impressed me at the time, as other producers were not getting musicians fired up. There's a certain talent in that."[13]

Dylan liked that about Johnston, too. In his 2004 memoir *Chronicles*, he wrote of the producer: "He had that thing that some people call 'momentum.' You could see it in his face and he shared that fire, that spirit. . . . He was born one hundred years too late. He should have been wearing a wide cape, a plumed hat and riding with his sword held high."

Not everyone saw Johnston in that light. Kooper characterized him to rock historian Clinton Heylin as "the kinda guy that just pats you on the back and says you're fantastic, and just keeps you going."[14]

Tony Glover, Dylan's close friend from his Dinkytown days who was on hand during the recording of *Highway 61 Revisited*, described the new producer's approach to Dylan biographer Robert Shelton in this way: "As far as I could tell, Bob Johnston was from the John Hammond school of production: call out take numbers, keep the logs, make phone calls, and stay out of the way."[15]

It's true that Dylan's new producer was a protege of Hammond, the legendary Columbia A&R man who had brought not only Dylan to the label but also Bessie Smith, Billie Holiday, Pete Seeger, and Aretha Franklin, and would later sign Leonard Cohen, and Bruce Springsteen. Johnston considered him "the greatest music man that ever lived."[16] Speaking of Hammond to Marcus years later, he said, "He was my mentor all the way down the line. He was the one I would go to for help."

After hearing Wilson was to be replaced, Johnston sought out his mentor. "I went to John Hammond and asked him to please help me 'cause I wanted [to work with] Dylan more than I ever wanted [to produce] anybody in my life," the producer told *On the Tracks* magazine.[17]

Johnston also shared his desire to produce Dylan with Bob Mersey, head of pop A&R for Columbia. As Johnston recalled in an interview with *Mix*, Mersey asked him, "Why do you want to work with him? He's got dirty fingernails, and he breaks all the strings on his guitar."[18]

Although he had the support of not only Hammond but also Gallagher and Mersey, Johnston was considered a long shot to replace Wilson as Dylan's producer. Nobody in Dylan's camp knew who he was. The favorite was L.A.–based staff producer Terry Melcher, the son of film star Doris Day. Day, who was signed to the label as a recording artist, had an album coming out that summer. Her son was on the cutting edge of folk rock, having produced the Byrds' cover of Dylan's "Mr. Tambourine Man," which had hit number one on the *Billboard* Hot 100 the last week in June.[19] The album by the same name released on June 21 contained three other Dylan covers with folk rock arrangements—"Spanish Harlem Incident," "Chimes of Freedom," and "All I Really Want to Do"; in August the last of these would also hit the Top 40.[20]

Johnston may have been the underdog, but he had "momentum," as Dylan himself pointed out. Part of what gave him momentum was the musical miracle he had performed a few months earlier, not long after he had joined Columbia as a staff producer, a feat that earned him his first Top 10 hit as a producer.

Born William Donald Johnston in Hillsboro, Texas, the thirty-three-year-old producer had music in his blood. His grandmother was a songwriter and his great uncle was a concert pianist. His mother, Diane Johnston, also was a songwriter who had songs recorded by Gene Autry, Bob Wills and His Texas Playboys, and Asleep at the Wheel, among many others. Johnston grew up in the Fort Worth area, where he remembers being in the studio during his mother's demo sessions at an early age, and even then, he was trying to do a little producing. "I was running around there when I was little; five, six, eight, ten, all those ages. I'd tell her guitar player to play something," he recalled to Jason Wilbur on *In Search of a Song* in 2012.[21]

After a stint in the navy during the Korean War, Johnston returned to Fort Worth to pursue a musical career of his own. He got his first real break in 1956 when Robert Mellin, a New York–based music publisher, heard some of his song demos. "I did some stuff in Fort Worth and sent it to him, and he loved it," Johnston explained.[22]

Mellin signed Johnston to his company and introduced him to songwriter-producer Clyde Otis, who cut two sides with Johnston that were released on Mercury Records in October 1956 under the name Don Johnston. The A side was an Elvis Presley–influenced rockabilly number Johnston had penned called "Born to Love One Woman," backed by the ballad, "How Many," which he cowrote with his mother,

Diane.[23] He released another single the following August on Mellin's own Algonquin label, "Whistle Bait" / "The Whipmaster," which was almost immediately picked up for wider distribution by Chic Records, a hot independent label out of Thomasville, Georgia.[24] In 1958, he signed with Dot Records and released one more single, "Luigi Pasquale," backed by the Jerry Lee Lewis–style piano rocker "I'm Hypnotized," both of which he cowrote with his mother. On that 45, he was billed as Don Johnson, not Johnston, but it's unclear if that was due to a typographical error or by design.[25]

With three singles that failed to chart to his credit, Johnston had an epiphany during an appearance in Los Angeles opening for Ricky Nelson. All the young girls in the audience were shouting, "We want Ricky! We want Ricky!" Johnston recalled to *On the Tracks*. "I got about halfway through and had to quit. It was embarrassing. I looked like shit 'cause I didn't have any money, and he looked like four million dollars. I thought, 'This isn't a good way to earn a living.' So I started to write and produce, and forget about the recording end."[26]

In 1959, a mutual friend introduced Johnston to a young Charlie Daniels, who was passing through Fort Worth with his Top 40 cover band, the Jaguars.[27] Their meeting resulted in Johnston writing and producing four instrumental sides for the band that were released as a pair of singles on Epic Records, including one that had some success called "Jaguar," which he cowrote with Daniels.[28]

By 1960, Johnston was traveling regularly to Nashville to produce demos of his songs for Mellin Music at the legendary Bradley Film and Recording Studios.[29] After a short stint as manager of Clyde Otis's publishing companies, Otis helped him land his first job in A&R in October 1961, as pop producer for Kapp Records.[30]

A few months later, Johnston heard a recording by a young Aretha Franklin of "Rock-a-Bye Your Baby with a Dixie Melody" featuring a string arrangement he really liked by Mersey, who at that time was a staff arranger and producer for Columbia.[31] The following spring he got in touch with Mersey and asked him to arrange strings on two sides for Helen Troy, a soul singer he was producing for Kapp. Despite his staff position at Columbia, Mersey agreed to do the arrangements and is credited with directing the orchestra on Troy's single, "I'm Always Dreaming" / "How Could You."[32]

Later in '62, Johnston teamed with Otis, then with Liberty Records, on what would become his first hit, Timi Yuro's "What's a Matter Baby (Is It Hurting You?)."[33] The single, which reached number twelve on the *Billboard* pop chart and number sixteen on the R&B chart, was coproduced and cowritten by Otis and Johnston, but the songwriting credit went to Otis and Joy Byers, Johnston's wife. Johnston had had a falling out with Robert Mellin but was still under contract to the publisher. So he pulled an end run, and for a number of years, despite never writing a single word or note, Byers was credited with writing and cowriting numerous songs that were actually written or cowritten by Johnston.[34] "What's a Matter Baby (Is It Hurting You?)" was published by Otis's company, Eden Music, but it wasn't long before Johnston had scored a deal with Hill and Range, the largest independent music publisher in the country, to write songs to be credited to Byers. Under this arrangement, Johnston had sixteen Elvis Presley cuts, including the 1964 Top 40 hit "It Hurts Me," cowritten with Daniels.[35] He also had songs recorded by Brenda Lee, Solomon Burke, Irma Thomas, Jerry Lee Lewis, Gene Vincent, Bill Haley and His Comets, Patsy Cline, Professor Longhair, Otis Blackwell, Del Shannon, and Ricky Nelson.

By the spring of 1964, Otis was working for Columbia, having been offered a job by his next-door neighbor Mersey, who by then had become head of pop A&R for the label. One day late that year Johnston dropped by the label's A&R offices on Seventh Avenue in Manhattan to play some of his new demos for Otis. As he was walking down the hallway, Mersey happened to open the door to his office. As Johnston related it to Wilbur, this is what happened next:

"What are you doing?" Mersey asked.

"I'm going to see Clyde Otis," Johnston said.

Noticing the tape boxes in his hand, Mersey continued, "What have you got there?"

"A couple of demos," he told him.

"You got anything for Barbra Streisand, or Andy Williams, or Tony Bennett? I'm doing them."

"No."

"Well, let me hear what you've got."

Mersey invited Johnston into his office, where he listened to the two songs. Johnston was known for producing master-quality demos, and the Columbia exec was impressed with the production work he heard on the tapes; so impressed, he offered Johnston a job.

"Do you want to go to work for me?"

"No," Johnston told him. "I'd like to go to work *with* you, not *for* you."

After setting up the new staff producer with a small office and a secretary, Mersey told him, "I need you to have an artist. I'll be back in a minute." He returned shortly and tossed an LP on Johnston's desk. It was a Christmas album by Patti Page.

"See what you can do with her," he said, then turned and walked down the hallway laughing.[36] Mersey was amused because he had just handed Johnston what he considered a doomed assignment, but one fitting for the department's new guy. Page had been hugely successful in the 1950s, but her appeal had sagged in a market increasingly dominated by younger acts. She had moved from Mercury to Columbia in 1962 and had yet to crack the Top 40 with any of her releases.

But Johnston had the last laugh. With the help of some connections he had made in Hollywood through Hill and Range, he got a line on a song that was about to receive a nomination for an Academy Award in the Best Original Song category. The song was "Hush . . . Hush, Sweet Charlotte," and it appeared in a film by the same name that had been rush-released at the end of 1964 in order to qualify for the upcoming Oscars. Al Martino sang the song by Frank De Vol and Mack David on the film's soundtrack, but he relegated it to the B-side of a single he released in January 1965, "My Heart Would Know," a song by Hank Williams that peaked at number fifty-two on the *Billboard* Hot 100.[37]

Johnston saw an opportunity and set about to seize it. First he had to convince Page to record the song, so he paid her a visit in Los Angeles. "It took two days to talk her into doing it because she hated the song," he later recalled.[38] Next, he scheduled sessions at Columbia Studio B in Nashville on February 17 and 18, where they not only recorded "Hush . . . Hush, Sweet Charlotte" but also much of the other material that would make up an album of the same name. Then it was on to New York, where strings, arranged and conducted by Mersey, were added.

Columbia released Page's rendition of "Hush . . . Hush, Sweet Charlotte" as a single on March 15. With the 45 in hand, Johnston soon headed back to Hollywood to meet with Seymour Poe, righthand man to Darryl F. Zanuck of 20th Century Fox, the studio distributing *Hush . . . Hush, Sweet Charlotte*. His goal was to convince the studio to let Page perform the song at the Academy Awards to the benefit of both the film and the record. Early one Friday afternoon a few weeks before the show, Poe told him he could give him two minutes.

"I put the record on his turntable, and you could see the opening string parts really got to him," Johnston recalled. "Thirty seconds into the song, I pulled the needle off the record and he said, 'What are you doing?' I said, 'Your two minutes are up.' He says, 'I'll call you Monday.' I said, 'You'll call me later today.'"[39]

Poe did call Johnston later that day with the news the studio had decided to let Page perform the song. Five days after the show, "Hush . . . Hush, Sweet Charlotte" made its first appearance on the *Billboard* charts in the "Bubbling Under the Hot 100" category at number 133. Six weeks later, it broke into the Top 40, then made a five-week climb to number eight. It had been nearly seven years since one of Page's singles had made it to the Top 10. The album by the same name did well, too, reaching number twenty-seven on *Billboard's* Top LPs chart during a seven-week run. Prior to the success of the single and album, Columbia had not planned to re-sign Page; "Hush . . . Hush, Sweet Charlotte" revived her career.

It had a major impact on Johnston's career, as well. In less than half a year with the label, he went from new guy to miracle worker. Without that hit, it's hard to imagine his bosses entrusting him with Dylan, their rising superstar. But that's exactly what they did.

When Dylan arrived at the studio that first day with Johnston at the helm, he wasn't just greeting the next guy in line. No, he was beginning a relationship with a producer who had seen him perform live multiple times in Greenwich Village, who considered him a prophet. Johnston was totally ready for the moment, a creative ally who would help Dylan reach the highest artistic heights. "I don't think there has ever been anyone like him and never will be again," Johnston told me.

The producer vividly remembers their first day in the studio—it was the first time they met: "I just walked up to him and said, 'Hi, I'm Bob Johnston,' and he just smiled and said, 'Hi, I'm Bob, too.'"[40]

During two three-hour sessions that day Dylan recorded master takes of "Tombstone Blues" and "It Takes a Lot to Laugh, It Takes a Train to Cry," both of which appeared on *Highway 61 Revisited*. He also cut the master take of his next single, "Positively 4th Street," which would be released six weeks later and eventually climb to number seven on the *Billboard* Hot 100 during a seven-week stay in the Top 40.

Back in the studio on July 30 for two more three-hour sessions, Dylan and the musicians got the master take of "From a Buick 6," included on *Highway 61 Revisited*, and also recorded early versions of "Can You Please Crawl Out Your Window" and "Desolation Row," the latter featuring Kooper on electric guitar. That was also the day Dylan first met Jerry Schatzberg, an in-demand magazine and fashion photographer who would go on to become a noted film director.

During a photo shoot the previous day, journalist Al Aronowitz had been at Schatzberg's studio with a disc jockey named Scott Ross. "They were talking about having been with Dylan the day before," Schatzberg recalls. "While I was working, I just sort of said, 'Hey, next time you see him, tell him I'd like to photograph him.'

"The next day, I got a call from Dylan's [girlfriend, Sara Lownds], who I had known before—actually, we'd dated some," he continues. "She was the first one to tell me about Bob Dylan. She kept talking about Bob Dylan, Bob Dylan, Bob Dylan, you know. She had an apartment that looked over the Village, somewhere where Dylan would play, and she would say, 'Dylan plays there.' And I'd say, 'Yes, yes, yes.' Finally, between she and Nico from the Velvet Underground, they kept hammering Bob Dylan. I finally listened to him and, of course, that's when I fell in love with his music."[41]

When she called that day, Lownds told Schatzberg, "I heard you want to photograph Bobby." He said he did, and she invited him to stop by the studio. "She gave me the address to where he was recording *Highway 61*, and I went over to meet him," Schatzberg says. "He's very suspicious of people, but because [Lownds] said I was cool, I had entrée to him and he treated me like an old buddy."[42] Many of the widely seen and iconic photos of Dylan in the studio from that era—wearing shades while standing at a music stand playing guitar or sitting at an upright piano—were shot by Schatzberg that day.[43]

After taking the weekend off, Dylan and the musicians returned to the studio on Monday, August 2, and completed master takes of "Highway 61 Revisited," "Just Like Tom Thumb's Blues," "Queen Jane Approximately," and "Ballad of a Thin Man." They also recorded a full-blown electric version of "Desolation Row" with Kooper on electric piano.

At some point during those first couple of days in the studio together, Johnston suggested to Dylan that he record in Nashville sometime. Gallagher and Grossman were there and overheard what Johnston said. Johnston recalled that moment to *Mix* magazine in 2003: "A little later, Grossman and Gallagher came to me and said, 'If you ever mention anything about Nashville again to Dylan, we'll fire you. The reason being, we're having too much success the way we're doing it now.' I said, 'Okay, you're the boss.'"[44]

But Johnston was just giving lip service to "the boss"—he still wanted to get Dylan down to Nashville to work with a group of young musicians he had been using on his demos for Hill and Range. "I thought they were brilliant musicians, I thought they knew what they were doing, and I thought if you put them together, it would all work out wonderfully," he told me.[45]

Following the session on August 2, Dylan received an acetate with the master takes for all the songs that would make up *Highway 61 Revisited*. After listening to it, he decided to end the album with an acoustic rendition of "Desolation Row" rather than use the electric take. A session was booked on August 4 to record the acoustic version. As it so happened, Johnston got a call on the morning of the session from Charlie McCoy, one of the young studio musicians he worked with quite a bit in Nashville.

McCoy and his wife were in New York to attend the World's Fair, and Johnston had promised to set him up with tickets to a Broadway show the next time he was in the city.

Only twenty-four, multi-instrumentalist McCoy already had an impressive track record as a session player, having worked with numerous music legends including Elvis Presley, Roy Orbison, Patsy Cline, Quincy Jones, and Johnny Cash. He was also a promising recording artist in his own right but had yet to score a hit. He released two rock singles on Cadence, the label that launched the Everly Brothers, before moving to Monument Records, home to Orbison. By the summer of 1965 he had released three singles on Monument backed by his band the Escorts, the most popular rock band in Nashville at the time.

As McCoy remembers it, when he called Johnston about the theater tickets that August morning, his timing couldn't have been better. "Are you free this afternoon?" the producer asked him. "I'm recording Bob Dylan, and I'd like you to meet him."

So McCoy went to the studio where he met Dylan and bassist Bill Lee. After the introductions Dylan told him, "I have one of your records. I really like your harp playing."

"It was a record I did for Monument that nobody had ever heard of," McCoy says of the single that had been released eight months earlier. "It was called 'Harpoon Man.'"[46] Songwriter Bob Neuwirth had given Dylan the 45.[47] While it may have been surprising Dylan knew of the record, it's certainly no surprise he liked it. "Harpoon Man" was an uptempo blues rocker featuring McCoy working out on harmonica—his best instrument—over a manic rhythm track courtesy of the Escorts. Dylan may well have liked the single's B side, a cover of the Muddy Waters R&B hit "I'm Ready," even more. McCoy's version featured the same sonic mix Dylan was experimenting with, a potent blend of guitar, harmonica, and organ.[48]

As McCoy prepared to leave, Dylan surprised him again. "Listen, I'm getting ready to do this song," he told the Nashville session ace. "Why don't you sit in?"

"What do you want me to play?" McCoy—who didn't have any of his instruments with him—asked.

"There's an acoustic guitar over there," Dylan said. "Just grab that."[49]

Less than an hour later, they had a master take of "Desolation Row" in the can, an eleven-minute acoustic version that would close out *Highway 61 Revisited*. McCoy improvised the flamenco-inspired guitar fills that became the track's musical highlight, saying later he tried to imagine what Grady Martin, the legendary Nashville session guitarist, would have played on the song.

After McCoy left the studio, Johnston told Dylan, "Now see how easy that was. That's how it would be in Nashville."

Dylan put his hand to his chin thoughtfully and said, "Hmmm."[50]

2

AIRBORNE
WITH THE HAWKS

WITH THE SONGS for *Highway 61 Revisited* in the can and scheduled for release on August 30, Dylan had more important things to think about than whether or not to record in Nashville—he had to immediately turn his attention to the task of taking his new electric sound on the road. First and foremost he needed a backing band for a pair of upcoming shows at big venues: August 28 at New York's Forest Hills Tennis Stadium, a fifteen-thousand-seat amphitheater, and the slightly larger Hollywood Bowl in Los Angeles on September 3.

He knew he wanted Al Kooper on keys, and he was thinking of using some musicians he knew in L.A. "I wanted Jim Burton, and Joe Osborn to play bass, and Mickey Jones," he told *Rolling Stone* a few years later. "They were all in California, though. And there was some difficulty in making that group connect. One of them didn't want to fly and Mickey couldn't make it immediately, and I think Jim Burton was playing with a television group at that time."[1]

James "Jim" Burton was an L.A. session guitarist best known at the time for his trailblazing guitar riffing and soloing on Dale Hawkins's 1957 seminal rock recording, "Susie Q," and for his work on Ricky Nelson's records. When he got the offer to play with Dylan, he was appearing on *Shindig!*, a musical variety TV series airing on ABC. Burton was playing guitar in the show's combo called the Shindogs, which included Delaney Bramlett (guitar, vocals), Joey Cooper (bass), Glen D. Hardin (piano), and Chuck Blackwell (drums). When he wasn't playing on *Shindig!*, Burton was working in the studio.

"I was very busy doing five sessions a day, seven days a week, and I was booked like a year in advance, so I really had no time to do anything," Burton says. "Al Grossman called me from New York, and he said Bob wanted me to do this tour, which was like a three-month tour, and there was no way I could get off and do a three-month tour, so I had to bow out. The timing was not right."[2]

Osborn, who had also worked with Hawkins and Nelson, was a first-call session bassist in the collection of L.A. studio players known as the Wrecking Crew. Because of his session work, Osborn also declined Dylan's offer. "I never did like to travel," he told *Vintage Guitar* magazine in 1998. "Bob Dylan made me a great offer . . . but I was happy with what I was doing."[3]

Jones was a drummer who got his professional start playing with singer-guitarist Trini Lopez in the late 1950s and whose muscular drum work would a few years later power the First Edition, a rock group fronted by Kenny Rogers and best-known for turning Mickey Newbury's "Just Dropped In (To See What Condition My Condition Was In)" into a top five hit. Jones wanted to accept Dylan's offer, but he was in the midst of a lengthy residency with Johnny Rivers's band at the Whisky a Go Go in West Hollywood, so like the others, he, too, had to say no.

Dylan needed some other options. The most expeditious solution was to use the musicians who had backed him on *Highway 61 Revisited*. Kooper was already on board, and electric bassist Harvey Brooks, a friend of Kooper's who had been the primary bass player on the album, signed on as well. Dylan hoped drummer Bobby Gregg, who had played on both *Highway 61 Revisited* and *Bringing It All Back Home*, would be available, too. But guitarist Mike Bloomfield, who was playing with the Paul Butterfield Blues Band at the time, declined. Kooper recalled in his memoir that he and Brooks learned of the guitarist's decision over lunch:

"You guys going on the road with Dylan?" he asked us.
    "Yeah, sure, aren't you?"

"I can't," he said. "You guys will be big stars, be on TV and in the movies, have your picture on the cover of *Time*, but I can't do it. I want to stay with Butterfield."

"Why?"

"All I want to do is play the blues, man. Ah *loves* tuh play de blues," he grinned.[4]

A decade later, Bloomfield would expound on his reasons for turning Dylan down to writer Larry Sloman. "I joined the Butterfield Blues Band, and Albert [Grossman] managed Bob and me," he told Sloman. "I figured he's the manager, he'll tell me what band he wants me to play with best, he'll tell what makes the most sense. So my druthers was to play with Butterfield, I mean I had absolutely no interest in playing with Bob 'cause I saw that I would be merely a shadow. First of all, I'm a bluesman and the music would take me in no direction that I wanted to go in, and I would be a shadow of this guy that I was beginning to see was an immensely popular star, and that held no interest for me at all."[5]

So Dylan still needed a lead guitarist. A young Canadian woman named Mary Martin who worked as a secretary for Grossman suggested he check out a band from Toronto called Levon and the Hawks. Levon was Levon Helm, and the Hawks were Robbie Robertson, Rick Danko, Richard Manuel, and Garth Hudson.

The Hawks got their start backing Ronnie Hawkins, a rockabilly artist from Arkansas who was Dale Hawkins's cousin. Hawkins had moved with his band to Toronto in 1958 after getting a tip that Canada was fertile ground for southern rock and roll from Conway Twitty, who was a rocker at that point, still seven years from making the switch to straight country. Twitty's tip turned out to be golden for Hawkins and the Hawks. Within a month of their arrival in Toronto they had become the city's hottest band, taking up residency at Le Coq d'Or Tavern on Yonge Street and packing the house.

Over time all but one of the original members of the Hawks got homesick and returned to the United States, the lone exception being Helm, the band's drummer. Hawkins eventually replaced the departing American members with Canadian musicians, figuring they were more likely to remain in the band.

The first Canadian to join the group was a piano player named Scott Cushnie, who Hawkins plucked from the Suedes, a Toronto-based combo that included Robertson on lead guitar. Although his stint with the band would be short, Cushnie convinced Hawkins to give the guitarist a tryout. Initially Robertson played a six-string electric bass for the band before switching to rhythm guitar. When Fred Carter Jr. left in 1960, Robertson replaced him on lead guitar. Bassist Danko was the next to come on board, in the spring of 1961; pianist Manuel joined later that summer. Sax man Jerry Penfound and organist/saxophonist Hudson were added in fall of '61.

Over the next few years, the Hawks honed their chops backing Hawkins at Le Coq d'Or and on the road, but as 1963 came to a close they were feeling limited by Hawkins's repertoire. "The band was becoming more and more knowledgeable about music, and the old stuff we were doing was getting on our nerves," Robertson explained to Barney Hoskyns, author of *Across the Great Divide: The Band in America*. "When the music got a little too far out for Ronnie's ear, and he couldn't tell when to come in singing, he'd tell us nobody but Thelonious Monk could understand what we were playing."[6] At the end of the year, fed up with Hawkins making most of the money and treating them like kids, the Hawks decided to quit working with the singer and go out on their own. They soon landed a regular gig at Friar's Tavern just down Yonge Street from Le Coq d'Or.

That's where Martin and her friend Toni Trow used to "spend a fair wad of time."[7] The Toronto native originally moved to New York City in 1963, attracted to the scene in Greenwich Village, and landed a job as receptionist at Albert Grossman's office through a friend who was secretary to one of Grossman's associates, John Court. Court, who managed folk duo Ian and Sylvia, convinced Martin she needed formal training in secretarial skills so she returned to Toronto and enrolled in Shaw's Business School.[8] While back home, she recalled during a 2009 interview with Jay Orr of the Country Music Hall of Fame and Museum, "we would go to the matinee, and probably we would hang out with [the Hawks]. We were groupies—it is the truth. And then we would go back for round two at whatever the place was."[9]

The band's agent was Harold Kudlets, who formerly had booked Hawkins. Kudlets helped Levon and the Hawks get the gig at Friar's Tavern, and he also arranged dates for them in the United States. In June of 1964 he booked them into the Peppermint Lounge in New York City. Before they headed down, Penfound left the group.

During the time they were working in New York, three of the Hawks—Helm, Hudson, and Robertson—played on a record with bluesman John Hammond Jr., son of the legendary Columbia A&R executive. Hammond had met Helm and the rest of the Hawks earlier that year when he was in Toronto appearing at the Purple Onion club. A friend took him to see the group at the Concord Tavern.[10] "I was just mind-boggled," he said. "These guys were one of the best blues-R&B bands I'd ever heard. They were so intense and so especially good."[11] After that, he would jam with the group whenever he was in Toronto.

Hammond suggested to his label (Vanguard) that the Hawks back him on his next record (*So Many Roads*), but they would only agree to hiring Helm, Hudson, and Robertson. They wanted Hammond to use bassist Jimmy Lewis, who had worked on his previous album for the company. Surprisingly, Mike Bloomfield played piano on the record—which spoke volumes about Robertson's growing prowess on guitar—and Charlie Musselwhite, who had come with Bloomfield from Chicago, contributed harmonica.

According to Hammond, Dylan stopped by the studio and was impressed by Robertson's guitar work. As he told biographer Howard Sounes, after hearing Robertson play a particularly wicked lick, Dylan said, "Oh, God. Listen to that."[12] Apparently, no introductions were made at that time, but several months later, as Robertson recalled in his memoir, he accompanied Hammond to one of the dates for *Highway 61 Revisited*, where he was introduced to Dylan and Grossman. During their short visit to the studio, Dylan played "Like a Rolling Stone" for them. "I'd never heard anything like this before," Robertson wrote. "The studio lit up with the sound of toughness, humor and originality. It was hard to take it all in on one listen."[13]

So while Martin recommended the Hawks to Dylan, it was Hammond who first introduced him to the band,[14] something Martin affirmed to author Jason Schneider for his book *Whispering Pines: The Northern Roots of American Music from Hank Snow to the Band*: "I've often been given credit for putting The Hawks and Dylan together, but I really feel, in retrospect, John Hammond [Jr.] was truly integral to all of that."[15]

With her degree from Shaw's in hand, Martin had returned to New York and Gross Court Management and become Grossman's secretary—but she still kept tabs on the Hawks. She also continued to push the band to Dylan because she knew how good they were, knew they might have what Dylan was looking for. "They were in their infancy, a really mature and dedicated bunch of boys who loved the music they were doing," she told Orr. "They executed it with passion."[16]

"She was a rather persevering soul, as she hurried around the office on her job; she was a secretary, did secretarial work, and knew all the bands and all the singers in Canada," Dylan said, describing Martin to *Rolling Stone* a few years later.[17] Martin had a definite ear for talent and was destined for an influential career in music as an artist manager and as a pioneering female A&R executive. She would become Leonard Cohen's first manager and help him land his initial recording contract with Columbia. She would also manage Van Morrison before becoming East Coast director of A&R for Warner Bros. in 1972, where she signed Emmylou Harris, among others.

Beginning in June, when they opened for Conway Twitty, Levon and the Hawks did several stints during the summer of 1965 at Tony Mart's in Somers Point, New Jersey, a small seaside town 125 miles south of New York City. During their residency in August to close out the summer season, Martin convinced Danny Weiner, one of Grossman's talent scouts, to go down to Somers Point with her to check out the band. Weiner agreed to go, and once there, liked what he heard, so a short time later Martin called the band and asked if they wanted to back Dylan on the upcoming shows at Forest Hills and the Hollywood Bowl. As both Robertson and Helm remember it, they were relaxing at the beach when they got the call from Martin.[18]

The band discussed it and agreed that Robertson should go up to New York to meet Dylan and explore the offer further. He was to meet Dylan at Grossman's office on East Fifty-Fifth Street. As Robertson recalled in his memoir, upon arrival he was escorted into a room full of new Fender guitars and amplifiers. As he was checking out the gear, Dylan came into the room, attired in a dark red polka dot shirt, blue striped trousers, and dark prescription sunglasses.

Dylan talked a little about his electric performance at the recent Newport Folk Festival; they also discussed the guitars Fender had sent over, and Robertson recommended Dylan try out a Telecaster. It was what he played, and he noted it was "lighter on the shoulder and stays in tune easier than the Strat, or any of the Fender guitars that come with a tremolo bar." Robertson suggested he ask for a black Telecaster with a white pick guard. Dylan, who was currently playing a Stratocaster, told one of the people in the office to relay that request to the Fender rep. Soon thereafter, Dylan would be playing Robertson's recommendation in concert.

At that point, as Robertson remembered it, they grabbed a pair of acoustic guitars and headed to Grossman's residence in Gramercy Park, where Dylan played him some of the cuts from *Highway 61 Revisited*, which would be coming out at the end of the month. After listening to a few selections, they tuned the acoustic guitars, and Dylan began playing one of the songs. Robertson watched his fingers to get the chord progression, then joined in, "floating between the vocal lines, swirling and stinging with fills when necessary."[19]

"To be honest, that was the first time I *really* heard Bob Dylan," Robertson told Hoskyns, discounting his earlier experience with "Like a Rolling Stone." "Sitting on a couch playing with him singing in this room. And that was the first time I said to myself, 'There's something to this, it kind of rambles a bit, but there is something about it.' I was playing a little loud, and I could see from his attitude that he *wanted* it to be rough."[20]

They played a few more songs, then Dylan offered the guitarist a job in his band and told him about the upcoming dates at Forest Hills and the Hollywood Bowl, and a possible tour to follow. Robertson explained that he wasn't really looking for a job, that he had his own band and they were starting to build some momentum. Dylan asked if he could at least do the two impending shows, and the guitarist said he might be able to do it if Dylan hired Helm to play drums. Dylan was open to the idea but thought they had already lined up Bobby Gregg.

"Well, let me know if we can do it with Levon, and I think we might be able to work something out," Robertson told him.[21]

The guitarist returned to Somers Point and told his bandmates about Dylan's offer, emphasizing that he wouldn't consider it if Helm wasn't involved but otherwise seeing it as an opportunity they should explore, considering Dylan's growing stature. Even with the caveat of his inclusion, Helm wasn't convinced; he wasn't looking to back someone else. The guitarist recalled in his memoir speaking to Helm privately about it, telling him, "We have to see what's behind this door."[22]

As it turned out, Gregg was busy with session work and didn't want to go on the road after all. Robertson soon received word that Dylan wanted to use Helm on drums, so the two of them went to Grossman's office for a meeting. "Bob was wearing mod-style clothes he had bought in England: a red op-art shirt, a narrow-waisted jacket, black pegged pants, pointed black Beatle boots," Helm said, recalling the first time he met Dylan to Stephen Davis, the cowriter of his autobiography.[23] At the meeting, Dylan told them they would be working with Al Kooper and Harvey Brooks, whom they would soon meet when rehearsals began mid-August at Carroll's Rehearsal Hall in Manhattan at 625 West Fifty-Fifth Street.

Kooper recalled the rehearsals for the Forest Hills gig in his memoir. "We rehearsed exhaustively every day over a two-week period, and the pieces fell together nicely," he wrote. "After rehearsing for two weeks, we were ready to take this new electric Dylan on the road."[24] But Robertson remembered the rehearsals differently, calling them "disorganized" in his memoir.[25] Helm described the rehearsals to Davis as "real ragged."[26]

At the soundcheck on the afternoon of the concert, Dylan told Robertson, "Just remember, tonight, don't stop playing, no matter what." "He said it like we were going into battle," the guitarist recalled.[27]

It was unseasonably cold and blustery on that August evening. The audience of more than fourteen thousand applauded Bob's forty-five-minute opening acoustic set and booed the second half when the band joined him on stage. They booed as if they thought booing was what was expected. The final song of the night was "Like a Rolling Stone."

As Kooper has noted in multiple interviews over the years, the audience sang along with the choruses and booed when it was over.

In the *New York Times* on August 30, 1965, Robert Shelton described the audience at Forest Hills as "rude and immature." In his definitive biography of Dylan, Shelton described the electric portion of the Forest Hills concert: "In a confused jangle of music and audience discord, someone yelled, 'Scum bag.' Dylan remarked, 'Aw come on now.' Some 'listeners' threw fruit, and some young rockers were evicted. One prankster got onstage and knocked Al Kooper off his chair."[28]

Six days later at the Hollywood Bowl the weather was not only warmer, so was the reception of the high-profile crowd. Johnny Cash and members of the Byrds were among the attendees that night, along with film stars Dean Martin, Gregory Peck, and Tuesday Weld.[29] Even so, there was still some booing. As he had at Forest Hills, Dylan opened with an acoustic set followed by a set with the band, the same songs both nights in a slightly different order.

Back in New York, Kooper received an itinerary for additional tour dates from Grossman's office. Two dates at the end of the month in Texas jumped out at him: September 24 in Austin and September 25 in Dallas. "Noting that the tour stopped in Texas, I began to give serious thought to making my exit from this traveling circus," he recalled in his autobiography. "I mean, look what they had just done to J.F.K. down there, and he was a leading symbol of the establishment. So what was going to happen when Bob Dylan, the most radical vision of the counterculture, paid them a visit? I wasn't sure I wanted to find out. Besides, what musician enjoys being booed on a consistent basis?"[30]

Robertson got a call from Dylan about the additional dates. Dylan wanted him and Helm to do the tour. The guitarist told him they couldn't, that he and Helm had their own band. But Dylan didn't want to take no as an answer and asked Robertson to meet him that evening at one of his regular haunts, the Kettle of Fish on Macdougal Street.

When he arrived at the bar, Robertson found Dylan sitting at a table in the back with his pal Bob Neuwirth. Once a round of drinks was ordered and received, Dylan asked Robertson again if he would do the tour, and again Robertson told him no, that the Hawks had their own plans, including a recording session the very next day. As Robertson recalled in his memoir, Neuwirth jumped in at that point, saying the guitarist could always come back later to "the Hawks thing," that at best, their prospects were a big "maybe."

Robertson disagreed with Neuwirth's assessment and told him so, but when he learned Dylan didn't plan to use Kooper or Brooks on the tour, he said he would consider the tour only if the Hawks, all of them, backed Dylan. "It's kind of an all-or-nothing situation," he said.

"Whoa, how do we know that these guys could even cut it?" Neuwirth asked. Robertson said they didn't know, that Dylan would have to come hear them perform. Dylan asked when he could do that, and Robertson suggested he come to Toronto the following week during their stint at the Friar's Tavern. Dylan said he would try to do that.

At the recording session the next day, Robertson told the rest of the Hawks about his talk with Dylan, and no one had any objection to exploring the possibility of touring with him. But the band was focused on their opportunity that day at Mira Sound. They cut two master sides that would be released by Atlantic Records on their ATCO subsidiary— the gospel-tinged "The Stones I Throw" and "He Don't Love You (And He'll Break Your Heart)," a totally infectious slice of hard-edged R&B featuring Manuel on lead vocal.[31]

Dylan joined the band in Toronto on Wednesday, September 15. *Variety* reported his visit to the city as follows: "Secrecy was the word last week when the folk composer and performer jetted into Toronto by private plane to rehearse with Levon and the Hawks, a local rock 'n' roll group that will back him on his current tour. In the city for two days, Dylan checked into a midtown motor hotel, said he wanted to work on his book *Tarantula*, and spent much of his evenings and early mornings at the Friar's Tavern, where the group was playing."[32]

Dylan was accompanied by his girlfriend, Sara Lownds. They arrived at Friar's Tavern at midnight and watched the Hawks' final set from an inconspicuous corner of the club. When the set ended at 1:00 AM, Dylan had a cab take Lownds back to their hotel. Before leaving, she told Robertson she had enjoyed their music and that she hoped that it would work out for them to tour with Dylan.

For the next four to five hours, Dylan and the Hawks ran through songs from his new album, as well as electric versions of the songs he previously had played acoustic. "We rehearsed with Bob after they locked up the place for the night," Helm recalled to Davis.

They rehearsed again the following evening after the Hawks' final set. According to Robertson, at the end of that rehearsal, Dylan said, "That sounds pretty good. So why don't we do this first tour and see how it goes. What do you think?" Although they didn't necessarily agree it sounded "pretty good," the band said they would do the fifteen-date tour.[33]

The following day, the band had lunch with Dylan and Lownds. To their surprise, Dylan's mother was there as well, and she took a liking to Danko. "Mrs. Zimmerman wanted to know where we had our suits tailored," the bassist recalled to Davis, "and eventually, we took Bob over to see Lou Miles, who made him that brown houndstooth suit, with the pegged waist. . . . It was photographed a lot."[34] Miles would become known as the "tailor to the stars," designing custom suits for not only Dylan, but for Frank Sinatra, the Beatles, and many other celebrities.

It's unclear exactly how many days Dylan was in Toronto rehearsing after hours with the Hawks. Altogether, it seems likely there were at least three or four nights of rehearsals. As Helm remembered it, "Bob stayed with us for maybe a week, hanging out, working on music."[35]

Dylan gave an interview during his first couple of days there to *Toronto Star* columnist Robert Fulford, part of which was used in a column published on September 18. "I know my thing now," Dylan told Fulford. "I know what it is. It's hard to describe. I don't know what to call it because I've never heard it before."[36] It would be another thirteen years before he found a description that worked—"that thin, that wild mercury sound."

In retrospect, the circumstances that led to the Texas shows, Dylan's first performances with Levon and the Hawks, seem altogether remarkable, the bookings being the result of a cold call to Grossman's office by a twenty-one-year-old promoter based in Austin named Angus Wynne. "I looked at the back of a Dylan album, and it said he was managed by Albert Grossman, so I called information in New York and got the number," Wynne told the *Austin American Statesman*'s Michael Corcoran. "When I called and made my pitch, someone yelled to the other room, 'Hey, do you want to go play in Texas?' and someone yelled back 'Yeah, sure.'"[37]

Wynne had decided to try to book Dylan into Austin and Dallas after hearing "Like a Rolling Stone" repeatedly on the radio in Texas after its release in July. "He was a king coming in," the promoter told the *Austin Chronicle*. "Dylan was very popular here because he'd sold a lot of records and was well-known for writing songs that other people recorded."[38]

Levon and the Hawks flew to Austin on a Lockheed Lodestar plane leased by Grossman for the tour. The plane was kind of a clunker—it was slow with intermittent air conditioning, and the band would come to call it "the Volkswagen of the Sky."[39] Dylan took a commercial flight to Texas's capital city and was met at the airport by Joe Mansfield, a Colombia promotions rep based in San Antonio. "I picked him up at the airport, he had this girl with him," Mansfield later recalled to the *Austin Chronicle*. "I said, 'Who's that girl?' He said, 'She's a photographer—Annie Leibovitz.'"[40]

Wynne knew Levon and the Hawks from their days backing Ronnie Hawkins, knew they were "badass," and he was not disappointed when he heard the electric portion of the show that first night in Austin.[41] "It was so in-your-face," he told Corcoran. "You couldn't really understand the words—quality concert sound systems were nonexistent back then—but you could feel the energy. It was like being knocked over by this huge burst of sound."[42]

As it turned out, Kooper had nothing to fear about Dylan's dates in the Lone Star State. Maybe it was southern hospitality, or maybe because it wasn't a folk audience, but both shows were well received, including the electric sets. Being from neighboring Arkansas, Helm was not surprised they got a positive response in Texas. "I was damn sure no southern audience would boo what Bob was doing, and I was right," he told Davis. "The Texas crowd loved Dylan's stuff, so our first show as Bob Dylan with Levon and the Hawks was a smash."[43]

Well-known New York–based writer-photographer Stephanie Chernikowski, who was living in Austin at the time, attended the concert that night at the city's Municipal Auditorium. "It never entered my mind—or heart—not to love the electric stuff," she told Corcoran. "Dylan and the Band were stunning. There were moments that felt like you were the only person in the room with them."[44]

Mansfield remembers a smattering of boos, but they were in response to the volume, not the fact Dylan was playing "electric." Wynne doesn't remember any booing, but he does remember Dylan telling the band to "crank it up" at one point. "Then everybody turned their amps up as high as they'd go and it overpowered the vocals," he said. "It was disconcerting, but also exciting."

The following night in Dallas at Southern Methodist University's Moody Coliseum, Dylan and the Hawks got a similar reception. A reviewer for the *Dallas Times Herald* described the audience as "an unusual mixture of beat pretenders, clean-cut teens, and adults" who "cheered and stomped the floor."[45] A review in the *Dallas Morning News* described the crowd's reaction to the show as "complete acceptance."[46]

From Texas, Dylan and the Hawks went to Woodstock, New York, where he had recently purchased a house, for a few more days of rehearsals, followed by a pair of dates in the Northeast: October 1 at Carnegie Hall in New York City, and then October 2 at the Symphony Hall Mosque Theatre in Newark, New Jersey. The Carnegie Hall concert stood in sharp contrast to the show at Forest Hills five weeks earlier. While the acoustic set was still more enthusiastically received, there was no booing during the electric set, and Dylan was obviously enjoying himself, so much so that he and the band even came back for an encore.

"At Carnegie Hall, a couple of hundred people rushed the stage at the end, shouting for more," Helm recalled. "I could see Bob standing at the microphone. He was exhausted, spaced out, but really beaming. 'Thank you,' he mumbled. 'I didn't think you'd feel that way.'"[47]

Dylan got a similar reception across the river the following night at the Symphony Hall in Newark, and that audience was treated to an encore, as well. Even with the more positive reception, Robertson remained skeptical. "I didn't know if it was ever gonna be special," he told Hoskyns. "Just making electric folk music wasn't enough, it needed to be much more violent than that, and I didn't know whether he would ever get it. There was a lot of strumming going on in this music, and for us, anyone who strummed just seemed to take the funkiness out of it."[48]

Robertson may have had doubts, but Dylan was excited by what he was hearing in his live performances with the Hawks and wanted to find out if they could capture it in the studio. So Johnston booked time in Studio A on three consecutive days, October 4, 5, and 6. As it turned out, only one of the dates was used; Dylan and the band did two three-hour sessions on the night of October 5, and those two sessions, produced by Johnston and engineered by Roy Halee, marked the official beginning of the *Blonde on Blonde* dates.

According to studio records, the first session ran from 7:00 until 10:00 PM, then after a break of an hour and a half, Dylan and the band returned for a second session at 11:30 PM that went till 2:30 in the morning. They tackled five songs, two of which were just a verse and a chorus. More than anything, it seemed as if Dylan wanted to try out some ideas with Levon and the Hawks, see how they performed in the studio, see where the music might take them.

They began with "Medicine Sunday," a piece of a song that was essentially the genesis of "Temporary Like Achilles," which Dylan would record a few months later. In terms of musical approach, the two songs were quite different—"Medicine Sunday" was a folk-rocker in the vein of "Like a Rolling Stone," although at a slightly slower tempo, while "Temporary Like Achilles" would be a slow blues. But "Medicine Sunday" contained the two-line chorus Dylan would rework slightly and use later as the chorus for "Temporary Like Achilles": "Well, I know you want my loving / Mama, but you're so hard." According to rock historian Clinton Heylin, a rough draft of the lyrics auctioned by Christie's in 2013 showed that "Medicine Sunday" had at least two verses. It's unclear if he had that draft with him at the studio, but whether he did or not, he didn't sing a second verse.[49] They recorded two takes featuring a verse and the chorus, both highlighted by Hudson's organ fills and neither more than a minute in length. If Dylan was looking for some inspiration to manifest while they worked on the song, it didn't.

From there, he moved on to "Jet Pilot," the other song snippet he brought to the studio that night; an uptempo blues rocker about a woman with "jet pilot eyes" that was totally in the Hawks' wheelhouse. Surprisingly, Dylan never revisited the idea. Propelled by a swinging shuffle beat laid down by Helm, the band really worked out on the one take they attempted, with first Hudson, then Robertson taking leads and demonstrating their fluency in the blues. Interestingly, the chorus ended with a twist, when Dylan revealed, ". . . she ain't no woman, she's a man."

According to label records, Dylan and the band next worked on "I Wanna Be Your Lover," which, when they started, he was calling "I Don't Wanna Be Your Partner." They gave the song a raw, slow blues treatment built around a nasty guitar riff courtesy of Robertson. After jamming on the riff for several minutes, they ran down the first verse and what was then the chorus, on which Dylan repeated the line, "I don't wanna be your partner, baby, I wanna be your man."

At that point, Dylan switched direction again and led them through two incomplete takes of "Can You Please Crawl Out Your Window," a song he had written during the summer and attempted to record previously on July 30 during the *Highway 61 Revisited* sessions. The final take recorded on July 30 was accidentally released on the first pressing of the "Positively Fourth Street" single but was quickly pulled when the mistake was discovered. Although Dylan was not satisfied with what was recorded in July, he clearly still believed in the song as a possible single and hoped to record a releasable version of it. On the first take, they tried a more relaxed tempo than what he had recorded at the July 30 session, but the music broke down less than a minute in. Then during a slightly faster second take, the music broke down again, and Dylan's frustration spilled out. "You can't hear anything in here, you know," he complained to Johnston in the control room. "Can you get us a monitor?" When neither Johnston nor Halee answered, he added, "Can you get us a monitor if it won't feed back?"

Using the talk-back mike, Johnston finally responded with an answer from Halee: "He said he couldn't. You want headphones?"

"No, there's just a dull sound in here, you know," Dylan said.

Dissatisfied with the situation, Dylan tabled "Can You Please Crawl Out Your Window" and went back to "I Wanna Be Your Lover." The song has been portrayed as a parody of the Beatles' "I Wanna Be Your Man" but might more accurately be described as an act of one-upmanship. Dylan had a complex relationship with the Beatles. They were his peers and friends, but they were also his musical rivals, and some of their recent releases had been undeniably Dylanesque. In a 1968 interview with *Rolling Stone*, Mick Jagger said Dylan once told Keith Richards he could have written "I Can't Get No Satisfaction," but Richards couldn't have written "Tambourine Man."[50] Dylan may have been communicating a similar message to John Lennon and Paul McCartney with "I Wanna Be Your Man," taking their simple idea and populating it with a colorful cast of characters: a rainman who dons a wolfman's disguise, a judge who denies Mona bond, an undertaker in his midnight suit, jumpin' Judy, Rasputin, and even Phaedra.

On the first official take, they continued with the raw, bluesy approach they had rehearsed earlier, only at a slightly faster tempo. After running it down for a minute, Dylan asked Johnston, "You ready to tape this?"

"We're rollin'," Johnston told him.

Then Dylan said to the musicians, "One verse, then we'll play it back."

Apparently Dylan didn't like what he heard on the playback because by take two, they had changed their approach to the song. They kept Robertson's guitar riff but abandoned the slow blues arrangement for a more uptempo, straight-ahead rock treatment in the vein of "From a Buick 6." Dylan also decided to more blatantly confront the Beatles, changing the first line of the chorus from "I don't wanna be your partner, baby, I wanna be your man" to "I wanna be your lover, baby, I wanna be your man," which matched the opening two lines of "I Wanna Be Your Man" word for word.

The second take broke down after a couple of minutes. Then after running through the song some more, Dylan and the band launched into a tighter third take, on which he introduced the last line of the chorus,

"I don't wanna be hers, I wanna be yours." By the fourth take, he had finalized the chorus.

There were ultimately seven takes of "I Wanna Be Your Lover," and apparently the seventh was the keeper take, although it didn't make the cut for *Blonde on Blonde*, nor was it released as a B-side on any of Dylan's singles from that period. When it was finally released twenty years later on the box set *Biograph*, Dylan said in the liner notes, "I always thought it was a good song, but it just never made it onto an album."

Columbia studio logs show they closed out the evening with two takes of an instrumental number, the second of which was a complete take featuring a relaxed, four-minute workout highlighted by organ and guitar fills from Hudson and Robertson respectively. From a musical standpoint, it was the highlight of the evening, not only the most polished recording they made all night, but also the one that showed the most potential, suggesting something special could be in store at Dylan's next session with the Hawks.

"There was one song idea, or at least a chord progression Bob had started with no vocals yet," Robertson wrote, recalling the instrumental in his memoir. "I think Bob called it '#1.' Garth played some beautiful little melodies and background on that, but we never came back to it."[51]

Although Dylan never did anything with it at the time, by the late '60s take two began appearing on Dylan bootlegs, and it was ultimately released in 2015 on the six-CD and eighteen-CD editions of *The Bootleg Series, Vol. 12: The Cutting Edge 1965–1966*.

———————————

While Dylan didn't accomplish a lot on that very first night of sessions for *Blonde on Blonde* (in no small part because he didn't bring that much material to the studio), the evening did provide a few hints as to where he was headed, the biggest being that he intended to make a record about women. Beyond that, the two complete songs he attempted that evening, "Can You Please Crawl Out Your Window" and "I Wanna Be Your Lover," both involved a love triangle, a dynamic that would appear in a number of the songs that would make it onto the album. And the choruses of both those songs, as well as the chorus of "Medicine Sunday," were centered around sexual longing, another theme that would be prominent on the record. So despite not recording anything that would make the cut for the album, Dylan set the tone for what was to follow, and undoubtedly was looking forward to getting back in the studio with the Hawks during the next break in his touring schedule.

3

MEET THE NEW DRUMMER, SAME AS THE OLD DRUMMER

DESPITE THE GENERALLY POSITIVE RECEPTION of the five concerts that followed Forest Hills, if Dylan thought he had gotten past the booing, he was mistaken. Four days after their first session together, Dylan and the Hawks hit the road again, performing twenty-one shows over the next fifty-one days, beginning with a date in Atlanta on October 9 and ending with a show in Washington, DC, on November 28.[1]

When they made stops in the cities that were part of the folk circuit, the electric portion of the show was met with choruses of boos and shouts of "Go back to England" and "Lose the band."[2] "Once we got out of the South, people started booing a lot," Rick Danko told *On the Tracks* in 1996.[3]

The "Dylan's gone electric" hysteria made no sense to Robbie Robertson, who was raised on rock and roll and R&B and had never experienced the emphasis folk musicians and folk music fans placed on acoustic authenticity. "It seemed kind of a funny statement to me at the time, that somebody's *gone electric*," Robertson told Michael Laskow, founder of independent A&R company TAXI, at the group's 2006 Road Rally conference. "It was like, jeez, somebody's bought a television.

"We didn't understand exactly what was going on," he continued. "We didn't understand that this was a musical revolution happening and that we were part of it. We just thought it was just a weird gig. You would go to a place, set up your equipment, people would come in, you'd play, they would boo you and throw shit at you, and then you'd pack up your equipment and you'd go on to the next place, and they would boo you again and throw more shit at you."[4]

Dylan genuinely appreciated the band's willingness to keep going onstage with him every night. "We were putting our heads in the lion's mouth, and I had to admire them for sticking it out with me," he said in the documentary *No Direction Home*. "Just for doing it, in my book, they were gallant knights just for even standing behind me."[5]

The road-hardened Robertson had a slightly less dramatic perspective on it all. "We were just doing what we said we would do, and whatever happened when we got there was beyond our control," he said. "It happened, it seemed really silly and bizarre at the time, but I guess for the people who were really feeling it, it wasn't silly at all. They meant it.

"After these jobs we had plenty of time because nobody wanted to hang out with people that were being booed. So we would go back and listen to these tapes from the gigs, and we'd say, 'That's not that bad.' I mean, you don't need to throw shit. Actually, we got to really like what we were hearing."[6]

The booing bothered some of the Hawks more than others. "I didn't take it personally, because I knew they were booing Bob. I was just a sideman," Danko told the *Morning Call* in 1993.[7]

Levon Helm took the booing the hardest. "It was real strange," he wrote in his memoir. "We'd never been booed in our lives. As soon as they saw the drums set up during the intermission, it was like, 'Light the kerosene.'"[8]

He told the *New York Post* in 2000: "I wasn't made to be booed. It's funny, it doesn't sound like much when you're talking about it, but when you're playing a song, and you get through it, and everybody goes 'boo,' you just can't imagine. It sounds awful. It made me crazy after a little bit. I was laughing on the outside, but crying on the inside."

According to his memoir, Helm told Richard Manuel he planned to stay with the tour through the end of the American dates, but he wasn't willing to go overseas. Besides the booing, he simply didn't want to be "anybody's band anymore." He still had aspirations that the Hawks would make their own records, have their own tours.[9]

Helm may have intended to stick with the tour through the end of the American dates, but he wasn't able to last that long. The end of the line was their concert in Washington, DC, on Sunday, November 28. "There'd been a lot of booing and a couple of fights," he recalled. "The vibes were pretty weird."[10]

With a five-day break in the tour schedule, Dylan and the band flew back to New York after the show. The band was staying at the Irving Hotel, and later that night, Helm went to Robertson's room and told the guitarist he was leaving. "It just ain't my ambition to be anybody's drummer," he said. "I've decided to just let this show go on without me for now. Tell the boys that I wish 'em well, and I'll see 'em when it's time to put this thing back together again."[11]

As far as Dylan was concerned, Helm's departure was especially ill-timed. Johnston had booked studio time for Dylan and the Hawks for November 30, leaving little time to schedule a replacement.

Prior to the October 5 session on which Helm had played drums, the only drummer Dylan had ever worked with in the studio was Bobby Gregg, so Gregg got the last-minute call to man the drum kit again on that last day of November. Born Robert Grego, Gregg came out of an R&B and jazz background and had been a recording artist in his own right, fronting the instrumental group Bobby Gregg and His Friends. In the spring of 1962, the group's single "The Jam," which featured Roy Buchanan on guitar, went to number twenty-nine on the *Billboard* Hot 100 and all the way to number fourteen on the magazine's R&B chart.

Not knowing how musically compatible Gregg and the Hawks would be, Johnston also called some of the other musicians from the *Bringing It All Back Home* and *Highway 61 Revisited* sessions—organist Al Kooper, pianist Paul Griffin, and guitarist Bruce Langhorne. Guitarist Joe Souter, better known as Joe South, a musician Johnston knew from Nashville, was also on hand.

When the session got started at around 2:30 that Tuesday afternoon, the extra musicians remained on the sideline as Dylan ran down his new song for the Hawks and Gregg. The song was marked "Freeze Out" on the recording sheet—that's what Dylan originally was calling "Visions of Johanna"—and was allegedly written three weeks earlier, on November 9, during the great northeast blackout that knocked out electric service in eight states.[12]

"Visions of Johnna" is considered by many to be Dylan's finest composition. The title was probably inspired by the title of the Jack Kerouac novel, *Visions of Gerard*; the influence of the Beat writers on Dylan is well documented, something he acknowledged in a 1978 interview with *Playboy* magazine. "It was [Allen] Ginsberg and Jack Kerouac who inspired me at first," he told Ron Rosenbaum.[13]

But the lyrics of "Visions of Johanna" also showed Dylan's deep acquaintance with the poetry of T. S. Eliot. On "Desolation Row," Dylan had depicted Eliot as fighting Ezra Pound in the captain's tower of the *Titanic*, and over the years, he has talked on the record about Eliot on numerous occasions, including a 1985 *20/20* interview in which he was asked if he considered his lyrics to be poetry. "I don't know what a, you know, Robert Frost or Keats or T. S. Eliot would really think of my stuff," he told interviewer Bob Brown.[14] While he has acknowledged Eliot's influence, Dylan also at times has disparaged his poetry. But even his criticisms revealed familiarity with Eliot's work.

"There is no denying Eliot's fingerprints are all over the song," poet and author David Daniel, who heads the creative writing department at Fairleigh Dickinson University, says. "It's really typical of people of Dylan's generation to have a complex relationship with Eliot. He was such a giant figure that artists simultaneously rebelled against his influence, while being influenced by him."[15]

Eliot's influence can be seen throughout the five verses of "Visions of Johanna." For example, in Eliot's "Rhapsody on a Windy Night," the street lamp "sputtered" and "muttered," while in "Visions of Johanna," the heat pipes "cough." "Muttering" can be found in a number of Eliot's poems; there are "muttering retreats" in one of Eliot's most acclaimed poems, "The Love Song of J. Alfred Prufrock." In the third verse of "Visions of Johanna," "little boy lost" is "muttering small talk at the wall." Dylan may have thought the word "muttering" was too Eliot-esque because by the final take they recorded of the song that day, he had reworked the line, singing, "With his small talk hitting the wall."

There are other apparent nods to Eliot in the song, such as the "empty lot"—there is a "vacant lot" in Eliot's "Preludes." Then there are the all-night girls in "Visions of Johanna" who "whisper" of escapades out on the D train. Eliot's poems feature a lot of whispering—in "Rhapsody on a Windy Night," twelve o'clock itself is "whispering" lunar incantations.

The touches of Eliot incorporated into "Visions of Johanna" are integral to the nocturnal atmosphere Dylan creates. Eliot was enamored with the evening: "Rhapsody on a Windy Night" begins at "twelve o'clock" midnight and ends at "four o'clock" in the morning; "Preludes" opens as the "winter evening settles down"; in "The Love Song of J. Alfred Prufrock," "the evening is spread out against the sky"; and his epic masterpiece, "The Waste Land," contains many references to the night and the evening. "Visions of Johanna" opens with, "Ain't it just like the night to play tricks when you're tryin' to be so quiet," while the third verse ends with, "And these visions of Johanna, they kept me up past dawn."

The identity of Johanna is a mystery that has been pondered for half a century now. If for no other reason than the similarity of the names, Joan Baez, with whom Dylan had been romantically involved, is often suggested as the inspiration for the song. Four days after the session, Baez was in the audience at the Berkeley Community Theatre when Dylan performed the song live for the first time during the acoustic portion of the first of his two concerts there.

"First of all, he had never performed it before, and [Bob] Neuwirth told him I was there that night, and he performed it, and that was very odd," Baez told author Anthony Scaduto in an interview for his 1971 biography of Dylan. "I was listening to the song and sort of inwardly wanting to feel flattered, but wondering whether—you know, I mean, everybody in the world thinks Bobby's written a song about them, and

I consider myself in the same bag. But I would never claim a song. But certain images in there did sound very strange.

"Then Ginsberg came up at one point and said, 'What do you think "Visions of Johanna" is about?' And I said, 'I don't know, Ginsberg, your guess is as good as mine.' He said, 'No, no, what do you think it's about? Bobby says . . . ' and then he reeled off this pile of crap that had nothing to do with anything. And I said, 'Did Bobby say that or did you make that up, Allen?' I had a feeling the two of them were in cahoots to make sure I never thought the song had anything to do with me. . . . Ginsberg was trying to get me to say I thought the song was written about me, and I would never say that about any of Bobby's songs."[16]

But Baez did say that, sort of, in a song she wrote in 1974 after hearing the news that Dylan planned to return to touring. The song, "Winds of the Old Days," seems to be about Dylan, referring in the first verse to the "prince" who had "returned to the stage." On the final chorus, she sang:

And get you down to the harbor now
Most of the sour grapes are gone from the bough
Ghosts of Johanna will visit you there
And the winds of the old days will blow through your hair[17]

Author, historian, and collector Jeff Gold, however, is "leery about trying to interpret what [Dylan] was thinking about or meaning" in his songs. Gold, who has seen and appraised thousands of Dylan's handwritten pieces and lyric sheets, including manuscript material at the Bob Dylan archive in Tulsa, Oklahoma, considers Dylan's writings to be "inscrutable" and thinks "people are so wrong in their interpretations of so many things" concerning his songs.

"It's a fool's errand to try and get into the mind of Bob Dylan and figure out why he did something or what he was writing about or what he was thinking about," Gold says. "He's just riffing constantly and writing constantly and what ends up on the final page bears no resemblance to what he started out doing. He would type all that stuff out and there might be half a line that shows up somewhere. The amount he writes relative to the amount that makes it out is really extraordinary."

He continues, "Having had all this experience looking at all this stuff, and a lot of it was him writing to himself and thinking out loud writing, and then looking at the colossal amount of stuff he threw away to get to where he ended up, and how he would take a little bit of this and little bit of this—just like his music, I am really loathe, more than ever before, to adopt or to play with the kind of fast-and-loose retroactive analysis that you see a lot of people doing.

"In all the stuff I've looked at, the one thing I come away with is you can never know what is happening in Bob Dylan's mind."

Gold, however, does concede "you can sort of figure out what the germs of some of these things are," but beyond that, "it's nothing more than speculation."[18]

Whether the song was inspired by Baez or not, on "Visions of Johanna," Dylan demonstrated the poetic possibilities for elevating songwriting from craft to art, and in the process, obliterated the very conventions of popular music, taking his songwriting to a place way beyond the sophisticated putdowns that had launched him to rock stardom earlier that year.

In advance of the song's release, fashion magazine *Glamour* published the lyrics to "Visions of Johanna" in its June 1966 issue. Reflecting on that in an essay for the *Guardian* in 2008, critic Greil Marcus noted: "What was unusual about this was that the lyrics worked on the *Glamour* page as they were presented: bare, without accompaniment, without a singing voice, as poetry."[19]

"Visions of Johanna" is written from the perspective of a man caught between his current love affair and memories of a past, more powerful relationship, and includes some of the themes and elements that recur on *Blonde on Blonde*. First, there is the helpless feeling of being blocked or stuck, which Dylan introduces in the second line of the song: "We sit here stranded, though we're all doin' our best to deny it." Then there are the "harmonicas" that "play the skeleton keys and the rain," the first of many musical instruments that would appear in the lyrics on *Blonde on Blonde*.

The song has five verses containing three rhymed sections: The first four have a three-line rhyme followed by a four-line rhyme, then a two-line rhyme, while in the final verse, the second section contains eight rhymed lines. The first verse, presented here as published, perfectly illustrates the verses' basic rhyme scheme:

> Ain't it just like the night to play tricks when you're tryin'
> to be so quiet?
> We sit here stranded, though we're all doin' our best to
> deny it
> And Louise holds a handful of rain, temptin' you to defy it
>
> Lights flicker from the opposite loft
> In this room the heat pipes just cough
> The country music station plays soft
> But there's nothing, really nothing to turn off
>
> Just Louise and her lover so entwined
> And these visions of Johanna that conquer my mind

With the rhymed couplet at the end of the verses, the song's rhyme scheme feels a bit like a sonnet, although both English and Italian sonnets have more total lines. "He's really concerned with the rhyme," Gold observes.

Including rehearsals, false starts, and breakdowns, Dylan and the musicians recorded fourteen takes of "Visions of Johanna" that day, and Dylan was tweaking the lyrics in subtle but sometimes significant ways throughout, working his way toward the song's final set of lyrics. In some instances, he was still searching for the right words; in others, he reworked lines so they flowed better when sung.

For example, he made multiple revisions to the pair of lines in the second verse involving the "night watchman." The complete fourth take was the first where they reached the second verse, and on that take, he sang the pair of lines as follows:

> We can hear the night watchman
> Ask himself if he's insane

On the next take, he gave the watchman some illumination and by take seven, the couplet had become:

> We can hear the night watchman click his flashlight
> And ask himself if he's really insane

In the same verse, there were five lines about the new lover, "Louise," that underwent a series of small changes, and aside from taking out the reference to "muttering," Dylan made only minor revisions to the third stanza concerning the aforementioned little boy lost over the course of the afternoon and early evening.

The fourth verse was essentially finished from the start, and it opens with what is surely one of the most profound lines he ever wrote—"Inside the museums, infinity goes up on trial"—and includes some of his funniest lines, too: "But Mona Lisa musta had the highway blues/You can tell by the way she smiles" and "When the jelly-faced women all sneeze/Hear the one with mustache say, 'Jeeze, I can't find my knees.'"

The fifth and final verse was also more-or-less together from the start, with only minor changes over the course of the fourteen takes. Initially, it was "the princess who's pretending to care for him," but on take seven, he changed it to "the countess."[20]

"Visions of Johanna" has been British rocker Robyn Hitchcock's favorite song for half a century, and he released his own version of the song on the 2002 live album *Robyn Sings*. For Hitchcock, the concluding line of the second section of the fifth verse contains one of the most powerful lines Dylan ever penned. "When he puts a line like 'my conscience explodes,' you sort of suddenly think, 'Oh, fuck, he knows what's going on—he's not fooling himself,'" Hitchcock says.[21]

In terms of the arrangement of Dylan's brilliant new composition, there were problems from the start, especially when it came to the drums. Considering the other members of the Hawks had never worked with

Bobby Gregg, that wasn't altogether surprising, but Gregg couldn't get on the same page with Dylan regarding the song's tempo. After their first run-through, on which Gregg played double time, Dylan told the drummer, "I don't want to get it too fast like that, man, because it's gonna be strong enough, you know?"

Despite Dylan's direction, Gregg went right back to double time on the second run-through. "Cowbell," Dylan shouted across the studio to him, in hopes of getting the drummer off the double-time beat. The musicians restarted the song—Dylan told Danko to start it—but even with the cowbell, Gregg maintained the double-time tempo.

"That's not right," Dylan said, then strummed his acoustic guitar at a slower tempo to show what he wanted. When they started up again, Dylan immediately stopped them. "No—that's not the sound, that's not it," he said. He strummed his guitar again at the tempo he was hearing. "It's not hard rock," he continued. "The only thing in it, man, that's hard is Robbie."

As Dylan continued to try to get the tempo locked in with Danko, Johnston lent support from the control room, telling Gregg, "Bob, lay off your cymbal more—and more cowbell."

After rehearsing the song for a few more minutes, Dylan and the players recorded their first complete take, slated as take four—Johnston had recorded the run-throughs, which were marked as takes one through three. Gregg began the song keeping time with just a tambourine, but a few lines into the first verse he added the full drum kit. Although the tempo was a little slower than in the run-throughs, the drummer stuck with his double-time approach on the take that topped seven minutes in length, clocking in at 7:41.

On the next take, another complete one, Gregg sped up the tempo again and played double time from the beginning of the song. Still dissatisfied, Dylan had the musicians run down the song again at a slower tempo for several minutes, stopping them multiple times, saying, "No," then restarting at a slower tempo. The Hawks were getting it, but Gregg's playing was still too busy.

Take seven was another complete take, and on it, they played the song at a slower tempo—it ran over nine minutes—but Dylan was still not happy. At the end of the take, he said, "That's not right at all. I just wanted to hear what it sounds like."

After some more work, they finally found a groove that worked for him on the next take (eight), not only convincing Gregg to abandon his double-time approach for a more relaxed tempo, but also getting more cowbell. Even so, the drummer was still approaching the song with too heavy a hand, ignoring its inherent dynamics. Although it wasn't included on *Blonde on Blonde*, take eight was released in 2005 on *The Bootleg Series, Vol. 7*.

There were six more takes slated that night, but only the fourteenth and final pass was a complete one. By the end of that take, Dylan felt they had gone as far as they were going to go with "Visions of Johanna" that evening and was ready to move on to another song. Considering all the problems Gregg had, Dylan may well have been wondering what they could have done with "Johanna" if Helm had stuck it out. He did add the song to his live shows from that point forward, but in the acoustic portion, not with the band.

––––––––––––

Next, Dylan returned to a song he had attempted in the studio twice before with less-than-satisfactory results, "Can You Please Crawl Out Your Window."

"Can You Please Crawl Out Your Window"—"Crawl Out the Window" on the track sheet—is the third in a trilogy of vicious put-down songs written by Dylan in the summer of 1965 that began with "Like a Rolling Stone" and included "Positively Fourth Street."

Session records show there were ten takes recorded that evening, but the first four were rehearsal takes that broke down as Dylan was working through the chord changes with the musicians. At one point while they were running the song down, Dylan's frustration flared again—this time with the bass part.

"If you don't know it, man, don't stay in front, you're not playing the right chords," he said in a scolding tone to Danko before strumming the chords for the verse. "Does everybody know the song? 'Cause the right chords aren't coming across." He strummed the chords again, then added, "I'll go through it, man, if everybody doesn't know it."

"Play me the verse again," the bassist said. Dylan ran through the first verse again, and Danko and a couple of the other musicians played along with him. Danko stumbled again a few minutes later in the same spot, the chord change at the beginning of the next-to-last line of the first verse. Dylan stopped the music and chided, "Rick, Rick, Rick, Rick, you've got to remember," then strummed the correct chords for him. "You've got to really remember."

After a few more false starts, they finally got a complete recording of the song on the sixth slated take. After another false start, they also got a full take on the eighth try. The tenth and final take they recorded of the song that day was the keeper. In a brilliant bit of ad-libbing at the end of the song that was absent from the earlier complete takes, Dylan drew attention to the fact the song was a sequel to "Positively Fourth Street" by reprising that song's opening lines, singing, "You've got a lot of nerve, to say you are my friend," before concluding with "if you won't come out your window."

Satisfied that he finally had a version of the song suitable for release, Dylan called it a night at around 10:00 PM. Three days later, he was in California with the Hawks and Gregg to kick off a run of eleven shows in the state between December 3 and December 19, beginning with back-to-back shows at the Community Theater in Berkeley on Friday, December 3, and Saturday, December 4, the first of which was the performance Baez attended.

On the afternoon of Sunday, December 5, Dylan took Robertson along to a large gathering of Beat writers arranged by Allen Ginsberg at poet Lawrence Ferlinghetti's City Lights bookstore in the North Beach area of San Francisco, an event that would later be christened "The Last Gathering of the Beats."

At one point, Dylan, Robertson, Ginsberg, and playwright Michael McClure went into the alley next to the bookstore, an alley since named for Jack Kerouac, to pose for a series of now-famous photos taken by a pair of young photographers, Larry Keenan and Dale Smith, who had become part of the Beats' inner circle through McClure. Dylan was dressed that day in a dark jacket and pants, a black shirt with white polka dots he had purchased earlier that year on Carnaby Street in London, and dark shades.

"We had them stand against a wall," Smith recalled to the *San Francisco Chronicle* in 2006. "They just started chatting with each other casually, as anyone would among friends. Later on, Dylan got to seem like a real wired-up guy. But that day he was so relaxed, confident and self-assured. People flowed in and out of our shoot: Robbie Robertson, Ferlinghetti and Julius Orlovsky—the brother of Ginsberg's lover, who had just gotten out of a mental hospital.

"Another photographer, Jim Marshall, suddenly appeared at the end of the alley and snapped a shot," Smith continued, "but Ginsberg held up his hand and shouted, 'You can't, it's their gig.' Then Dylan said, 'Okay, that's enough.' And it was over."

Smith's girlfriend at the time, Therese Chudy, also spoke to the *Chronicle* about that day at City Lights. "I sensed that Dylan was tickled pink to hang out with the Beats at this cool spot in San Francisco," Chudy told the newspaper. "He knew and accepted that he wasn't the big cheese at this particular scene. And Ginsberg in particular really enjoyed having him there."[22]

Dylan performed at the Masonic Memorial Auditorium in San Francisco that night, then the following day he rode to Los Angeles with Ginsberg, McClure, and Peter Orlovsky in Ginsberg's Volkswagen bus. Dylan and the Hawks checked into Chateau Marmont Hotel and made it their base for the six shows they would perform in Southern California between December 7 and December 19. According to Robertson, producer Phil Spector, who was interested in working with Dylan, had a spinet piano delivered to Dylan's bungalow for him to use during his stay in L.A.[23]

On December 21, just three weeks after Dylan had recorded it, "Can You Please Crawl Out Your Window" was released as a single (backed by "Highway 61 Revisited"). Columbia ran a full-page ad in the December 25 issue of *Billboard* to promote the release, declaring it "another Bob Dylan smash."[24]

On December 28, a week after the release of the single, Dylan did a photo shoot at the Park Avenue studio of photographer Jerry Schatzberg, who had become Dylan's go-to lensman after photographing Dylan at Columbia Studio A back in the summer. "They saw the photographs from the shoot at the recording studio, and they liked them, and I took the opportunity to ask them if he would come to the studio after that," Schatzberg recalls. "Because, you know, in his domain of the recording studio, he pretty much has his way, and I felt I'd like to have a little more control over the sitting. But they liked the shoot, and our arrangement was that they could use whatever they want, and I could use whatever I want. So they did come to the studio, and we got some spectacular things in the studio."[25]

At the shoot on December 28, Dylan played "Can You Please Crawl Out Your Window" for everyone who was there, including singer-songwriters David Blue and Phil Ochs. As Ochs recalled to Anthony Scaduto, before playing it, Dylan told them, "This is the one I've been trying to do for years, this is the record that's really got it."

When the record ended, Dylan said, "What do you think?" Blue loved it; Ochs not so much. "It's okay," he said.

"What do you mean," Dylan roared. "Listen to it again." After playing it again, he said to Ochs, "Well, what do you think?"

"It's okay," Ochs said, "but it's not going to be a hit."

"What do you mean, it's not going to be a hit?" Dylan challenged. "You're crazy, man, it's a great song. You only know protest, that's all."[26]

Recalling the confrontation, Schatzberg says, "In front of everybody, Phil was just as honest as he always [was], and Dylan didn't take too kindly to it."[27]

Later that evening, Ochs and Blue were riding with Dylan in his limo to a nightspot—possibly Ondine, the jet-set discotheque Schatzberg co-owned. On the way to the club, Dylan was still stewing over Ochs's comments. They hadn't traveled far before Dylan told the limo driver to pull over and ordered Ochs out of the vehicle, telling him as he got out, "Phil, you're not a writer, you're just a journalist."

Although that moment has achieved mythological status with his fans, it was not the first time Dylan had hurled such a taunt at Ochs, and it probably didn't even carry much sting. After all, Ochs had billed himself as "The Singing Journalist," so he likely didn't consider it much of an insult. But whether writer or journalist, Ochs's prognostication regarding the hit potential of "Can You Please Crawl Out Your Window" was spot on. While it did reach number seventeen on the UK singles chart, in the United States, it failed to make the *Billboard* Top 40, peaking at number fifty-eight on the Hot 100 chart dated January 29, 1966.

4

"IT WAS THE BAND"

Dylan returned to the studio on January 21, 1966, with the four members of the Hawks, but instead of Bobby Gregg, Sandy Konikoff, a friend of the Hawks' from Canada, was on drums. Konikoff was taking over for Gregg on the tour, and, like the members of the Hawks, he was an alumnus of Ronnie Hawkins's band. As Robbie Robertson recalled in his memoir, Konikoff had gotten deep into jazz, so the guitarist gave him some friendly advice at the beginning of the session: "Rule number one, don't swing. Never swing. Flighty fills and jazzy grooves don't work here."[1]

They spent twelve hours in the studio that Friday, working the entire time on "She's Your Lover Now," the first of three new songs Dylan would record over the next six days, all seemingly inspired, at least in part, by Edie Sedgwick. Sedgwick was one of the original It girls, an heiress and debutante who came to fame in the mid-'60s as an actress who starred in several of Andy Warhol's short films.

Lyrically, the song is about a love triangle that would seem to be inspired by the real-life situation between Dylan, Sedgwick, and Bob Neuwirth. Although he has never publicly acknowledged it, Dylan had been romantically linked to Sedgwick prior to his marriage to Sara Lownds on November 22. According to various published accounts, the news of his nuptials hit Sedgwick hard, but she quickly rebounded into the arms of his friend Neuwirth.

Through that lens, it's tempting to read the lyrics of "She's Your Lover Now" as a recounting of some crazed confrontation involving Dylan and Sedgwick at which Neuwirth was present, with the verses directed to her, and the choruses mostly aimed dismissively at him, as in the third chorus: "An' you, just what do you do anyway?" In the first chorus, Dylan refers to "her iron chain," a possible reference to Sedgwick's now well-documented issues with drug and alcohol abuse. The final line of the chorus alternates each time it's sung—"She's your lover now" on the first and third choruses, "You're her lover now" on the second and fourth—but the message remains the same: She's your problem now.

Whether "She's Your Lover Now" was inspired by Sedgwick and Neuwirth or not, when Dylan embarked on his 1966 world tour a few weeks later, Neuwirth was conspicuously absent, despite having served as his road manager/right-hand man for the past year.

Dylan and the musicians spent twelve hours working on "She's Your Lover Now" that afternoon and evening. Musically, the song has a dynamic, majestic quality to it, not unlike "Visions of Johanna." But while drummer Bobby Gregg struggled to find the right approach on "Johanna," Konikoff had a good feel from the beginning on "She's Your Lover Now," even though Dylan experimented with varying tempos over the sixteen tracks slated that day.

Prior to the first take, Johnston asked Dylan from the control room, "What do you want to call this for now?"

"This is called," Dylan started, but before he could continue, Robertson jokingly offered, "You Can Have Her." Dylan laughed, and said, "Yes, that's good," then laughed again. To Johnston, he said, "We'll call it 'Just a Little Glass of Water.'"

"Take one, we're rolling," the producer said.

Dylan, who started out the session on guitar, ran down the song with the musicians at a fairly brisk tempo, and from there, he tried increasingly slower tempos over the next eight takes and tinkered with the arrangement, clearly searching for the best approach to capture the song's inherent dynamics.

When the third take broke down about forty seconds into the song, at the beginning of the tenth line of the verse, Dylan told the band, "When we get to that part, everybody break, and just me and Garth [Hudson] will do that." He sang the beginning of the line, "Now you stand here . . .," then added, "Just voice and Garth."

They tried that approach on the next two takes, but when they got to that line in the first verse on take six, only part of the band—guitarist Robertson and pianist Manuel—laid out, with bassist Danko and Konikoff joining Hudson in a sparse accompaniment behind Dylan's vocal.

In many respects, take six was the best take of the song they would record that day, featuring some standout guitar work by Robertson before breaking down in the fourth verse when Dylan fumbled a line.

Dylan switched to an upright piano on the seventh take, while Richard Manuel remained on the studio's grand piano. About a minute into the ninth take, the music broke down again and Dylan said, "It's not right, it's not right." He decided to try a faster tempo on take ten—even faster than take one. When that take broke down, they tried some slightly slower tempos on the eleventh. At one point during that take, Johnston said over the talkback mic, "Bob, you wanna try it once like you had it out there with that double beat?"

"I don't know, yeah, OK," Dylan said, then told Konikoff, "Play the beat. The double beat."

"With the four-four drum," added Johnston, singing and tapping out the beat on the console.

With Konikoff playing double time, they resumed take eleven, which was still rolling, but the music quickly broke down again. With frustration straining his voice, Dylan said, "Somebody's not, it's not together, man. Just play it together, just make it all together. You don't have to play anything fancy or nothing, just together, OK. Let's just get one together." Then he asked, "Do you need earphones to hear it?"

A couple of the musicians said no before Robertson expressed the frustration the musicians also were feeling. "Hey, man," he said, "it's not our fault. It's not untogether, man. It's just different every time, you know."

Dylan ignored Robertson's comment and asked again, "Do you need earphones?"

Take twelve was slightly faster and had more swing to it but broke down in the second verse; then on the thirteenth take, he returned to a faster tempo and stuck with it through the next two takes. At the end of take thirteen, Dylan expressed some frustration with Manuel, who had been having trouble with one of the chord changes. Take fourteen broke down in the second verse, but the fifteenth take was another nearly complete take, breaking down in the fourth verse. This is the take that would be released in 1991 on *The Bootleg Series Volumes 1–3 (Rare & Unreleased) 1961–1991.*

Still not satisfied, Dylan switched back to electric guitar, and they rehearsed the song some more at a slower tempo. It wasn't long before Dylan's frustration spilled out again. "Aw, it's ugly," he said, with pain in his voice. "I can't, I can't even," he added, before angrily striking a chord on his guitar. "It's not that way at all."

They resumed playing, but the music quickly broke down again, prompting Dylan to give further direction to Manuel. "Just do that, Richard, please do that, please," he said of a certain lick. "Just do that, just, just—"

Manuel interrupted him. "I know, but sometimes you're doing a long break."

They ran through the song some more, but Dylan soon stopped the music and said, "I can't, I can't do this." From the control room, engineer Roy Halee said, "Why don't you take a break."

When they restarted, they barely made it through the first verse and chorus before Dylan stopped and said, "I can't hear the song anymore."

It was two in the morning, and Dylan realized whatever spark they had earlier was not to be rekindled, so he told the musicians to call it a night. Then he let Johnston know he wanted to take one final pass at the song, just him, piano and vocal.

Once tape was rolling, the producer said, "Last take, anytime."

"OK," Dylan responded. "It's not going to be exactly really right."

He arranged his lyric sheets on the piano, then haltingly played the opening chords of what was slated in the control room as take sixteen. He began the take with a long, rambling intro during which, even solo, he was still searching for the song's elusive groove. He finally found it about a minute in, at which time he launched into the first verse. Seven and a half minutes later, he had made it through all four verses and choruses; after twelve hours, it was the first complete take of the day. "Huh," he said to himself, as if surprised he actually made it all the way through the song. Then to the control room, he said hopefully, "Did you get that down?" They had.

––––––––––––

Disenchanted with trying to record with the Hawks as a unit, when Dylan returned to the studio four days later on January 25, only Robertson and Danko were in attendance. Bobby Gregg was back on drums, and Paul Griffin was on keys. In addition to working with Dylan on his two previous albums, Griffin had played on a number of pop and R&B hits, including the Shirelles' number-one smash "Will You Still Love Me Tomorrow" and the Isley Brothers' first big hit, "Twist and Shout."

The session got underway that Tuesday at 2:30 in the afternoon, and the first song they tackled was a new one called "Leopard-Skin Pill-Box Hat." According to German vocalist and Warhol protege Nico, "Bob's song 'Leopard-Skin Pill-Box Hat' is written about Edie. Everybody thought it was about Edie because she sometimes wore leopard." Nico went on to call it "a very nasty song."[2]

By Dylan's standards, the song was actually fairly mild. It's a hilarious, satirical commentary on the folly of fashion and its accompanying lifestyle—and an ex-lover enslaved by it. In addition to the ex-lover, the song's cast includes a doctor and her new boyfriend, and like "She's Your Lover Now," it's easy to read the lyrics as being about Sedgwick and Neuwirth.

Three years later, however, when Rolling Stone editor Jann Wenner asked what the song was about, Dylan told him, "I think that's something I mighta taken out of a newspaper. Mighta seen a picture of one in a department store window. There's really no more to it than that."[3]

Legendary critic Robert Christgau said that on Blonde on Blonde, Dylan "represents himself as being part of the pop demimonde," and that "Leopard-Skin Pill-Box Hat" was "a perfect example" of that. "That is really a song about being among fashionable people—and that was new," Christgau explained in the 2012 documentary *Bob Dylan and The Band: Down in the Flood*. "And there's a lot of that on that record. He was no longer in your world—and that was made clear again and again and again on *Blonde on Blonde*."[4]

Both musically and lyrically, the song's structure was largely derived from Lightnin' Hopkins's "Automobile Blues," which appeared on the album *Lightnin'*—released in 1961 on the Bluesville label, a subsidiary of Prestige Records. Hopkins originally recorded the song in 1949 as simply "Automobile" for the Gold Star label. That version, which was reissued first on Jax Records and then later on the Arhoolie label, had dramatically different lyrics after the opening verse.[5] The version for Bluesville is the one Dylan used as a jumping-off point, and on that recording, Hopkins sang the first verse as:

> I saw you riding 'round in your brand-new automobile
> Yes, I saw you ridin' around, babe, in your brand-new auto-
> mobile
> Yes, you was sitting there happy with your handsome driver
> at the wheel
> In your brand-new automobile[6]

When compared to the first verse of "Leopard-Skin Pill-Box Hat" as Dylan sang it that day on take one, the connection to Hopkins's composition is obvious:

> Well, I see you got your brand-new leopard-skin pill-box hat
> Yes, I see you got your brand-new leopard-skin pill-box hat
> Tell me now, baby, how's your head feel under that
> Under your brand-new leopard-skin pill-box hat

Dylan also drew on the second verse of "Automobile Blues" for the second verse. While Hopkins called the woman's car pretty and wondered if he might drive it sometime, Dylan called the former girlfriend's hat pretty, then detoured into the absurd, asking not if he could wear it, but rather if he could "jump on it sometime?"

Whereas the Bluesville version of "Automobile Blues" had four verses, Dylan had seven verses on the first take of "Leopard-Skin Pill-Box Hat," although he would ultimately discard the last two. On the sixth verse, he sang:

> Well, I don't drink whiskey, no, I don't drink gin
> But I'm so dirty, honey, I've been working all day in the
> coal bin
> Right now I wanna see you, honey, will you let me in
> Your brand-new leopard-skin pill-box hat

The seventh verse would seem to owe a debt to "Me and My Chauffeur Blues" by Memphis Minnie, on which she sang:

> Won't you be my chauffeur, won't you be my chauffeur
> I wants him to drive me, I wants him to drive me downtown

On the final verse of take one, Dylan offered to do the driving:

> Well, can I be your chauffeur, honey, can I be your chauffeur
> Well, you can ride with me, honey, I'll be your chauffeur
> Just as long as you stay in the car, if you get outside to walk
> You just might topple over in your brand-new leopard-skin
> pill-box hat

Musically, they approached the song on take one as a straight-up twelve-bar blues, with Dylan on electric guitar and harmonica. Griffin was on Hammond B3 and his playing on the take was stellar. Robertson also stood out on the take, handling all the soloing, while Dylan laid down a sassy, churning rhythm. And unlike his last session with Dylan, Gregg had no problem locating the groove—he was in sync with Danko from the first note, and together they gave the take a fat bottom.

A slightly faster take two had a little more swing to it and was highlighted by Griffin's swirling, strutting B3 work and the twin guitars of
Robertson and Dylan.

Dylan tried a completely different third verse on the second pass.
On take one, he sang:

> Well, if you wanna see the sun, honey, I know where
> Well, if you wanna see the sun, we'll just sit there and stare
> Me with my belt wrapped around my head
> And you sittin' there in your brand-new leopard-skin pill-
> box hat

Whereas on take two, the third verse went as follows:

> Well, you don't feel no trouble, no, you don't feel no pain
> Well, you don't feel no trouble, you ain't scared when it
> starts to rain
> Well, you look pretty good riding a camel, honey, but how
> you ever gonna hop a train
> In your brand-new leopard-skin pill-box hat[7]

There were other lyrical variations on the second take. At the beginning of the fifth verse on take one, Dylan sang, "Well, I see you got a new
boyfriend, well, I don't want to see him no more." Then on take two, he
changed it to: "Well, I see you got a new boyfriend, no, I never seen him
before." In the same verse, "You think he loves you for your *money*" on
take one becomes "You think he loves you for your *body*" on take two.

Dylan clearly was still tweaking the lyrics, so despite recording two
promising takes, he chose to move on to another song.

Before they started working on the next song, Al Kooper stopped by
the studio. "I just came to visit that night," he recalls. "I wasn't hired on
the session. . . . I just came to visit and ended up playing."[8]

The lyrics for the song Dylan wanted to record next also were unfin-
ished. The song would become "One of Us Must Know (Sooner or Later)"
over the course of the evening, but it initially was slated that night as

"Song Unknown" because he had not yet decided what to call it; not surprising when you consider he had yet to settle on the chorus.[9]

On "One of Us Must Know," Dylan continued with the lyrical theme he had explored on "She's Your Lover Now" and "Leopard-Skin Pill-Box Hat"—the aftermath of a breakup. Taken together, the three songs would seem to trace an emotional arc from unwelcome confrontation to mocking dismissiveness followed by hedged apology.

The engineers would log twenty-four takes of "One of Us Must Know (Sooner or Later)" that afternoon and evening, the first fourteen being rehearsal takes during which Dylan worked out the arrangement and tempo with the musicians. While he and the players were ironing out the musical wrinkles, he also was working on the apology. That was something new for Dylan—"One of Us Must Know (Sooner or Later)" apparently was the first time he offered anything close to an apology in one of his songs. On "Ballad in Plain D" from *Another Side of Bob Dylan*, he pointedly sang, "The words to say I'm sorry, I haven't found yet." It took him two more years to do so, and when he did, it was on a song with a more mature perspective on personal relationships than anything he had previously recorded.

He already had the song's three verses—each a pair of quatrains—more or less mapped out, but he was just getting started on the chorus and didn't even have a clear idea what the hook would be.

With Kooper taking over on organ, Griffin moved to the studio's grand piano and played a few chordal flourishes with a beautifully light touch, foreshadowing what was to come.

Dylan asked Kooper, "How's the chorus?"

"And the chorus is the lines?" Kooper replied.

"Yeah, yeah, the four lines," Dylan said.

Griffin played the chords to the chorus on the grand piano, then Dylan played the chords himself on the upright piano. Danko fell in with him for half a minute or so, then Dylan said, "OK, we'll just play it, and we'll go as far as we can on it."

From the control room, Johnston said, "OK, you're rolling anytime, Bob."

Dylan played a few measures and the band joined him, but around thirty seconds in, he stopped the music and said, "That's not right, Al. I don't get it."

"We're playing three-quarter notes," Kooper explained.

"Well, how do we play—what's the tempo?" Dylan asked.

Kooper hummed the tempo, and the other musicians came in on their instruments, playing a few measures, at which point Dylan said, "Oh, OK," and jumped in himself. The take broke down in the middle of the first verse when he flubbed a line. "No, no, I'm sorry," he said. Accompanying himself on piano, Dylan picked up where the song broke down but abruptly stopped and asked Kooper, "Are you sure that we played it at that tempo?"

"It may have been a drop slower, but that was the groove we were in," Kooper told him.

Dylan said, "Oh, yeah, that was too fast."

Johnston interrupted from the control room, "Rolling on two," after which Dylan added, "That's just too fast."

They started again at a slower tempo, and Dylan took it from the top of the first verse. When they got to the chorus, he sang four lines with no resemblance to what the final lyric would be, concluding with a variation on the song's opening line:

> Now you're glad it's through
> And aren't feeling so mad
> Now I think you tried
> But I didn't mean to hurt you so bad

Knowing he didn't have the chorus together, Dylan was unable to contain a laugh while singing the final line. The music broke down a few bars after that, and Dylan said wearily, "Ah, hey, I'm ready to go home." But he quickly gathered himself and said, "Uh, that's one."

Before the third take, Dylan left the upright piano and strapped on his Fender Stratocaster for the remainder of the session. On take three, they tried a bluesier arrangement, but they went back to the original approach on take four. On that take, Dylan picked up with the second verse and when they got to the chorus, he still had nothing definite, singing four more lines he would ultimately discard. When he got to the chorus on the fifth take, he was zeroing in on the hook line—"Ah, yes, sooner or later, one of us will know"—but he was still figuring out the rest of the refrain. By take eight, the entire chorus was taking shape:

> Sooner or later, one of us will know
> That you just did what you had to do
> Sooner or later one of us will show
> That I really wasn't that bad to you

On take nine, when he got to the first chorus, he had made a small but important change to the chorus, substituting "must" for "will" in the hook line:

> Sooner or later, one of us must know
> That you only did what you had to do
> Sooner or later, one of us must show
> That I really wasn't so bad to you

Dylan blew a little harmonica at the end of the chorus, then he stopped the music and said, "I don't think that's the right way, do you think so? I think we ought to do it quieter—it's kind of loud. And raise it."

On the next take, they took it again from the top in a higher key and at a more relaxed pace. When Dylan sang the first line, he had softened the apology, substituting the word "treat" for "hurt" to make it, "I didn't mean to *treat* you so bad." He stopped the music again after his voice cracked reaching for a note near the beginning of the second line. "God, that's too high," he said. "Put it in G. Oh, my Christ! Hah!" He began retuning his guitar, then continued, "Nobody sings these songs in A. Know any people who sing in A?"

Temporarily satisfied with the key, Dylan said to Johnston in the control room, "Why don't you record this."

"I'm gettin' it all," the producer told him. Johnson didn't want to miss anything Dylan might do or say, so he usually had tape rolling continuously.

When they resumed, Dylan took it from the top but quickly realized the key was still too high and stopped the music. "No, that's no good," he said. "I'm sorry. Lower than G." They finally settled on F.

The next take, slated as the fifteenth, was the first time they even attempted to get a complete take. The first verse was almost finished, but he was still searching for the second line, trying "You were just going for a fall" on that take. He made another small but significant refinement to the verse: he changed the pronoun in the next-to-last line, making it "you'd be back in a little while," rather than "he'd be back in a little while"—which not only was a better fit with the final line, but also obscured the gender of the "friend" mentioned in the fifth line.

When he got to the chorus, he had the hook line set, but was still tweaking the second and fourth lines.

> Ah, sooner or later, one of us must know
> That you just did what you had to do
> Sooner or later, one of us must know
> That I really didn't play so cruel to you

After the first verse and chorus, Dylan told the band, "I'm gonna sing the whole song." When they got to the second chorus, he tried a slight variation on the second line and a different fourth line:

> Sooner or later, one of us must know
> That you only did what you had to do
> Sooner or later, one of us must know
> That I really wasn't so bad to you

When they got to the third chorus, Dylan made another slight but significant refinement, changing the second line from what she "had" to do to what she was "supposed" to do. He also made an important change to the last line of the chorus, getting off the negative ("wasn't") and on to the positive ("was").

> Ah, but sooner or later, one of us must know
> That you only did what you were supposed to do
> And sooner or later, one of us must know
> That I really was so close to you

After false starts on the next two takes, Johnston asked from the control room, "Bob, can you bring it in on harmonica on the intro? Have that riff going, but play it with your harmonica?"

"Oh, yeah, OK," Dylan told him.

"Rolling on eighteen," Johnston said. The musicians started playing and Dylan said to them, "OK," then launched into the harmonica intro suggested by his producer. After the third verse, he sang what would be the final set of lyrics for the chorus:

> Sooner or later, one of us must know
> That you just did what you were supposed to do
> And sooner or later, one of us must know
> That I really did try to get close to you[10]

The seemingly minor changes Dylan made to the chorus during the two three-hour sessions they logged on the song that night, especially the changes he made to the final line of the chorus, were actually quite consequential, shifting the mood of the song in a subtle way from its original apologetic tone to more of an explanatory one, letting the guy off the hook for the hurt the woman felt—and maybe letting himself off the hook, too. He took the chorus's final line from "But I didn't mean to hurt you so bad" on take one to "That I really wasn't that bad to you" on take nine and finally to "That I really did try to get close to you."

This shift from apology to explanation also was enhanced by similar changes Dylan made to the verses over the course of the evening. For example, on take two he had the opening lines of the first verse as "I didn't mean to hurt you so bad / I didn't mean to be that, that small."

By take nine, he had begun to shift responsibility to the woman, changing the second line of the first verse to "You were just in line for a fall." By take fifteen, he again subtly eased the burden of blame on the guy and shifted more to the woman by changing "hurt" to "treat": "I didn't mean to treat you so bad / You were just going for a fall." By the final take, the shift was complete: "I didn't mean to treat you so bad / You shouldn't take it so personal."

As with a number of songs on *Blonde on Blonde*, there has been much discussion over the years as to whom "One of Us Must Know" was written about, and speculation has centered largely on Sedgwick, in part because of the song's thematic proximity to "She's Your Lover Now" and "Leopard-Skin Pill-Box Hat," a pair of songs associated with the debutante-turned-actress. But the last line of the first verse—"I didn't know you were sayin' goodbye for good"—suggested to author Andy Gill the song was about Joan Baez. In his book, *Don't Think Twice, It's All Right: Bob Dylan, The Early Years*, Gill contended the line "could refer to her final departure from the hotel room in the film *Don't Look Back*, after which the pair (Dylan and Baez) didn't speak for several years."[11] Biographer Robert Shelton, however, conjectured Dylan "may have been talking to the folk world, a lover that turned on him" in the song.[12]

After the eighteenth take, Johnston left the control room and went into the studio, where the musicians were discussing some refinements to the arrangement. Dylan said to him, "How long is it? Did you time it?"

"Yeah, it's about five minutes now," the producer told him.

"Oh," Dylan replied, somewhat surprised.

"Five forty-five," engineer Roy Halee informed Dylan from the control room.

"Let me—I'm gonna cut the harmonicas out," Dylan said, then added, "until the end."

"OK," Johnston said.

They struck up the song again, but after the second line of the verse, Dylan stopped the music after noticing something with Griffin and said to the pianist, "What?"

"How come we never play the same chord there?" the pianist asked.

"I don't know," Dylan said, and strummed the chord progression. Griffin played along on piano, and then the other musicians joined in, but Dylan soon stopped the music again.

"No, no, I don't like that bass run," he told Danko.

"Is it too low?" the bassist asked.

"No, no, that's modal," Dylan told him.

When they resumed with what was mistakenly slated as the nineteenth take (it was actually the twentieth) Dylan had a finished set of lyrics, so it became a matter of getting a keeper take, which they did four takes later. Before that take, the twenty-fourth, Johnston told them from the control room, "It's gotta be that soul feel."[13]

As he had on "Like a Rolling Stone," Gregg kicked off the keeper take of "One of Us Must Know (Sooner or Later)" with a rimshot on the snare drum, albeit one with less of a pop, which Dylan followed with his harmonica intro. The master take had many highlights: Kooper's organ figures, Robertson's ringing guitar fills, Gregg's drum rolls during the choruses. But it was Griffin's exquisite piano work that shined above all. The church is where Griffin first learned to play, and he was especially feeling the spirit on take twenty-four, but he displayed his classical training, as well. All that came together just after midnight in the early hours of January 26, resulting in a brilliant piano part on which Griffin traveled from the church to the concert hall and brought the rest of the musicians along for the ride. He kept the rhythm rolling with a bouncy, two-handed gospel approach in the verses before building to a crescendo that led into the choruses and a beautifully majestic cascade of notes punctuated by Gregg's drum rolls.

Kooper says he was "flabbergasted" by Griffin's performance during the actual recording of the master take and told Andy Gill, "The piano playing on 'One of Us Must Know' is quite magnificent. . . . It's probably Paul Griffin's finest moment. He was an amazing player."[14]

Immediately after the session, Dylan, along with Kooper and a couple of the other musicians, went to the studio of WBAI, a listener-supported

FM radio station in New York City housed in a converted church on East Sixty-Second Street near the Queensboro Bridge. He stopped by the studio for an appearance on *Radio Unnameable*, an all-night show hosted by Bob Fass, legendary pioneer of free-form radio.[15] Dylan, who had appeared on the overnight show many times, arrived around 1:30 and took calls from thirty-eight listeners over a two-hour stretch.

Fairly early in his appearance, Dylan asked Fass to play the Lightnin' Hopkins record "Drive My Car," actually meaning "Automobile Blues," a song fresh on his mind since only twelve hours earlier he had been recording his own reworked rendition of the song. As it turned out, Fass didn't have that particular cut by Hopkins and played a different one instead.

At some point during the time he was at the station that night, most likely while the Hopkins record was spinning, Dylan played Fass a tape copy of the song they had just recorded, "One of Us Must Know (Sooner or Later)." Near the end of the appearance, Fass thanked Dylan for playing the new song for him and asked when it would be released.

"It's a rush job," Dylan told him. "We just made it. It's a single; we're into making an album, you know, and this one's the only thing we came out with in like three days. So—so, like, gonna have to forget about the album for right now.

"It's very good, the single," he continued, unable to suppress his excitement over it. "It's better than the last two, you know, and it's just as good as 'Like a Rolling Stone.'"

"One of Us Must Know (Sooner or Later)" was indeed a rush job, hitting the streets just nineteen days later on February 14. When *Rolling Stone*'s Jann Wenner asked him in 1969 about his sessions with members of the Hawks, Dylan brought up "Sooner or Later." "That's one of my favorite songs," he said.[16]

The studio was booked for the following day from 2:30 in the afternoon till 2:30 AM, but possibly because of the late hour when they finally left WBAI, the session was canceled. By the time they returned to the studio on the afternoon of Thursday, January 27, a nor'easter was already bearing down on the city, the beginning of what would come to be known as the blizzard of 1966.

Robertson and Danko were on hand that afternoon, as were Kooper and Gregg. There is some uncertainty regarding what they worked on first that snowy winter day, but Columbia's reference numbers suggest it was "Keep It with Mine," a song recorded a few months earlier by Judy Collins and released as a single on Elektra Records. Collins said she "recorded it primarily because Dylan said he had written it for me," a statement he would affirm decades later.[17] But according to Nico, Dylan wrote the song not only for her, but also about her.[18] When biographer Robert Shelton had asked Dylan a month earlier if the song referred to his wife, Sara, and their soon-to-be-born child, Bob Neuwirth corrected Shelton. "You don't know where it's at," he said. "That song was for Nico, man. Just for Nico."[19]

As rock historian Clinton Heylin delineates in his book *Revolution in the Air: The Songs of Bob Dylan, 1957–1973*, Dylan previously demoed the song in June 1964 for his publisher (Witmark Music), then recorded it again seven months later during the January 1965 *Bringing It All Back Home* sessions (slated that day as "Bank Account Blues"). Both of those versions were piano and vocal, so Dylan made his first attempt to get it down with a band that snowy afternoon.[20]

Dylan played guitar as he taught the song to the musicians, but after they found a laid-back, melancholy groove, he switched to piano and they tried recording a take of the song. Dylan sang the verses in a different order than on the two earlier recordings of the song, switching the second and third stanzas—probably a mistake, considering the official lyrics match the earlier versions. Musically, from Gregg's tasteful brush work to Kooper's melodic organ fills, the one take of the song they recorded— which would be released a quarter century later on *The Bootleg Series Volumes 1–3*—had a certain elegance to it, culminating in some beautiful interplay between Robertson, Kooper, and Dylan on the outro.

They also worked on "Lunatic Princess," a dummy title Dylan had employed previously, using it the first time he attempted to record "From a Buick 6." The song snippet given that name at the January 27 session had a a similar tempo to "From a Buick 6" and one promising couplet:

Now you lost it all, I see, and all you got is
Your two dollar bill and your hatful of gasoline

When the take ran out of steam after just over a minute, Dylan said, "I'm scared, man, I'm scared," presumably of the lunatic princess.

Dylan concluded the session by resuming work on "Leopard-Skin Pill-Box Hat." He strummed the chords on his electric guitar and sang the first line in his folk style, which drew a laugh from some of the musicians.

"'Leopard-Skin Hat' take one," Johnston said over the talk-back mic.

Dylan told Robertson, "Go ahead," and the guitarist counted off the song and played some Dixie-fried blues licks to kick off the song, but as soon as the other musicians joined in, the music broke down.

"That's good, go ahead," Dylan told him.

From the control room, Johnston quickly announced, "Take two."

Robertson counted off the song, then played the same bluesy parts to start the song, with the rest of the band jumping in on cue. The take was more reserved than the two takes they recorded on January 25. When they got to the third verse, Dylan sang the alternate set of lyrics he had tried two days earlier:

Well, I see you don't feel no trouble, I see you don't feel
no pain
Well, I see you don't feel no trouble, I see you don't feel
no pain
Yes, you look pretty good riding a camel, honey, but how
you ever gonna hop a train
In your brand-new leopard-skin pill-box hat[21]

From there, he went into what was formerly the third verse and had refined the opening phrase, changing it from "If you wanna see the sun" to "If you wanna see the sun *rise*," another apparent reference to "Automobile Blues"—Hopkins mentioned the break of dawn in the third verse.

When they got to the end of that verse, the music broke down. "No, no, no, it's not as good as it was yesterday," Dylan said. "Hey, why don't we just make a couple of verses and just dub 'em in. Can we do that, Bob?"

"Yeah," the producer replied, but the question seemed to catch him off guard.

"Let's just do this last verse," Dylan told the band.

They launched into the groove, and after a few measures Dylan picked up the song with the fourth verse. Again, he changed the third line, as he had on each of the two earlier takes, making it: "You might think he wants you for your *loving*, but you're wrong, I know what he really wants you for."

After he sang the verse, they vamped on the groove for a few extra measures, then Dylan stopped the music and said to Johnston in the control room, "Just put that in the last verse."

"The last verse?" the producer asked.

"I just messed up the words, you see."

"On the last verse?" Johnston asked again.

"Yep," Dylan told him.

"OK," Johnston said.

While it was technically possible to insert the new fourth verse into one of the takes they had recorded two days earlier, it wouldn't be a simple edit, in part because none of the takes were recorded at exactly the same tempo—this was in the days before studio drummers played to click tracks. There was also the matter of a different lineup: Neither Griffin nor Bloomfield were there that day, so the arrangement and instrumentation also were slightly different. It would take some considerable time, skill, and ingenuity on the part of the engineer to seamlessly insert the new fourth verse into an earlier take. It's unlikely Johnston considered that a realistic option for producing a master take of the song. Dylan may not have either, considering he told Bob Fass he was "gonna have to forget about the album for right now."

With the "Leopard-Skin Pill-Box Hat" insert in the can, the session came to an end, and although Dylan didn't realize it at the time, it was the last session he would have at Columbia's New York Studios for more than four years. Johnston had booked the studio for the following Monday, January 31, but that session was canceled. Due to begin the American leg of a four-month world tour in Louisville on February 4, Dylan had decided to take Johnston up on his suggestion and move the sessions for the album to Nashville during a short break in his tour mid-month, and have Kooper join him there.

Dylan knew the sound he was seeking, could hear it clearly in his head, but he also knew he hadn't found it during his sessions in New York with the Hawks. Six weeks later, when Robert Shelton joined Dylan for a leg of his tour, they talked about why the New York sessions for the album hadn't been productive. "Oh, I was really down," Dylan told him. "I mean, in like ten recording sessions, man, we didn't get one song." He continued, "It was the band. But you see, I didn't know that. I didn't want to think that."[22]

PART II

NASHVILLE

5

THE NASHVILLE CATS

ONCE DYLAN DECIDED TO GIVE Nashville a shot, Bob Johnston immediately sprang into action. He block-booked Nashville's Studio A for the open dates in Dylan's itinerary and began getting the studio ready for him. He also began lining up the musicians he wanted to use on the sessions.

Although it seems counterintuitive, Studio A was the secondary studio at Columbia's Nashville facility; Studio B was the in-demand room, the iconic Quonset Hut, ground zero for Nashville's emergence as a recording center, where numerous well-known pop, rock, country, and R&B hits had been cut, including "Jingle Bell Rock" by Bobby Helms, "You Can Make It If You Try" by Gene Allison, "The Battle of New Orleans" by Johnny Horton, "Teen Angel" by Mark Dinning, "El Paso" by Marty Robbins, "Turn On Your Lovelight" by Bobby Blue Bland, "I'm Sorry" by Brenda Lee, and "Crazy" by Patsy Cline.

When Columbia purchased the facility at 804 Sixteenth Avenue South early in 1962 from legendary producer Owen Bradley and his brother, session guitarist Harold, for a price "between $300,000 and $350,000," they not only got a great-sounding studio where their own Nashville artists could record (most of whom already did), they also got a real cash cow—a room that never lacked for bookings.[1]

The Bradley brothers had opened Nashville's second professional recording facility in 1952, renting and refurbishing a space inside the

Joel A. Battle Lodge at Second and Lindsley just south of downtown in an area known as Rutledge Hill. After only a year at the location, the owner of the building tripled their monthly rent (from twenty-five to seventy-five dollars). As Harold Bradley explained to writer Jessi Maness, they were insulted by the rate increase, so they moved their operation to a building in the Hillsboro Village area near Vanderbilt University. Two years later, with a promise from Decca Records executive Paul Cohen that he would guarantee them one hundred sessions a year, they bought the property on Sixteenth Avenue South for $7,500. That was the flagship property in an area of the city where record labels, studios, and music publishers would soon be concentrated, the world-famous Music Row, which the music trades first dubbed "Record Row."

The Bradleys put their studio in the house on the property, and not long thereafter, they purchased a surplus army Quonset hut and put it at the rear of the lot with a plan to shoot musical performances there for film and television. "We put the Quonset hut in the back, and that was going to be our film studio," Bradley said. "But then somebody wanted to record in the Quonset hut—and once they started recording in the Quonset hut, we were recording in both of those studios."[2]

Studio A, which was inside the house, was a smaller space, and it wasn't long before the Quonset hut became the preferred destination for their growing list of label clients, which included not only Decca Records, but also Columbia, Capitol, and Mercury.

After Columbia bought the property from the Bradleys, they quickly learned the downside to having an in-demand room: it often wasn't available for their own artists. So in 1964, the label announced plans for an expansion of their Nashville facility that included a new, state-of-the-art studio that would become Studio A—the old A room would be demolished in the construction.

The new studio was fifty-eight feet long and thirty-seven feet wide with a twenty-five-foot ceiling. It featured a floating parquet floor and thirty-eight movable glass-fiber sound-absorbent panels, which at the time made it "the most versatile and modern recording studio in the country," according to studio manager Harold Hitt, who made that claim in an interview with *Billboard* in advance of the grand opening of the room on October 22, 1965.[3]

"The 'floating floor' is on heavy springs with concrete and hardwood floors over it," Hitt said in the interview. "The floor will shield off outside vibrations, much in the way auto shock absorbers work. In the next year or so, there will be much interstate highway construction work in the area.

"The floor idea came from the CBS TV center in New York, and the fiberglass panel idea from Columbia's Hollywood recording studio."[4]

Like the Columbia studios in New York and Los Angeles, Nashville Studio A was equipped with a mixing console and studio monitors designed and built by Columbia's own research and development department, headed by Eric Porterfield.

Despite the glowing hype, there were problems with the studio from the start. "The first session was Ray Price, and Don Law was the producer," Hitt recalled to me. "He came up to my office and said, 'Harold, what in the hell have you done. . . . The bass drum is getting in every mic.' So basically what had happened was the floor was vibrating.

"So he took the session down to Studio B," Hitt continued, "and I got with my maintenance guy, and we took the panels up and screwed all of those springs down tight so that the floor wouldn't vibrate. And from that time forward, it was OK. Don Law came back up there and finished the album in Studio A."[5]

Studio A may have been "OK" after that, but "OK" was not what labels, producers, and artists were looking for, especially when down one flight of stairs there was a studio that had magic in its walls, where hit recordings were the norm, not the exception. For that very reason, Studio B was not available for Dylan on the days when he had a break in his tour, but Studio A could be block-booked days on end.

In the limited time he had spent at the label's Nashville facilities over the past year, Johnston had made himself unpopular with some of the staff there, a situation that was about to worsen with the arrival of Dylan. Some of the Columbia employees considered the producer self-important and demanding, taking liberties he shouldn't, making a big deal out of everything he was doing. Even so, they all knew it *was* a big deal that Dylan was coming to record in Nashville.

Uncertain whether word would leak out Dylan was in the city, Johnston arranged to have off-duty Metro Nashville police officers stationed at the back entrance to the Columbia building where the musicians entered, just in case any fans showed up and tried to get in.

In multiple interviews over the years, Johnston claimed he had the isolation booths in Studio A ripped out by studio maintenance man Ed Grizzard because Dylan wanted all the musicians to be able to look at one another while they played. He told author Michael Kosser, "We stripped it, took everything outside and had the fire department burn it."[6] But Hitt and others say that never happened. Either way, one thing is certain: the isolation booths were not used by the musicians during the *Blonde on Blonde* sessions.

––––––––––

Johnston wasn't taking Dylan into the A room cold—he had worked with Simon and Garfunkel there for two days in mid-December, sessions that yielded a pair of hit singles: "Homeward Bound" and "I Am a Rock." He wanted to use the same core of musicians who backed Simon and Garfunkel on the upcoming Dylan dates. Not surprisingly, the first person he called was Charlie McCoy, tapping him to be the session leader on all Dylan's upcoming sessions. McCoy, of course, had already worked with Dylan in New York on the master recording of "Desolation Row." Johnston admitted to me he had orchestrated McCoy's appearance on that recording to help entice Dylan to Nashville.

When Johnston first moved to Nashville in the early '60s as a writer for Hill and Range, he tried using the legendary A-team of musicians (guitarist Grady Martin, bassist Bob Moore, drummer Buddy Harman, pianist Floyd Cramer, etc.) on his demo recordings, but he found them to be less than cooperative.

"They were all wonderful musicians, and they played on so many hit records," Johnston told me. But when he asked them to play a song a certain way, "Every one of 'em declined in their nice professional way, that they knew what they were doing and everything.

"Otherwise, they were wonderful people," Johnston continued. "They had nothing against me; I had nothing against them. I'd just never run into musicians who knew what to play, and 'Well, no, I can't play that.' And I thought that was bullshit."

Johnston's wife, Joy, was friends with recording artist and session vocalist Priscilla "Prissy" Mitchell and happened to mention to her that Johnston was looking to work with some other musicians. "She told my wife about these great musicians in town—Ray Stevens, Charlie McCoy, Jerry Kennedy, Wayne Moss, and Kenny Buttrey—people like that," Johnston recalled. "So I got them in the studio and used them one time, and then [after that], I used them on all my demos."[7]

McCoy was the ringleader of a younger circle of musicians in Nashville—"the quarterback," as bassist-producer Norbert Putnam puts it.[8] Although he was only twenty-five years old, the multi-instrumentalist had made a meteoric rise in the Nashville session world, regularly getting calls to work with the legendary A-team of studio cats, most of whom were a decade or more older than him.

"Charlie McCoy was the most dangerous musician in Nashville," Putnam says, "because once he walked into the room, your job could be in jeopardy."[9]

By the time Dylan went to Nashville in 1966, McCoy was doing four hundred sessions a year—and that was on top of performing live on the weekends with his own band, Charlie McCoy and the Escorts.

McCoy had initially visited the city in the summer of 1959 after meeting rising country star Mel Tillis in Miami at the Old South Jamboree. "It was a country music dance, and they had rock and roll ten minutes an hour for the young people—and that was me," McCoy says of the Saturday night gig he and his band had when he was a senior in high school. "I met Mel Tillis [there], and he said if I'd come to Nashville, he could get me a record contract. Well, he couldn't really do that, but I was eighteen years old and gullible, and I believed it. So the day after school was out, I took off for Nashville."

When McCoy got to Music City, he learned Tillis was out on the road. Undeterred, he looked up Tillis's manager, Jim Denny. As luck would have it, Tillis had told Denny about McCoy. "He said, 'I know who you are. I'll call and set up some auditions for you,'" McCoy recalls. "He had never even heard me. He was taking Mel's word for it."

Later that same day, McCoy was doing guitar-vocal renditions of Chuck Berry's "Johnny B. Goode" for a pair of Nashville music icons:

Owen Bradley at Decca Records and Chet Atkins at RCA. They both thought he had talent, but neither Bradley nor Atkins was looking to sign the next Chuck Berry. Although Bradley didn't offer McCoy a contract, he did give the eighteen-year-old musician a life-altering experience.

"Owen invited me to a session, and I went and watched Brenda Lee record," McCoy recalls. "And the whole idea of what I wanted to do changed. At that moment, I didn't care if I ever sang another song—I wanted to be a studio musician. Because what I saw in that studio was amazing, you know—and of course, what I heard was amazing, too." The song McCoy watched Lee and the musicians record that day was her first big hit, "Sweet Nothin's."

McCoy returned to Miami and enrolled at the University of Miami that September, where he planned to get a degree in music education. "I had mainly music courses, and I liked a couple of them," he says. "And I liked one of my teachers. But to be honest, I was not all that thrilled about school."[10]

Some of his professors didn't approve of him playing rock and roll on the weekends, thought he shouldn't be involved in "lower forms of music," as he would later tell *Billboard*.[11] Plus, he couldn't get that Brenda Lee session out of his head. "What I had seen had just knocked me out," he says of his visit to Bradley's already famous Quonset hut studio a few months earlier.

The following April, McCoy got a call from Kent Westberry, a guy he knew from Florida who had moved to Nashville to be a songwriter. "He called me and said he had a job for me as a guitar player if I could come on up there," McCoy says. "That's when I made the decision to drop out of school and go to Nashville. I broke my father's heart because it was his dream for his son to go to college."

After arriving in Nashville for the job, McCoy was met with a rude surprise. "The singer, a guy named Johnny Ferguson, told Kent, 'Man, you never called me back. I've already hired somebody,'" McCoy recalls with a laugh. "So here I am, I've dropped out of school, drove all night, and I don't have a job. That was pretty devastating.

"This guy Ferguson was such a nice guy, and he felt so sorry for me, he said, 'What else can you play?' And I said, 'Well, I can play harmonica.' He said, 'I don't need harmonica—can you play drums?'

"I knew a little bit about it, and I thought, 'Say no and you're done,'" McCoy continues. "So I said, 'Yes, but I don't have any.' He said, 'We'll get you some.' So, there I was, my first job in Nashville—as a drummer!"

Ferguson cosigned a note for him to procure a drum kit from a local music store. When the group returned from the gig (two weeks at a hotel lounge in Toronto), McCoy took most of the money he earned and paid off the drums. "Then two weeks later, [Ferguson] calls up and tells everybody, 'Well, I don't have any more jobs, so I guess the band is over,'" McCoy says and laughs; then adds sarcastically, "Thanks a lot!"

It's ironic that McCoy's first job in Nashville was as a drummer because it wouldn't be long before he would be playing in a band with one of the greatest drummers in the history of popular music, a percussion wunderkind who would also get the call for the Dylan sessions— Kenneth Buttrey.

In the fall of 1960, McCoy met Buttrey when he was asked to sub for the bass player in the group Bobby Williams and His Nightlifters. The bass player, Snuffy Smith, was another person McCoy knew from Florida, and Smith recommended him for the gig. He got a call from the band's guitar player, Wayne Moss.

"Wayne called me and said, 'I'm a friend of Snuffy Smith's, and we have this band, and Snuffy is the bass player, and I wanted to see if you would sub for him,'" McCoy recalls. "I said, 'You know, I don't really play electric bass.' He said, 'But you play guitar, and it's just like the bottom four strings of a guitar.' I said, 'Well, I don't own one.' He said, 'We've got one, don't worry about it.'

"So I went over to Wayne's house—it was the first time I'd met him—and he showed me all these songs that they were doing, and I was trying to figure out what to do with the bass, you know. That's how I started playing electric bass."[12]

As it would turn out, McCoy would play with four future bandmates that first night he subbed on bass for Bobby Williams and His Nightlifters. In addition to Moss and Buttrey, he worked for the first time with keyboardist Bill Aikins and saxophonist Jimmy Miller. Aikins still remembers the night vividly; it was a gig at the Fort Campbell Airmen's Club.

"We're playing, and Charlie is playing bass—no big deal, he's just a guy," Aikins recalls. "He's not *Charlie McCoy* yet—he's just a guy. So Bobby says to him, 'Snuffy says you play harmonica. Do you play harmonica?' And he says, 'Yeah, I play harp.' 'Well, why don't you come up and do a blues tune and blow some harp.'

"When he stepped up to that mic and started playing blues harp, he picked the band up about ten notches," the keyboardist continues. "It went from being a gig to being a party, man. When he hit that harp, I'd never experienced anybody in the flesh that good."[13]

While his future bandmates were being wowed by McCoy, he was noticing Buttrey. "I'd never heard a drummer like Kenny, you know," he says. "I was just blown away—he was about sixteen or something, at the time. I'd never really heard anybody play R&B like that."[14]

Like McCoy, Aikins will always remember when he saw Buttrey play for the first time. It was before he joined the Nightlifters, when he was working with a group called the Skipper Hunt Combo. "One night, Skipper and I went out to a place called the King of Clubs in Bordeaux, and Bobby Williams and [His] Nightlifters were playing," the keyboardist recalls. "You couldn't go out into the crowd—I was under age. You could walk on a little pathway through the kitchen and get to the back of the bandstand. You could stand behind [the band] and watch them perform, almost like you were backstage.

"Kenneth Buttrey was playing drums," he continues. "I'm standing there, and the drummer's always at the back, so I'm really focusing more on the drummer. When I heard him play, my jaw hit the floor. I could not believe how good this kid was. Instant recognition of a talent. Boom! It was just in your face. It was like meeting Van Gogh or something. You just go, 'Oh, wow! This guy's special.'

"He had the nicest feel, the best shuffle I probably ever heard—and he was just a kid. I can remember saying to myself, 'I don't know when, and I don't know how, but that's who I want to play with.' Kenneth was the best drummer in Nashville, man. There was no one better." Not long thereafter, Aikins became the keyboard player for the Nightlifters.[15]

Sax man Miller also saw Buttrey for the first time at the King of Clubs, a two-story roadhouse just outside the Nashville city limits on the

Clarksville Highway that had live music and dancing downstairs, illegal gambling upstairs, and illegal booze on both floors—liquor by the drink was not allowed in Davidson County in those days. "He was a red-hot drummer, even at that age," Miller says of Buttrey, who was only fourteen and had to have a letter of permission from the sheriff's office to legally perform at the joint. "Anyone who ever worked with Kenneth Buttrey will tell you that he's the best they ever worked with. He just made you want to play. He could bring out the best in you. Everything just felt so good when he was on drums."[16]

A Nashville native, Buttrey started working professionally at age eleven, and by the age of thirteen he was touring with guitar legend Chet Atkins. He grew up in a poor neighborhood north of downtown, not far from the historic strip of R&B clubs on Jefferson Street. As a kid, he could hear the hot drummers over on the strip night and day—some of those clubs never closed—and he would play along with them, hitting sticks on cans. So he grew up loving black music and was an R&B drummer at heart.

"He was very heavy into tempo," songwriter and guitarist Mac Gayden says of Buttrey. "Kenny was adamant about tempo and the groove. To him, keeping good tempo was like making love to a woman."[17]

Buttrey's timing was impeccable. "You cut from the intro to the end of the song and it would be the same tempo," says producer Elliot Mazer, who worked with Buttrey on a number of records. "I never met another musician who could do that."

Buttrey didn't tolerate any sloppiness when it came to tempo. "If someone wasn't with him, he would give them hell," Mazer says.[18]

Gayden got a taste of that the first time he ever worked with the drummer in 1962. "He let me know right away that if I didn't stay with him, he and I would be having problems," the guitarist recalls with a laugh.[19]

On sessions, Buttrey wanted a copy of the lyrics of the songs they were recording. "Kenny didn't play parts, he played the song," Mazer explains.[20]

By the time he worked with Dylan on the *Blonde on Blonde* sessions, Buttrey had garnered studio credits with the likes of Elvis Presley, Simon and Garfunkel, and Arthur Alexander.

After that first gig with the Nightlifters, McCoy subbed for Smith "five or six times," as he remembers it. "I was enjoying it because all I was doing was hanging out at Jim Denny's office, and I was playing on some demos," he says. "But I was twenty years old, and I was still into rock and roll and Top 40, what's on the radio, and these guys were playing it. So it was fun for me to go and play that kind of music."

That same year, McCoy cowrote a fateful song called "Cherry Berry Wine" with Westberry and Gil Metters for Denny's historic publishing company Cedarwood Music. Metters had shared the original idea with McCoy back in Miami, and he and Westberry finished it in Nashville. Westberry, who was a Cedarwood writer at the time, had always sung lead on his demos, but "Cherry Berry Wine" was a bluesy rocker, which was a little outside his comfort zone. "He said, 'You need to sing this demo, this isn't my style at all,'" McCoy recalls. "So I went in and sang the demo."

In October, McCoy received some surprising news. "Jim Denny called me and he said, 'I played this song for Archie Bleyer of Cadence Records, and he wants to record you,'" McCoy remembers with a laugh. "So there I was singing again, you know, it was the furthest thing from my mind. But I said, 'Hey, why not. I'll do it.'"

In January 1961, Cadence, which was home to all the Everly Brothers big hits, released "Cherry Berry Wine" as a single backed by the blues shuffle "My Little Woman." "Cherry Berry Wine," which featured haunting guitar by Harold Bradley and a calypso-inspired beat, was favorably reviewed by *Billboard* and hit the magazine's Hot 100 in late February, reaching number ninety-nine.

Around that same time, the Nightlifters found out Williams had been shorting them on the earnings from their gigs, so they decided to go out on their own. Initially, they were fronted by a woman named Pat Campbell and billed as Pat Campbell and Her Escorts, but by late spring, the band had recruited McCoy and changed its name to Charlie McCoy and the Escorts. McCoy sang lead and played bass, harmonica, and sometimes trumpet, backed by Buttrey on drums, Moss on guitar, Miller on tenor sax, John Sturdivant on baritone sax, and Aikins on piano and occasionally trumpet, joining with the sax players and McCoy to create a four-piece horn section. Soon Charlie McCoy and the Escorts were the most popular band in the area, in demand for club gigs at Fort Campbell, frat parties at Vanderbilt University, and club residencies in Printers Alley. After hearing them perform, Bleyer had the Escorts accompany McCoy on his second single for Cadence, a pair of covers: "I Just Want to Make Love to You" backed by "Rooster Blues."

In June 1961, McCoy landed his first two master recording sessions as a sideman. "Kent [Westberry] was writing a lot and he would let me sit in on his writing sessions," he explains. "I would get my harmonica out and play along while he was singing his songs. So he did this song called 'I Just Don't Understand' that he and Marijohn Wilkin wrote together, and I was playing along with it, and he said, 'Boy, I'm going to ask Denny if you can play on the demo of this song.'"

So McCoy played some signature, mournful harp on the demo recording, and not long after that, he got a call from Denny. "Chet [Atkins] just called," the publisher said, "and he's recording a new girl singer from Sweden named Ann-Margret, and he wants you to play exactly what you played on the demo."

The week after he played on his first record, McCoy played on his second. After Bob Moore, the bassist on "I Just Don't Understand," heard McCoy blow, he had booked him to play harmonica a few days later on a session that yielded Roy Orbison's "Candy Man." Not a bad start to his career as a studio cat: two sessions, two Top 40 hits, both powered by his harmonica work.[21]

After playing on those two hit records, McCoy started to get a lot of calls for sessions. Jerry Kennedy, who by the time Dylan came to town had risen from top session guitarist to label executive and producer, says, "There were a lot of years that Charlie McCoy was called for every session I produced. Not knowing whether I would need him or not, but I wanted him there."[22]

"I got called a lot that way—just show up with all your stuff," McCoy says. "Of course, back then, there were fewer guys working, and I was *the* utility man, which was a great asset for me. They knew I could play vibes, they knew I could grab another guitar if they needed it. I even played organ on some pretty big hit records, you know."[23]

Whenever possible, McCoy recommended his bandmates for sessions, mostly Buttrey, Moss, and Aikins—producers weren't using a lot of horns in Nashville at that time.

Like Buttrey, guitarist Moss had "red hot" chops. At the age of fifteen, he had traveled with his mother from his home in Charleston, West Virginia, to audition for Chet Atkins in Nashville. After the audition, Moss's mother said to the RCA A&R executive, "Isn't he amazing?" Atkins told her, "No, he's average." Undeterred, she asked if he had a future in music. The A&R man told her, "Lady, I don't know, he looks like he'd make a good plumber."

Looking back on that experience, Moss recalled what a motivational speaker he heard once had noted. "He said, 'You're either going to spend your life trying to prove somebody right or prove somebody wrong.' I was doing both. I was trying to prove my mother right and Chet wrong."[24]

By the end of the 1950s, Moss had moved to Nashville and become the lead guitarist in the city's first rock and roll band, the Casuals, a group that would go on to back Brenda Lee under the name the Casual Teens. He had already left that group when he was invited to play with the Nightlifters. By 1966, he had become a protege of Atkins as well as a session player, contributing prominent guitar parts to a pair of number-one hits recorded in the city—Tommy Roe's "Sheila" and Orbison's "Oh, Pretty Woman." Moss was comfortable moving between rock, country, and R&B, and he was best known for his precise timing and technique.

Keyboardist Aikins moved with his family from the New York City area to Nashville when he was fifteen. Aikins, whose playing was influenced by Johnny Johnson (of Chuck Berry's band) and Jerry Lee Lewis, got his start professionally while still in high school, performing with the Skipper Hunt Combo, a four-piece that played blues and rock and roll. He still was working with Skipper Hunt when he began playing with the Nightlifters. Aikins had a good ear for harmony and was a strong rhythm player with good timing. "He could nail a groove," Gayden said of the man who's nickname was "Groover."[25]

Aikins got called for a lot of demo sessions, and that's how he met Johnston, but when it came to master sessions, he was third on the depth chart, stuck behind two Music City keyboard icons: Floyd Cramer and

Hargus "Pig" Robbins. Aikins, however, did get the call from Johnston to play organ on the two hits Simon and Garfunkel recorded in Nashville in December.

Early in his career as a studio musician, McCoy got a call to work a session with the legendary vocal group the Jordanaires. As they were working up the song to record, he noticed that Jordanaires lead singer Neal Matthews Jr. used a musical shorthand to quickly write out the vocal parts. McCoy immediately realized Matthews's shorthand could be adapted to chords, and in that epiphanic moment, the now world-famous Nashville Number System was born.

Because Nashville session musicians rarely played to charts, McCoy started using the numerical shorthand to quickly sketch out a song's arrangement. "When I first came here, most of the music that was being done was relatively simple," McCoy explains. "Very logical, you know, straight-ahead country music. And it was easy to memorize that stuff. And that's the way the A-team did it; they memorized it right off the shoot, you know. But then, as the music got more complicated, we found the number system could make things better—and a whole lot more logical. So, as time passed, then the numbers became much more important because of the complexity of the music."

McCoy told Moss about his discovery, and the guitarist wanted to learn to use the number system, too. From there, it spread organically to other Nashville musicians. "Wayne asked me if I could explain it to him," McCoy recalls. "So he and I started talking about it, and on sessions, he would try to write the number chart. He'd say, 'Hey, come over and look at this, and see if it is right.'"

One day at a recording date, session leader Harold Bradley saw McCoy and Moss talking—McCoy was checking to see if Moss had numbered the chord progression correctly. "I walked over there and said, 'Hey, what's going on?'" Bradley recalls. "One of them said, 'We're writing some numbers.' They were not writing it in Roman numerals, like the Jordanaires did—they used regular numerals."[26]

McCoy credits Bradley with helping spread the number system to the city's other session cats. "All of a sudden, I was becoming leader on a lot of sessions," Bradley explains, "and when I saw what they were doing,

I saw it was saving us about fifteen minutes on each [song]. So I saw it would be a great way to save time."[27]

Soon everyone in the Escorts was using the number system, and by the time Dylan came to town in 1966, its use was fairly ubiquitous on Nashville recording sessions.

Whenever McCoy was the session leader, he liked to work with two different sets of musicians in the studio, and Johnston asked him to line up the men in both groups for the Dylan dates. One of the studio groups McCoy worked with featured members of the Escorts. He would play bass, Buttrey would be on drums, Moss would play guitar, and Aikins would be on either piano or organ.

The other group McCoy liked to use on sessions included Buttrey and Moss, along with pianist Hargus "Pig" Robbins and bassist Henry Strzelecki, with McCoy on either harmonica or rhythm guitar, or one of the other instruments he could play, such as trumpet, vibes, or organ.

To Jerry Kennedy, Robbins was "one of the best, if not *the* best, musician" in the city.[28] A native of Spring City, Tennessee, who was blinded in a knife accident at the age of three, Robbins entered the Tennessee School for the Blind in Nashville at the age of seven and studied classical piano. He also became acquainted with pop and jazz piano styles through recordings by Floyd Cramer, Ray Charles, Papa John Gordy, and Owen Bradley. Although he began playing sessions in 1957, Robbins's career as a studio player took off in 1959 after he contributed the lively piano parts to George Jones's number-one country hit "White Lightning." When Cramer's career as a solo recording artist flourished after his instrumental "Last Date" went to number two on the *Billboard* pop singles chart in 1960, Robbins slid into his spot as first-call keyboardist with the city's acclaimed A-team of session musicians. "He learns a song quicker than anybody I've ever known—complicated stuff, too," McCoy says of Robbins. "It was incredible to me, the way he could organize that stuff in his head."[29] By 1963, Robbins had become a recording artist in his own right, but did not duplicate the pop success Cramer had.

Robbins met Johnston through McCoy and got the call to work on a number of the producer's demo recordings for Hill and Range. He also worked with him on Patti Page's *Hush, Hush, Sweet Charlotte* sessions in Nashville. Robbins remembers Johnston as being unconventional. "He was different from the other [producers] I was used to," the pianist says. "Just his ideas and way of going about things, you know. I didn't know what to think about it. Hell, I was just going along for the ride to see where it would take me."[30]

Bassist Strzelecki moved to Nashville in 1960 from his hometown of Birmingham, Alabama, to play bass with celebrated guitarist Hank Garland's jazz outfit, replacing local legend W. O. Smith. Garland had a residency in Printers Alley at the Carousel Club and invited Strzelecki to come to Nashville and sit in with him. The bassist said about receiving that invitation: "I thought, 'Man, he is the best guitar player I have ever heard in my life, I'm coming up [there].' I came up and sat in with his band, and he said, 'I'm thinking you move up here.' And I said, 'How 'bout next week?'" Strzelecki recalled to me with a laugh.

In September of the following year, Garland was involved in an automobile accident that cut short a promising career as a jazz recording artist. After that, Strzelecki joined Chet Atkins's touring band and began to get calls for session work, most notably working sessions with Atkins, Presley, Orbison, and Bobby Bare.

Like most of the other session cats who got the call for the upcoming dates with Dylan, Strzelecki had worked on Johnston's demo sessions for Hill and Range. "I think Bob is a great producer," he said. "And I'll tell you why. . . . He didn't get in the way of anything. A lot of producers get in the way. Bob Johnston didn't do that. He let us do what we could do, which was the best thing a producer can do for a record, I think."[31]

Guitarist Mac Gayden was another musician who worked on Johnston's demos. By the beginning of 1963, Moss had left the Escorts because he had become too busy with studio work. He was replaced by Gayden, who, according to Aikins, gave the group a "funkier" sound. Like Buttrey, Gayden was a Nashville native and into R&B. He would get the call from

McCoy for session work when Moss was unavailable, and sometimes they would both get the call, as was the case on at least one of the *Blonde on Blonde* dates.

By 1966, Gayden had begun to blossom as a songwriter, having penned a number of the songs McCoy recorded with the Escorts for Monument Records. One of Gayden's songs was "Harpoon Man," the single Dylan had with the cover of Willie Dixon's "I'm Ready" on the flip side; that seven-inch record provided Dylan with two concrete examples of the kind of sound he might get in the city working with McCoy and his bandmates.

Johnston also tapped guitarist Joe South for the Dylan sessions. At the time, he was best-known as a songwriter and producer. The iconic rock pioneer Gene Vincent had recorded two of his songs, "I Might Have Known" and "Gone Gone Gone." He had written and produced "Untie Me," a hit for the Tams on the R&B charts in 1962, and had written Billy Joe Royal's breakout hit on Columbia, "Down in the Boondocks," which had gone all the way to number nine on the *Billboard* Hot 100 the previous summer. South had moved to Nashville three years earlier after the publishing company he wrote for, Atlanta-based Lowery Music, opened an office there. Besides South, Lowery's roster of writers included two other future music legends, Ray Stevens and Jerry Reed.

South was not an in-demand session guitarist during the years he lived in Nashville, describing himself as a member of the B-team in a 1988 interview with Dutch music journalist and radio host Jan Donkers, but C-team was probably more like it.[32] That's not to suggest that South wasn't a good studio guitarist: "He could always come up with a good lick," says Putnam, who first worked with the guitarist in Muscle Shoals.[33] But he couldn't necessarily do it quickly, which was a requirement in Nashville's fast-paced studio world, where the players were expected to knock out anywhere from three to six master sides in a three-hour session. So, he mostly did demo sessions, and that's how he got to know Johnston. "Bob was a pal of mine that I used to work with at some dates when I used to live in Nashville," South told WFMU FM's Michael Shelley in 2010.[34]

Although he knew he might not be available, the producer also reached out to Jerry Kennedy regarding working with Dylan. Originally from Shreveport, Louisiana, Kennedy followed in the footsteps of stellar axemen like James Burton and Fred Carter Jr. as lead guitarist in the *Louisiana Hayride* house band, joining the show at the age of eighteen. But he got his start professionally seven years earlier, when he landed a record deal with RCA at eleven, resulting in his first trip to Nashville where he recorded several sides under the direction of Chet Atkins. He moved to Nashville in 1960 at the urging of Mercury Records executive Shelby Singleton, who thought Kennedy's bluesy chops would add something a little different to the city's sonic tapestry.

Mercury was recording a variety of artists in Nashville, and Kennedy not only got the call for the label's country sessions but was also on hand whenever one of its R&B acts came to town, recording with Brook Benton, Ruth Brown, Clyde McPhatter, and Fats Domino. He also worked with an array of pop and rock artists, including Elvis Presley, Dusty Springfield, Patti Page, and Roy Orbison. Kennedy was one of the three guitarists, along with Moss and Billy Sanford, who played the monster guitar hook on Orbison's final number-one hit, "Oh, Pretty Woman."

Not long after Kennedy arrived in Music City, Singleton had him wearing multiple hats, not only using him on sessions as a guitarist but also giving him his first work as a producer and making him an A&R executive for the label. As Johnston had expected, because of those duties, Kennedy was available for only one of the Dylan dates, the evening session on the first day of recording.

Dylan's tour started in Louisville on Friday, February 4, then he performed in White Plains, New York, on Saturday and Pittsburgh on Sunday. He returned to New York City for a few days before heading to Memphis for a show on Thursday, February 10. While back in the city, he went to Jerry Schatzberg's studio on the afternoon of February 8 to do a photo shoot for the cover of his forthcoming album.

Recalling the shoot, Schatzberg says, "That came from Grossman, because he now had seen a number of photographs and they liked them very much. I know they were using one on the cover of *Tarantula*—and they started to use different photographs—and he just called me up one day and asked me if I would be interested in shooting the next album . . . and I said, 'Absolutely!'"

Dylan had done several sittings at Schatzberg's studio at 333 Park Avenue South, including the one where Phil Ochs said he didn't like "Can You Please Crawl Out Your Window," and that's where they began on that bitterly cold Tuesday in February. "I started off [at the studio], 'cause I didn't really know what I was gonna do, but I thought I would do color in the studio, and we did some, but I just didn't . . . " Schatzberg's voice trails off. "Some of them were beautiful shots, and I used a lot of them at different times, but I just thought I would like to get something a little different with him. And I hadn't been out of doors with him, and I've always liked the meatpacking district."[35]

They rode together in Dylan's baby blue 1966 Ford Mustang to the meatpacking district, which was only a couple of miles from Schatzberg's studio.[36] The photographer didn't have a particular destination in mind—he would know it when he saw it, and he saw it at the corner of West Street and Morton Street where a building stood that was home to the Brooks Transportation Company. The afternoon sun was hitting the side of the brick building in a way that caught his eye.[37]

"I found this location, and we were taking the pictures, and the majority of them are sharp and clear, and everything," Schatzberg says. "But there were four or five where we are moving around, and I guess the camera was shaking, and we got this movement."

Decades later, he would tell Bob Egan of PopSpots, "It was pretty cold out. I know all the critics, everybody tried to think, 'Oh, they were trying to do a drug shot' or something. It's not true. It was February, and he was wearing just that jacket, and I was wearing something similar, so we were really cold."[38] As it would turn out, it was New York's coldest day of 1966, with a low of four degrees, twenty degrees below the city's average temperature for that day.

Dylan would soon be in the warmer climes of the South. In two days, he would fly to Memphis for the show there, then over to Virginia for dates in Richmond and Norfolk before traveling on to Nashville for three days of recording, and hopefully, the completion of the album.

6

HURRY UP AND WAIT

THE NASHVILLE THAT AWAITED DYLAN'S arrival in 1966 was not the booming It city of today. At the time, the city's population was under half a million people, and the local music industry had yet to blossom into the multibillion dollar force it would later become. In fact, to many of the city's blue bloods back then, it was still something to be frowned upon.

Dylan's first Nashville session was scheduled for 2:00 PM on Monday, February 14. The day was unseasonably warm, even for a southern city like Nashville—the high was around sixty degrees, with scattered light rain. Of course, it was a coincidence that Dylan's first sessions in Nashville to record an album of songs mostly about romantic relationships fell on Valentine's Day, but in retrospect, it was a good omen.

The Nashville musicians who had gotten the call from Charlie McCoy had already loaded in and were setting up their gear in Studio A by the appointed time. Besides McCoy, drummer Kenny Buttrey, guitarist Wayne Moss, guitarist/bassist Joe South, and pianist Bill Aikins were all on hand.

Al Kooper was there, as well. He had flown in separately from Dylan and almost missed his flight to Nashville. Kooper's band the Blues Project had played a concert the previous Saturday night at Antioch College in Yellow Springs, Ohio. When the rest of the band returned to New York on Sunday, he had remained in Ohio so he could catch a flight into Nashville Monday morning from Columbus. "I tagged along while some school kids drove the whole entourage to the airport, gave the boys five, said, 'See ya in a week,' and hopped a ride back to the school with two women on the concert committee," he recalled in his memoir, *Backstage Passes and Backstabbing Bastards: Memoirs of a Rock 'n' Roll Survivor*.

> I never made it to the school. I just barely made it to the plane the next morning. It was the first time I had ever been with two women at once and only the clarion call of Bob Dylan could've got me to that airport on time. Well, almost on time. When I got there, the plane was taxiing toward the runway and it was snowing like *Dr. Zhivago*. All of a sudden the plane stopped and this tiny jeep pulled up carrying yours truly, looking a little worse for the previous night's shenanigans. They dropped the stairs down, and I, unaware that the flight had originated in New York City, boarded the plane only to be greeted by much laughter and fingers pointed in my direction. Many of the passengers were music business people that I knew from New York. . . . And they couldn't understand what I was doing in a jeep on the runway during a snowstorm in Columbus, Ohio, at nine o'clock on Monday morning. And I wasn't telling either. I believed in the magic of rock 'n' roll![1]

Bob Johnston picked Kooper up at the airport in Nashville, so the keyboardist was already at the studio when the Nashville musicians began to arrive. While it has been written the Nashville cats didn't even know who Dylan was, that certainly wasn't the case for McCoy, Buttrey, Moss, South, or Aikins. That's not to suggest they were intimate with his entire body of work, but they all knew "Like a Rolling Stone" and were familiar with some of his songs that were hits for other artists, such as "Blowing in the Wind" by Peter, Paul and Mary and "Mr. Tambourine Man" by the Byrds. Still, they weren't awed by that; there were a lot of great songwriters in Nashville, including some who had influenced Dylan, such as Johnny Cash.

Not long after the musicians arrived at the studio, Johnston informed them Dylan's flight from Norfolk had been delayed in Richmond, Virginia. They continued setting up for the session while the engineer—probably

Charlie Bragg, but possibly Tom Sparkman, who was the label's chief engineer in Nashville at the time—miked the drums and the amplifiers for the electric instruments and worked on getting the recording levels. Once the setup was complete, the musicians headed downstairs to the lounge to await Dylan's arrival.

They spent the next few hours hanging out, drinking coffee, and killing time. Some of the musicians played Ping-Pong. Aikins remembers a few of the guys playing Rich Uncle, a Monopoly spinoff. At five o'clock, their first three-hour session officially ended and they all signed union time cards. It was the first time any of the Nashville musicians could remember getting paid for a session without hitting a single note, much less getting paid master scale.

Aikins had gotten the call that day because Hargus "Pig" Robbins, who would handle piano duties on most of the album, was booked on other sessions and wouldn't be available until later in the evening. "It was one of the most unusual dates I ever worked," he recalls.[2]

The Nashville studio musicians were accustomed to precise, three-hour sessions where a minimum of three songs would be tracked, and possibly four or five or even six, if luck was with them. But during their first six hours at Studio A that day, they didn't play a single lick. Aikins remembers thinking, "I'm sitting around on my ass making money, no pressure—this is a great gig."[3]

By the time Dylan arrived at the studio with his manager, Albert Grossman, around 6:00 PM, the sun had already set and the temperatures were beginning to drop outside. Dylan was wearing a polka-dotted shirt with dirty cuffs. "He was kind of a weird, offbeat guy," Aikins says.[4]

After he was introduced to the musicians, Dylan told Johnston he still had some work to do on one of the songs he wanted to record that day. "Johnston came to us," McCoy recalls, "and said, 'Hey, if you want to go to dinner, go on and come on back. He's not finished writing a lyric, so go ahead and do your dinner and get on back because I don't know when he's gonna be ready.' So we all left and came back, and then sat around for eternity," he adds with a laugh.[5]

The waiting they did on that first day of sessions was like nothing they had ever experienced, as if they had stepped into an episode of *The*

Twilight Zone. Several of the musicians remember seeing Dylan sitting at the piano with a legal pad. "I can remember him sitting at the piano in deep, deep, meditative thought," Aikins says. "He was creating, writing. So we were just on-hold as musicians, on the payroll, on a master session, and we were just hanging out. That's the kind of budget they had for him."[6]

It's not entirely clear what time it was when word finally was sent down to the musicians' lounge that Dylan was ready to record, but it definitely was after 9:00 PM, because a number of the musicians remembered signing time cards for two three-hour sessions that day before they ever played a note.

"I think he was excited to be here," McCoy says, recalling that first session. "He was a little apprehensive at first, wondering, 'Oh, how are these Nashville guys gonna take me?' I think right away, everything was great."[7]

The song Dylan chose to kick off the sessions was the one he had just spent several hours finishing, "Fourth Time Around," a song that was musically unlike any other he had ever recorded. A light, acoustic number in a fast 3/4 waltz time, he may have considered it a good song to start with, something that would be right in the wheelhouse of the Nashville players—and it was.

Depending on the source, "Fourth Time Around" is either the original inspiration for the Beatles' "Norwegian Wood (This Bird Has Flown)" or an acerbic answer to it. Both melodically and lyrically, the song is unquestionably similar to "Norwegian Wood," which had been released the previous December on *Rubber Soul.* In his book *Bob Dylan in America,* Sean Wilentz described the song as "Bob Dylan impersonating John Lennon impersonating Bob Dylan."[8]

Dylan's growing influence on the Beatles, both lyrically and musically, was evident not only on *Rubber Soul,* but also on the two albums that preceded it, *Beatles for Sale* and *Help.* Some observers thought he purposely echoed "Norwegian Wood" on "Fourth Time Around" to send a friendly warning to Lennon in particular that some of his recent material was sounding a little too Dylanesque—introspective songs featuring acoustic rhythm guitar, such as "I'm a Loser," "You've Got to Hide Your Love Away," and of course, "Norwegian Wood."

As Dylan ran down the song for the musicians, Kooper immediately noticed the similarity between "Fourth Time Around" and the Beatles' song. "I thought it was very ballsy of Dylan to do 'Fourth Time Around,'" he told author Andy Gill. "I asked him about it. I said, 'It sounds so much like "Norwegian Wood,"' and he said, 'Well, actually, "Norwegian Wood" sounds like this. I'm afraid they took it from me, and I feel that I have to, you know, record it.' Evidently, he played it for them, and they'd nicked it."[9]

But according to Paul McCartney, Lennon had begun the song in January or February of 1965 while on a skiing vacation in the Swiss Alps with his wife and Beatles producer George Martin, a fact confirmed by Martin.[10] "I was very careful and paranoid because I didn't want my wife, Cynthia, to know that there really was something going on outside the household, so I was trying to be sophisticated writing about an affair," Lennon told Playboy in 1980.[11]

There is nothing to suggest Dylan had written or even begun work on "Fourth Time Around" prior to when Lennon began writing "Norwegian Wood"—no label or publishing records or lyric sheets. In fact, he wrote all or most of the song in the studio during the hours immediately prior to recording it, so Dylan likely was speaking in general terms when he told Kooper "they took it from me," referring to the appropriation of his style, rather than the specific song.

Dylan took Lennon's story of an affair and raised the bar, crafting a longer, more graphic, and more sophisticated tale featuring an assignation much darker than the one the Beatle described. When asked by Jonathan Cott of Rolling Stone in 1968 what he thought of "Fourth Time Around," Lennon said, "I was very paranoid about that. I remember he played it to me when he was in London. He said, 'What do you think?' I said, 'I don't like it.' I didn't like it. I was very paranoid. I just didn't like what I felt I was feeling—I thought it was an out-and-out skit, you know, but it wasn't. It was great."[12]

"Fourth Time Around" may not have been an "out-and-out skit" as Lennon originally thought, but Dylan clearly was having fun with it. He playfully used the word "come" with its inherent sexual innuendo in the second and fourth verses. He began the second verse with an apparent reference to oral sex: "I stood there and hummed / I tapped on her drum and asked her how come." Then he opened the fourth verse with, "Her Jamaican rum / And when she had come, I asked her for some."

Unlike "Norwegian Wood," which included only the two people having the affair, Dylan added a third person (you) to the dynamic of his tale, someone to whom he spoke directly. One might presume it was another woman, and Dylan may have intended that. But considering what he told Kooper about the song, it seems Dylan took Lennon's tale of an affair, rewrote it, and put Lennon himself in the new song as the person to whom the song was sung.

The song consisted of five nine-line verses sung back to back, without a chorus or bridge, and the first verse ended with the admonition, "Don't forget / Everybody must give something back / For something they get." Dylan introduced the third person in the third verse, and the fifth and final verse was entirely about the third person. In the third verse, the man having the affair tries "to make sense out of that picture of *you* in your wheelchair."

Was Lennon the person in the wheelchair, the implication being he wasn't standing on his own artistic vision? It's a thought reinforced by the last two lines of the final verse: "I never asked for your crutch / Now don't ask for mine," which might be translated as, "I didn't cop your style, don't cop mine."[13]

George Harrison offered his take on the song in an interview with Vic Garbarini in 1992 that was published nine years later in *Guitar World*: "To my mind, it was about how John and Paul, from listening to Bob's early stuff, had written 'Norwegian Wood.' Judging from the title, it seemed as though Bob had listened to that and wrote the same basic song again, calling it 'Fourth Time Around.' The title suggests that the same basic tune kept bouncing around over and over again."[14]

According to studio records, twenty takes were slated that evening despite the fact the arrangement was essentially in place from the get-go.[15] Like "Norwegian Wood," "Fourth Time Around" featured a circular melody. The delicate arrangement they worked up featured Dylan on harmonica, Buttrey on drums using brushes, Moss and McCoy on acoustic guitars, South on electric bass, and Kooper on organ. (On his organ part which ultimately didn't make the final mix, Kooper used a clavichord sound that often has been misidentified as a bass harmonica part played by McCoy.)

Seventeen of the slated takes were either rehearsals, false starts, or breakdowns, most of which were related to finding the right tempo, but some of which were related to technical issues. The technical issues weren't altogether surprising considering it was the first song on the first day of the sessions.

The first complete take was the fifth one, but after listening to the playback, Dylan resumed work on the song. There was an ongoing problem with the bass sound, and Johnston stopped take seven to address it. "Hold it just a minute, let's save your voice, Bob, just a second," the producer said from the control room; then to South, "Try that other bass." But the problem persisted with the other bass, too, causing Johnston to interrupt the slightly faster eighth take. South and engineer Tom Sparkman worked on the problem some more, then recording was resumed. "Standby, rolling on nine," Johnston told Dylan and the musicians in the studio. Dylan hummed the melody and strummed his guitar to set a slower tempo. After a couple of false starts, they got another complete take on the eleventh try, but like take five, it wasn't the *one*.

When the music broke down on take fifteen, McCoy said, "I think we were rushin' a little bit. Were we rushin'?"

"Yeah," Johnston answered. "Count it off one more time for 'em, Bob." After Dylan hummed the melody and strummed his guitar again, McCoy counted off take sixteen at a slightly slower tempo.

There were a few more false starts as the musicians locked into the slower tempo. At the end of take eighteen, South told Moss, "Sounds like the guitars are dragging."

"All right, let's pick it up a little bit, then," the guitarist replied.

They began again at a slightly faster tempo, but Johnston interrupted Dylan once more in the middle of the second verse. "I'm sorry," he said. "Joe, you're breaking up on that bass again, distorting all over the place."

"I don't know what to tell you, man," South told him.

Once more, Johnston, South, and Sparkman worked on the problem with the bass. When they were done, Dylan and the musicians recorded their twentieth take, and it would be the keeper.

The master take was highlighted by Dylan's plaintive harmonica parts and Buttrey's tasteful brush work, but especially by the Spanish-flavored, arpeggiated lines performed on acoustic guitars by Wayne Moss and Charlie McCoy. Moss played the higher, dominant figures on his Jose Ramirez gut-string, while McCoy contributed the lower, simpler, counterpoint lines on his steel-string acoustic.

After the take, Dylan went into the control room to hear the playback with Johnston and Grossman. Songwriter Billy Swan was there as well, and Dylan stood next to him while they all listened to the take. Swan was working for Columbia at the time as an engineer's assistant, not to be confused with an assistant engineer. Once the playback was finished, Dylan turned to Swan and asked, "You like that?" and Swan told him, "Yeah."

As it so happened, Swan, who had already scored a Top 10 pop hit with Clyde McPhatter's recording of his song "Lover Please" and would later hit number one as a writer and artist with 1974's rockabilly-inspired "I Can Help," was working his final week at Columbia and would be succeeded the following week by another aspiring songwriter destined for fame, Kris Kristofferson. Kristofferson often has said he worked for Columbia as a "janitor," but they actually were "engineer's assistants," according to Swan.

"When Kris and I worked there, it was getting food for the engineer, maybe erasing tape, helping keep tape in the studio, helping clean up in between sessions, stuff like that," he says of the job. "Whatever they [the engineers] needed, we would go do it."

After working there for about a year, Swan decided to pursue some other opportunities in the music business. "I went in to give my two-week notice to Harold Hitt, who was the general manager of the studio at the time," he recalls. "He said, 'OK. If you know of anybody who might be looking for a job, bring 'em in. Or tell 'em to come in.' And I said, 'Fine.'

"Well, after I gave him my notice, I'm leaving the building, and as I'm going out the door, Kris is coming in. And he says, 'Hey, do you know where I can get a job?' I said, 'Yeah, I just quit mine. Come on.' So he and I went back into Harold's office, and I said, 'Harold, he's looking for a job.' And Kris took my place at the end of my two weeks."[16]

Dylan had to be pleased with the results of "Fourth Time Around": right off the bat, he had challenged the Nashville players with the most delicate song he had ever attempted to record, and they had responded with a beautifully elegant arrangement that matched the song's delicacy. So next, he decided to introduce the musicians to his masterpiece, "Visions of Johanna."

By then, it was midnight or later, and guitarist Jerry Kennedy, who had arrived while they were recording "Fourth Time Around," joined the other musicians in the studio and plugged in his Gibson 335. Dylan ran down the song, and the Nashville cats notated the chord progression. Sparkman slated four takes of "Visions of Johanna" that night, but only the final take was a complete one. The first and third takes were false starts and the second take broke down just before the hook line at the end of the second verse. But take four was the one—seven-and-a-half minutes of perfection considered by many to be Dylan's finest work.

Dylan had further tweaked the lyrics since attempting the song in New York. In the couplet about the night watchman in the second verse, he introduced an element of doubt as to who's actually insane:

> We can hear the night watchman click his flashlight
> Ask himself if it's him or them that's really insane

In the same verse, he further refined the sixth line, about Louise, changing "She's steady, seems like the mirror" to "She's delicate and seems like the mirror."

In the third verse about little boy lost, Dylan added the word "muttering" back in, maybe deciding it was not too Eliot-esque, after all, changing "with his small talk hitting the wall" to "muttering small talk at the wall."

He made a few other significant changes to the fifth and final verse. On the New York date in November, the "fiddler" spoke to the countess and the "peddler" stepped to the road, whereas two and a half months later in Nashville, they had swapped places. Also, in New York, "ev'rything was gone which was owed," whereas by the time he arrived Nashville, he had decided "ev'rything's been returned which was owed."

As performed at the New York session, the fifth verse was four lines longer than the other verses, but that night in Nashville, Dylan deleted one of the extra lines in that verse, a much-pondered passage: "He examines the nightingale's code." He has never offered a clue to the line's meaning, but it would appear to be a reference to poet John Keats's "Odc to a Nightingale."[17]

Aikins recalls trying to understand what Dylan was saying in the song. "I thought it was really *far out* would be the term I would have used at the time, and still today, it was a very *out-there* song," he says.[18]

McCoy echoes Aikins's assessment. "The lyrics were—we'd never heard lyrics like that before," he says.[19]

For British rocker Robyn Hitchcock, who now lives in Nashville, the song was a revelation.

> "Visions of Johanna" for me is the matrix; it's where I come from as a songwriter. To me, that defined what a song could be. It was why it was worth trying to write songs. Whereas in the past, you know, as a child, I had always thought that songwriting was basically writing pop songs, and that wasn't something I was going to do. I loved pop music, and I loved the Beatles, but it didn't occur to me that it was something I might want to do.
>
> Bob Dylan on *Blonde on Blonde* and on "Visions of Johanna" particularly, showed me, "OK, that's the job I want to have." When I grow up and I'm employed, I want to have a job writing songs like "Visions of Johanna," in some way. Not that sound like them or even feel like them, but I want to get to a position where I'm writing songs in that league. Songs that make you

laugh and make you cry in the same sentence. Things that take you up and bring you down simultaneously. Things that go in two opposite directions. Things that achieve the impossible.

And for me, that song has given me something to aim at and miss. I'll never write a song as good as that, but it set the bar high. And I've certainly written some interesting stuff in an attempt, not to rewrite "Visions of Johanna," but to write songs with an understanding, with some of the understanding of life that "Visions of Johanna" has.[20]

Former UK poet laureate Andrew Motion told the *Guardian* in 1999 he considered "Visions of Johanna" the best song lyric ever written, calling the song "clear evidence of Dylan's brilliant use of language."[21]

On "Visions of Johanna" that first night in Nashville, Dylan showed he wasn't abandoning balladry with his new direction, he was just adding a band, and in the process, furthering the rock ballad as an art form. Whereas Bobby Gregg had a problem finding the song's groove during the November 30 session, Buttrey was locked in from the start, combining with South's "hillbilly funk" bass (as Kooper described it) to give the song its soulful swing. Reflecting on the song years later, Kooper told Gill, "If you listen to it very critically, it's very important what Joe South's bass is doing in that. He's playing this throbbing thing which rhythmically is an amazing bass part."

As for his own contribution to the track, Kooper added, "On my part, I was responding to the lyrics—like when he says 'the ghost of 'lectricity howls in the bones of her face,' it was very challenging to play something after that line."[22] What Kooper chose to play were some high, haunting lines that captured the intensity of the lyric.

All the performances were superb on the master take, including Dylan's vocals and harmonica breaks. Kennedy's lead guitar fills especially stood out, the guitarist matching Dylan's expressions of yearning with wrenchingly soulful blues licks in the pauses and spaces. Kennedy's contribution to this game-changing side has often been misattributed to Robbie Robertson, but while Robertson was on hand when Dylan attempted "Johanna" in New York, he wasn't present in Nashville on the night the definitive take was recorded.

Clocking in at more than seven minutes, "Visions of Johanna" was two to three times longer than what the Nashville musicians were used to. "Up until then, I'd probably never played on a song that was more than four minutes long before," McCoy says. "And in that day and time, a four-minute song recorded here was unheard of. I mean, you just didn't do it."[23]

"They were used to playing a session and making one song two minutes and thirty seconds long," Johnston told me. "Nobody made one over three minutes. There wasn't any such thing."[24]

Johnston was exaggerating slightly, but not by much. "The longest song ever recorded in Nashville before [the *Blonde on Blonde* sessions] was probably 'El Paso,'" McCoy says, referring to the number-one smash hit by Marty Robbins from 1959. "And that was just over four minutes."[25] Four minutes and nineteen seconds to be exact, which still was shorter than "Fourth Time Around" at 4:33.

With "Visions of Johanna" done, they moved on to another song Dylan had attempted in New York, "Leopard-Skin Pill-Box Hat." Dylan had completed the lyrics in the three weeks since the New York session and had every reason to expect to get a master take of the song before calling it a night.

Hargus "Pig" Robbins had gotten to the studio while they were working on "Johanna," so he took a seat at the studio's grand piano. From Johnston's vantage point behind the console in the control room, the setup in the studio looked like this: Robbins was center left at the piano; Buttrey was on the drums against the left wall facing the center of the room from behind four-foot baffles; just beyond the drums, Kooper manned the organ facing back toward the control room; to his left was South on bass; the guitarists—in this case, McCoy on acoustic and Moss and Kennedy on their electrics—were lined up across the center of the room toward the right wall; and Dylan was center right inside several tall baffles with glass windows built into them, which allowed him to see the other musicians but still prevented any major bleed from their instruments into his vocal and harmonica mics.

From the control room, Johnston announced, "83184, 'Leopard-Skin Pill-Box Hat,' take one." McCoy asked about the song's intro, and the producer told him, "The intro is just the drums and Bob."

Dylan started off the take with some harmonica soloing, then Buttrey came in with a funky beat on just the kick drum. When they got to the beginning of the verse, Buttrey hit the snare drum twice and the rest of the band joined in, but almost immediately, Dylan stopped the music—he was having some trouble with his harmonica.

McCoy, of course, had his collection of harmonicas with him, so he asked Dylan, "You want another one?"

Eyeing McCoy's harps, Dylan said, "Is there another B?"

McCoy pointed at one and said, "See if that's not a B right there."

Dylan checked it out and said, "Yeah."

Dylan tried out the harmonica and when he was satisfied, Johnston said, "Rolling on two." Three bars into the intro, Johnston stopped them and said, "I'm sorry, we didn't have Wayne up high enough."

On the third take, they got past the intro and into a laid-back variation on the twelve-bar blues groove Dylan had experimented with in New York. The result was not only a complete take, but a potential keeper. Dylan's words flowed easily on top of Buttrey's swinging drums, South's crunchy bass, and the boogie rhythms laid down by Moss and McCoy. Robbins reinforced the rhythm section when he wasn't sprinkling in flashy piano runs. And as he had on "Visions of Johanna," Kennedy delivered some nasty Delta blues licks, taking turns with Robbins and Moss filling the spaces around Dylan's vocals and harmonica breaks, the three of them showing off their considerable skills. In the break after the third verse, Dylan blew a furious solo around which Robbins wove some memorable piano fills, while during the outro, Moss and Kennedy swapped licks around Dylan's harmonica riffing.

When they got to the end of take three, which clocked in at nearly four-and-a-half minutes, they could have called it a night, right then and there; the take featured superb performances on the part of all involved, from start to finish, fulfilling the potential of the twelve-bar blues approach suggested at the New York session.

But they didn't call it a night. Instead, Dylan wanted to try approaching the song as an uptempo blues rocker, joining Moss and Kennedy on electric guitar. The song sounded good with that approach, but curiously, they kicked off the uptempo version with an intro more suited for a novelty record. Maybe it was because Kooper discovered some sound effects on one of the organs in the studio—or maybe it was because they were closer to daybreak than midnight and people were getting silly.

"They had a Wurlitzer organ there, as well as a Hammond," Kooper recalls. "And I didn't have much experience with the Wurlitzer, so I was very curious about it. One of the things it had on it was a doorbell, where you pushed the button and it went, 'bing bong.'"[26]

They started with that sound of a doorbell ringing, after which all the musicians yelled, "Who's there?" That was followed by the honk of a car horn, then the music kicked in. On take four, Johnston stopped the musicians just after the intro and said over the talk-back mic, "All right, hold it. Let me hear the bell," which drew a laugh from Dylan and a couple of the musicians.

With the signal from the doorbell boosted, they tried it again—and Johnston stopped them again. "All right, hold it," he said. "One more time, and everybody has to say 'Who's there?' real loud. That's the only thing not picking up. Scream it."

"It's a little too fast," Dylan told McCoy, who responded, "OK."

The tempo was still too fast on take five, so they tried it even a little slower on the next one. On that take, which broke down around a minute into the song, the doorbell and car horn were reprised in each chorus, and McCoy played harmonica.

They got a complete take on the eighth try, but it wasn't the keeper. When take nine broke down after the third verse, Johnston went out into the studio to make a few suggestions regarding the arrangement. Robbins asked him, "You know when the last verse will hit?" Johnston said, "There's three verses, then the solo, then two more verses, and that's the end," then added, "Come in there real strong, Pig." Then to Sparkman in the control room, he said, "On every turnaround, Tom, it's going to be the piano instead of this guitar here."

"OK," Sparkman said.

"And, Tom," Johnston continued, "there's going to be an instrumental on the piano, too, and I'll point at you when."

"Jerry not have an instrumental now?" the engineer asked, referring to guitarist Kennedy.

"No," Johnston told him.

The producer stayed in the studio, counting off the take and joining in loudly on the "Who's there?" part. It may have been Johnston's idea to use the sound effects because he's credited as *playing* the doorbell. Take ten was a false start and take eleven broke down after the third verse when Dylan accidentally sang, "and you just sittin' there, in *my* brand-new leopard-skin pill-box hat."

"Hey, no, no, no, I missed the words, man," Dylan said, sounding beat. "Hey, we're spending too much time on it. It's just a natural song, you know."

"You want to slow it down?" Johnston asked.

"Well, let's just get it this one last time," Dylan said. "Let's just make it."

They took the twelfth take at a slightly slower pace, but it quickly broke down. They kept the same slower tempo for take thirteen and made it all the way through. When it came to the piano solo, Robbins showed why Kennedy considered him the best musician in Music City. On the vamp-out, Kooper also flashed his improving organ chops.

After the lucky thirteenth take, Dylan called it a night with three songs attempted and presumably three master takes in the can. Returning to his hotel, he was excited about his first day of recording in Nashville, excited he may have found the musicians who could help him realize his artistic vision.

As they packed up their gear and made their way to their cars in the back parking lot, the Nashville cats had somewhat different impressions of their first day working with Dylan. It unquestionably had been one of the most bizarre set of sessions they had ever played on. As they drove from the studio to their homes just a couple of hours before daybreak, they could only imagine what the next day would bring.

7

AN ALL-NIGHTER WITH
THE SAD-EYED LADY

BACK IN THE STUDIO LATER that day—February 15—at 6:00 PM, the Nashville cats found out what "the next day would bring" them. More waiting.

Dylan wasn't there. He and Al Kooper were back at their hotel—probably the Capitol Park Inn at Fifth and Charlotte downtown—where Dylan was working on the song he intended to record that evening. "I spent a lot of time in his hotel room because he had a piano in there, put in the room," Kooper says. "He wasn't finished with the songs, so he would teach me the music of the song, and I would play the piano and he would work on the lyrics."[1]

While they waited for Dylan to arrive, Johnston had the Nashville musicians work for a couple hours on a backing track for "I'll Keep It with Mine," the arrangement for which apparently originated with Johnston himself. It didn't resemble the version of the song recorded in New York three weeks earlier, but it's easy to imagine Dylan singing the song's words and melody over the instrumentation they recorded that evening.

Johnston was actually out in the studio directing the musicians, even manning the piano on the ten takes they recorded that night, which suggests Pig Robbins was booked elsewhere from six to nine. At the end of the fifth take, the producer had the musicians make a change to the chord progression. "Hold it, take that G chord out that I put in," he said. "It's screwing it up."

The arrangement was reminiscent of "Fourth Time Around," with some beautifully melodic guitar interplay by Charlie McCoy and Wayne Moss, highlighted by the latter's finger-picking style guitar work.

They slowed the tempo slightly on take eight and kept it there on the next two takes, which were mistakenly slated as eight (again) and nine; both were complete takes. On take ten, Moss switched from his Jose Ramirez gut-string acoustic to his Martin D-18 steel-string, and Johnston judged that to be the keeper take.

Considering the quality of the final take, it's surprising Dylan never added vocals to the track. In fact, as of this writing, he has yet to revisit "I'll Keep It with Mine" at all, either live or in the studio.

Mid-evening, Billy Swan drove downtown in the blue station wagon owned by the label to pick up Dylan and Kooper at the hotel and bring them back to the studio. A light rain was falling, and Swan remembers the two musicians ducking the rain and leapfrogging puddles as they made their way to the studio's back entrance being guarded by one of the off-duty cops Johnston had hired.

Once in the studio, Dylan continued to work on the song he wanted to try next, keeping the musicians on ice until the dead of night. "We took a break and three hours later we signed a [union] card, and took another break," Moss recalls.[2]

The Nashville musicians had never experienced anything like it. Although they had worked late night sessions with artists like Elvis Presley, they weren't used to pulling all-nighters. They hoped the previous day's wait was primarily a result of Dylan's flight being delayed, but as the hours passed during the second night of sessions, they began to realize that was not going to be the case.

"There were quite a few days when he would go into the studio and sit at the piano himself and work on lyrics for hours," Kooper recalls. "I mean six or seven hours. . . . He would be in there extremely concentrating and never coming out of there until he finished."[3]

"Spending a lot of time didn't seem to bother him," Robbins says. "I guess that's the way he'd been used to working."[4]

But Kooper had never experienced anything like it either on sessions with Dylan in New York. "It was really brand new for me, too," he says.

As the wait stretched into the early morning of February 16, the Nashville musicians struggled to fight off sleep. Kooper remembers Moss quipping, "That hour of sleep I got last night is getting pretty lonely."[5]

"In a situation like that, okay, you can go take a nap, but you don't really because you think, 'Any minute now, they're going to be ready to go,'" McCoy told the *Tennessean* fifty years later. "Then when it comes, you know right out of the chute [it's] going to be a live recording; there's not going to be any overdubs, there's not going to be any repairs, even though we were recording on multitrack. . . . So it's especially important to keep your mind on the subject.

"We were just trying to stay in it and to be ready."[6]

There was a lot of Ping-Pong being played. According to McCoy, Buttrey was one of the best players. Swan excelled at table tennis, too. "That's basically how I got the job at CBS," Swan recalls with a laugh. "'Cause I'd hang out there so much and play Ping-Pong, you know. I'm a good Ping-Pong player."[7]

———————

The song Dylan kept them waiting for was "Sad Eyed Lady of the Lowlands." As he would tell biographer Robert Shelton not long after cutting it, he considered "Sad Eyed Lady" the best song he had ever written, and, unlike the rest of the material on *Blonde on Blonde*, there is no question whom Dylan was writing about. A decade later, he revealed it was about his wife in "Sara," a song from the album *Desire* that included the lines, "I'd taken the cure and had just gotten through / Stayin' up for days in the Chelsea Hotel / Writin' 'Sad Eyed Lady of the Lowlands' for you." While Dylan may have started the song at the Chelsea Hotel, there is no question where he finished it—in Nashville, at his hotel and at the studio.

Shelton described "Sad Eyed Lady of the Lowlands" as "virtually a wedding song."[8] In his introduction to the *Blonde on Blonde* songbook, music critic Paul Nelson called it a "celebration of woman as a work of art, religious figure, and object of eternal majesty and wonder."[9] In his book *The Poetry of Rock*, *Village Voice* critic Richard Goldstein had high praise for the song. "'Sad-Eyed Lady of the Lowlands' is one of Dylan's least self-conscious songs—the most moving love song in rock," he wrote. "Even its foibles conspire to convey the paradoxical reality of its heroine; this sad-eyed lady who can be so nonchalantly strong, and so predictably weak; so innocent, yet so corrupted. His sad-eyed lady is everyone's girl, and everyone's girl is what the love song is all about."[10]

Tom Waits, whose own songwriting has been heavily influenced by Dylan, said of the song, "For me, 'Sad Eyed Lady of the Lowlands' is a grand song. It is like 'Beowulf' and it takes me out to the meadow. This song can make you leave home, work on the railroad or marry a Gypsy. I think of a drifter around a fire with a tin cup under a bridge remembering a woman's hair. The song is a dream, a riddle and a prayer."[11]

Not long after he recorded it, Dylan himself acknowledged the song's reverent nature, describing it to journalist Jules Siegel as "old-time religious carnival music."[12] Three years later, he would tell *Rolling Stone*, "That song is an example of a song, it started out as just a little thing, 'Sad Eyed Lady of the Lowlands,' but I got carried away somewhere along the line. I just sat down at a table and started writing. At the session itself. And I just got carried away with the whole thing. I just started writing and couldn't stop. After a period of time, I forgot what it was all about, and I started trying to get back to the beginning. [laughs]"[13]

For Pink Floyd alum Roger Waters, the song was pivotal. "'Sad Eyed Lady of the Lowlands' changed my life," Waters told Howard Stern during an appearance on his satellite radio show in 2012. "When I heard that, I thought, 'If Bob can do it, I can do it.' . . . It's a whole album side! And it in no way gets dull or boring. It becomes more and more hypnotic."[14]

To Robyn Hitchcock, the song was "another world."[15]

Not everyone was so impressed. Music critic Lester Bangs disparaged the song's opening lyric in an essay titled "Love or Confusion?" that appeared in the collection *Studio A: The Bob Dylan Reader*. In regards to one of Dylan's later albums, Bangs wrote, "If in the '60s we were really ready to accept any drivel that dropped out of his mouth—a mercury mouth in the missionary times, say—then if he had released it in 1966, he might have been able to get away with *Street Legal*."[16]

Bangs wasn't the only critic to take exception to the concept of a "mercury" mouth; some contended in the English language, you can't simply take a noun like "mercury" and make it an adjective. In his comprehensive analysis of Dylan's lyrics, *Understanding Bob Dylan: Making Sense of the Songs That Changed Modern Music*, Tony Beck noted, "In 'Sad Eyed Lady,' he uses nouns as adjectives in a way that challenges the listener to figure out if [the] combination makes any sense."[17]

While it's not hard to question whether noun combinations like "mercury mouth," "matchbook songs," "geranium kiss," and "warehouse eyes" *make any sense*, making literal sense was not what Dylan intended on "Sad Eyed Lady of the Lowlands"—or for that matter, on any of the material he would record for *Blonde on Blonde*. As author Stephen Scobie pointed out in his book *Alias Bob Dylan: Revisited*: "Much of Dylan's poetry in the mid-1960s was indebted to his reading of the French Symbolist poets, especially Rimbaud, who were also influential in the development of French Surrealist painting in the 1920s. A central technique of Surrealism, the sudden juxtaposition of bizarrely unrelated objects, was derived from a line by Lautreamont: 'the chance meeting, on a dissection table, of an umbrella and sewing machine.'"[18]

Dylan's interest in Arthur Rimbaud was well-known. Dave Van Ronk, one of his early mentors in New York City, told Shelton he had asked Dylan if he had ever heard of the French poet, and Dylan had responded, "Who?" But later, on a visit to Dylan's apartment, Van Ronk realized Dylan may have been putting him on. "On his shelf, I discovered a book of translations of French symbolist poets that had obviously been thumbed through over a period of years," Van Ronk said. "I think he probably knew Rimbaud backward and forward before I even mentioned him."[19]

Dylan himself acknowledged Rimbaud's influence on his writing in a 1976 interview with Neil Hickey. "Rimbaud has been a big influence on me," he said. "When I'm on the road and want to read something that makes sense to me, I go to a bookstore and read his words."[20]

He put it more forcefully in his 2004 memoir, writing, "I came across one of [Rimbaud's] letters called, '*Je est un autre*,' which translates into

'I is someone else.' When I read those words, the bells went off. It made perfect sense."[21]

Dylan discussed the symbolist poets with French writer and director Antoine De Caunes in 1984: "I studied a lot of French poets when I was starting out. Apollinaire, Rimbaud, and those guys. . . . I drifted into it pretty natural; came out of the Beat poets and then drifted into the surrealistic poets. But I did that naturally. I didn't say, you know, I'm gonna do this or . . . it just happened."[22]

Despite the symbolic nature of the song's lyrics, it does contain a few fairly overt references to Dylan's new bride. For example, both the opening line of the second verse ("With your sheets like metal and your belt like lace") and the first line of the fifth and final verse ("With your sheet-metal memory of Cannery Row") seem to refer to the fact that Sara's father was a scrap metal dealer. The "magazine-husband" mentioned in the second line of the fifth verse is widely accepted as a reference to her first husband, Hans Lownds, a successful fashion photographer who did a lot of work for magazines. The third line of the first verse mentions "your silver cross," while the sixth line of the final verse includes "your holy medallion," and those, too, seem to be direct references to Sara, as there are photographs in wide circulation, albeit from a few years later, that show her wearing various necklaces bearing crosses. There is also the obvious similarity between *Lownds*, Sara's name from her first marriage, and *Lowlands*—the lowlands, of course, being frequently mentioned in Scottish balladry.

But beyond that, two of *Blonde on Blonde*'s prevailing themes—gates and waiting—are present in "Sad Eyed Lady," most notably in the final couplet of the chorus. A number of the musicians remember seeing Dylan consulting a Bible, looking for inspiration perhaps, as he worked on the lyrics, and in a few places, "Sad Eyed Lady" seems to echo some of the language and imagery found in the Old Testament book of Ezekiel, including the chorus's final couplet.

The third verse begins with a line about the kings of Tyrus and their list of convicts, Tyrus being the Latin name for Tyre, Lebanon. A Phoenician city in ancient times that was one of the most prominent cities in the world due to its strategic location as a port, Tyre was also

Dylan's electric set was booed at the Newport Folk Festival in July 1965, but it only strengthened his
lve to pursue a rock 'n' roll vision. *PHOTOFEST*

When Bob Johnston took over as Dylan's producer in late July 1965, he was already planning to take the budding superstar to Nashville to record with some young, red-hot session musicians there. *George Schowerer*

As he had on *Highway 61 Revisited*, Al Kooper contributed the organ parts on *Blonde on Blonde* that were so integral to the elusive sonic quicksilver Dylan was trying to capture on tape. *PHOTOFEST*

LEVON
and THE HAWKS

Levon and the Hawks backed Dylan on the very first sessions
for *Blonde on Blonde,* but ultimately only Robbie Robertson
(bottom right) and Rick Danko (bottom left) appeared on
the album. *Showtime Music Archives (Toronto)*

Dylan recorded thirteen of *Blonde on Blonde*'s fourteen tracks
over eight days at Columbia Records' Nashville studios in 1966.
Nashville Metro Archives

A recording artist in his own right, Charlie McCoy was the ringleader of a group of younger session musicians in Nashville, including members of his own band the Escorts, who helped Dylan create his magnum opus. *Country Music Hall of Fame and Museum*

Escorts drummer Kenneth Buttrey was only twenty years old when he anchored the Nashville sessions for *Blonde on Blonde*. *Cheri Buttrey-Jenkins*

Guitarist Wayne Moss, shown holding the Fender Jazzmaster he wielded on *Blonde on Blonde*, was one of the original members of Charlie McCoy and the Escorts. *Wayne Moss Collection*

addition to Charlie McCoy (far right) and Kenneth Buttrey (center), two other members he Escorts also would appear on *Blonde on Blonde*: trombonist Wayne "Doc" Butler left) and guitarist Mac Gayden (right rear). *Country Music Hall of Fame and Museum*

Already a hit songwriter and producer, Joe South played both guitar and bass on Dylan's 1966 Nashville sessions. *Bill Lowery Music*

To many of the Nashville session cats, Hargus "Pig" Robbins, who manned the grand piano at the *Blonde on Blonde* sessions, was the best musician in the city. *Country Music Hall of Fame and Museum*

Kennedy, shown with his Gibson 335, appeared on only one of the *Blonde on
de* tracks recorded in Nashville, but he still made his mark, contributing the achingly
utiful lead guitar fills on "Visions of Johanna." *Jerry Kennedy Collection*

Eight years before he would top the *Billboard* Hot 100 as a writer and artist with "I Can Help," Billy Swan worked at Columbia's studios in Nashville as an engineer's assistant and was on duty for Dylan's February sessions there.
Billy Swan Collection

When bass ace Henr Strzelecki joined the *Blonde on Blonde* sessions on Dylan's third day in Nashville it freed up Joe South concentrate on guitar
Country Music Hall of Fan and Museum

shown here during his show at the Academy of Music in Philadelphia on February 24, 66, Dylan played the black Telecaster with the white pick guard recommended to him Robbie Robertson on his 1966 world tour. *Charlie Steiner*

With Dylan looking on, Robbie Robertson took a solo during their performance at the Academy of Music in Philadelphia on February 24, 1966. *Charlie Steiner*

lan stayed at the Ramada Inn on James Robertson Parkway with his wife and infant
on his second visit to Nashville in March 1966. *Nashville Metro Archives*

Kris Kristofferson (left) was working at Columbia's Nashville
studios when Bob Johnston sent him to borrow a collection of
harmonicas from fellow songwriter Chris Gantry (right)
for Dylan to use on his March 1966 sessions in the city.
Chris Gantry Collection

① ~~xxxx~~ you Now the eagles
(Jail)

you eagle's teeth
yes i can see you in left ~~xxx~~ here for me
the promise you
left gone to me
trust
sell these

② i waited for you — half sick
~~xxxx~~ hated me
i waited for — frozen traffic
how ~~xxx~~ tho i had some other place to be
Now yes they are ~~xxx~~
but ~~xxxxxxx~~ (not many / perhaps not any)

③ ~~xxxx~~ six flying hours / you did promise
to bring down to the plantation
but to them ~~____~~ hound
You always say that you agree
So Now

(they are known ~~xxxx~~ Fate)
you gonna have to wait

④ i got
~~xxxx~~ Fever — in her pocket
The ____ follows me
i can take ____ i cant un
you see ____

⑤ i been in jail ~~xxxx~~ should
that a man cant give his address to bad company
standing in the ruins of your balcony
wondering when you are

Several manuscripts were recovered from Dylan's March 1966 Nashville sessions, including one for "Absolutely Sweet Marie" and one for "I Want You." *Jeff Gold Collection*

1. the lonesome undertaker sighs
the —— organ grinder cries
the silver saxophones say I should refuse you)
the cracked bell & crystal horn
that blow into my face with scorn
Tell me that I wasn't born to love you)

2. The drunken politician leaps
upon the street where mothers weep
with saviours walking in their sleep
who wait for you)
And with my broken heart / drinking from my broken cup
they tell me when to open up the gate (for you)

3-4 you dancing child in his Chinese suit
he spoke to me / I took his flute
an I wasn't very cute to him — (was I ?)
but I did it because he lied & because he took you for a ride
+ because time was on his side
+ because !)

(bridge)
now tell my fathers they gone down
true love —— them without it
—— sons + daughters put me down
cause I don't think about it

While working on the final mixes for *Blonde on Blonde* in early April 1966 at Columbia's West Coast facilities in Los Angeles, The Castle in the Los Feliz area of the city was home base for Dylan, shown here in the mansion's solarium. *Lisa Law*

Dylan in the dining room at The Castle in L.A. in April 1966. *Lisa Law*

Picture sleeve for the single
"Rainy Day Women #12 &
35" released in April 1966.

Daryl Sanders Collection

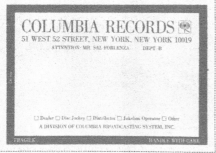

Radio promo piece for
"Rainy Day Women
#12 & 35" from 1966.

Daryl Sanders Collection

Trade ad for the single "I Want You" from the summer of 1966. *Daryl Sanders Collection*

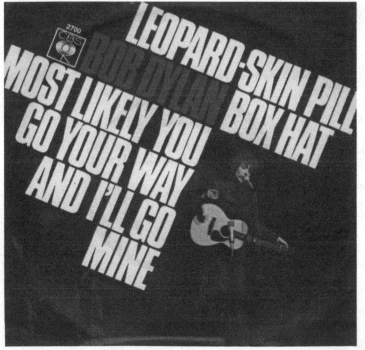

Picture sleeve for the final single released from *Blonde on Blonde*, "Leopard-Skin Pill-Box Hat," which dropped in March 1967. *Daryl Sanders Collection*

a city that was allegedly full of unscrupulous merchants and despised by its neighbors. Tyrus, as the city is called in the King James version of the Bible, was the subject of one of the prophet Ezekiel's most accurate prophecies, which foresaw the city's repeated destruction by its enemies, the word of God coming to him in chapter twenty-six and telling him Tyrus would be "laid waste" because it had broken "the gates of the people."

Gates are mentioned often in Ezekiel, but the most relevant reference for "Sad Eyed Lady" is the second verse of chapter forty-four: "Then said the Lord unto me: This gate shall be shut, it shall not be opened, and no man shall enter in by it." In the chorus of "Sad Eyed Lady of the Lowlands," Dylan seemed to draw on the imagery in that verse from Ezekiel, with a prophet, a reference to "no man," and a closed gate:

> Sad-eyed lady of the lowlands
> Where the sad-eyed prophet says that no man comes
> My warehouse eyes, my Arabian drums
> Should I leave them by your gate
> Or, sad-eyed lady, should I wait?[23]

Mind you, this is not to suggest "Sad Eyed Lady of the Lowlands" has anything to do with the subject matter of Ezekiel. If passages from Ezekiel did inform the song, Dylan was only mining them for some Biblical flourishes to give it that "old-time religious" feeling.

When Dylan finally had a complete set of lyrics, he went into the control room to find Johnston. "I don't know what time it was—2, 3, 4 o'clock in the morning," the producer recalled to the *Austin Chronicle*'s Louis Black. "Dylan finally came out, looked at me and said, 'Hey Bob, you still awake?'

"I said, 'Yeah.'

"'Is there anyone else awake down there?' he asked. 'Who is around you can get? I think I got something here.'

"'Yeah, man,' I said, going off to wake them."[24]

According to studio records, it was 4:00 AM when the Nashville musicians finally got their introduction to the "Sad Eyed Lady"—Kooper, of course, had heard the song back at Dylan's hotel room. The lineup was Dylan, McCoy, and Moss on acoustic guitars, Robbins on piano, Kooper on organ, South on bass, and Buttrey on drums. Although they had already recorded the seven-and-a-half-minute "Visions of Johanna," the Nashville players were not ready for "Sad Eyed Lady."

Over the years, a number of the participants at that session have remembered recording "Sad Eyed Lady of the Lowlands" in one take, and that has become part of the mythology surrounding the song, but there were actually four takes officially slated that morning, three of which were complete.

Although Dylan basically started with a finished set of lyrics, he did revise a few lines here and there over the course of the four takes, most notably the song's first line. On the first two takes, he sang it as, "With your mercury eyes and the months that climb," but prior to recording the third take he changed it to the now familiar, "With your mercury mouth in the missionary times." He made the other significant tweak on the fly during the first take, deciding after three verses that the prophet in the chorus was also "sad-eyed," after previously singing the second line as, "Where the prophet says that no man comes."

Buttrey recalled Dylan running the song down for them to biographer Bob Spitz: "'Okay,' he said, 'this going to be like a couple of verses and a chorus and an instrumental. Then I'll come back in and we'll do another couple of verses, another instrumental, and then we'll see how it goes.'"[25]

The first take, which clocked out at 10:07, undoubtedly was the one Buttrey had in mind when he recounted the recording of "Sad Eyed Lady" to rock historian Clinton Heylin. "Not knowing how long this thing was going to be, we were preparing ourselves dynamically for a basic two- to three-minute record. Because records just didn't go over three minutes," Buttrey explained. "If you notice that record, that thing after like the second chorus starts building and building like crazy, and everybody's just peaking it up 'cause we thought, Man this is it. . . . This is gonna be the last chorus and we've got to put everything into it we can. . . . After about ten minutes of this thing we're cracking up at each other, at what we were doing. I mean, we peaked five minutes ago. Where do we go from here?"[26]

The drummer told biographer Howard Sounes, "I was playing one-handed, looking at my watch. . . . We'd never heard anything like this before."[27]

"It was one of those deals, 'Please don't let me make a mistake,'" McCoy recalls.[28] "After you've tried to stay awake 'til four o'clock in the morning, to play something so slow and long was really, really tough."[29]

After they got over their initial shock at the length of the song and understood they were dealing with a marathon, not a sprint, the musicians set about getting the tempo and feel down. The song was in the key of D, and as Dylan strummed the opening chords on his acoustic, Robbins and Buttrey fell in with him. As they played around with it, Dylan asked McCoy, "Is that right, is that the right beat?" McCoy told him, "I don't know." To which Dylan replied, "Oh, wait now," then played the opening chord progression and hummed the melody at a tempo he liked. Satisfied, he said, "There it is."

From the control room, a sleepy-sounding Johnston announced the take, "Rolling on two."

Just to confirm he was clear, Buttrey asked McCoy, "You playin'," then hummed the beat as he understood it and also toe-tapped it on his bass drum.

"Yeah, we had a triplet feel awhile ago, didn't we?" McCoy asked the drummer in return.

Before they could discuss it further, Robbins joined in, asking McCoy, "Which one? Eighths or triplets?"

"It's supposed to be a triplet feel," he said.

Moss began to fingerpick the melody with that feel, and McCoy joined in. After a few bars, McCoy stopped playing and said, "It's eighths."

Moss continued with his fingerpicking and asked Dylan, "Is that what you want?"

Before he could answer, Robbins joined in on piano, playing some beautiful accompaniment to Moss's fingerpicking, and McCoy started strumming his rhythm part again, too. After several bars, McCoy said, "All right, eighths it is."

Sounding really tired, Dylan finally responded to Moss's question, "I think that's a little bit slow though."

"It is too slow?" Moss asked.

"Sing a little bit," McCoy said to Dylan, so Dylan sang the opening lyric.

After they worked out the tempo, McCoy ran down the song structure to make sure everyone was clear on how long it would be. "After five times around, he's gonna play the melody on the harp the sixth time around," he said. "At the end of that, uh, if we get that far before the fade comes, just hang a D chord. Six times around and hang a D chord."

"Why don't I come in with you on this and then you can just pull me off," Dylan said to McCoy. "I just want to set the tempo, OK?"

"All right," McCoy said.

"Rolling on two," Johnston said again from the control room.

They rehearsed the tempo a bit, then moved on to take three, which clocked in at more than twelve minutes. Take four was slightly faster but still topped eleven minutes, and it was the keeper.

Aside from his vocal, it was Dylan's harmonica playing and Buttrey's drumming that really stood out on the master take. Halfway through the song's instrumental intro, Dylan came in with a soulful harmonica solo that foreshadowed a longer solo he would deliver at the end of the song. And from the opening measure, Buttrey propelled the song along with a steady, repetitive mix of closed hi-hat licks and tambourine accents atop his kick drum pattern, deviating from that rhythm only during the choruses, on which he set up the third line ("My warehouse eyes, my Arabian drums") with a series of snare rolls that continued through the line before tapering back into the hi-hat groove as Dylan began to sing the next-to-last line of the refrain.

South played a softly swinging, in-the-pocket bass part, while McCoy, who had his steel-string guitar capoed up, strummed a high rhythm part, and Moss fingerpicked the song's lilting circular melody on his gut-string. Robbins added majestic chords on the piano that captured the song's stately manner, as did Kooper's organ lines, especially his countermelodies during the choruses.

Johnston later told *Sound On Sound* magazine when Dylan came into the control room and they listened to the playback, "It was one of the prettiest things I ever heard in my life."[30]

"To me, this is the definitive version of what 4 a.m. sounds like," Kooper said, describing "Sad Eyed Lady of the Lowlands" to *Mojo* magazine in 2005. "It may very well be because we recorded it at that hour—but many tracks have been transported to tape in the earliest of a.m.'s, and yet none actually proclaims its birthplace as saliently as this track does."[31]

By the time they called it a night, it was 5:30 AM, still around an hour till daybreak. Dylan headed back to his hotel, tired, but feeling extremely satisfied with his second day of sessions in Music City. For the Nashville cats, however, it had been another really long, strange day at the office. Regarding the song they had just recorded, other than realizing it concerned a sad-eyed lady, they had no idea what it was about. "I'm still trying to figure out what that song means," Moss says.[32]

8

NASHVILLE BLUES AGAIN

BACK IN THE STUDIO at 6:00 PM, the musicians continued their adventure in getting paid master scale to drink coffee and play games, time and a half after midnight. "We didn't mind playing Ping-Pong and signing a [union] card every three hours," Wayne Moss says, "but it wasn't what we were used to."[1]

Albert Grossman also was sitting around waiting, so occasionally he wandered downstairs to the musicians lounge where the Ping-Pong action was. "I played Dylan's manager," Billy Swan recalls. "I wouldn't just stay in the control room all the time, you know. I might go down and play a little Ping-Pong or whatever, so I played [Grossman] a few times. He was a good Ping-Pong player. The first time I ever heard the name Thelonious Monk, I was playing Ping-Pong with him."

As Swan remembers it, during one of their games, Grossman stopped before serving the ball and asked, "You ever heard of Thelonious Monk?"

"No," Swan told him. "No, I haven't."

"Well, he's a jazz player, but he's a good Ping-Pong player, too," Grossman told him, then resumed the game. Of course, Swan found out later Monk was a little more than just *a* jazz player.[2]

The musicians kept themselves occupied for ten hours while Dylan remained in the studio, finishing the lyrics for the next song. "I thought he was a junkie," Johnston told the *Nashville Scene* in 1996. "'Cause he never left the studio . . . and he kept ordering milkshakes and malts, candy bars. And I thought, 'Well goddamn, he's a junkie.' But he wasn't, he was just gettin' energy."[3]

Johnston's first thought was probably closer to the truth. Dylan told Robert Shelton the following month, "It takes a lot of medicine to keep up this pace."[4] Writing in his memoir about when the Hawks were touring with Dylan in 1965 and '66, Robbie Robertson noted, "He wasn't doing too much eating in those days," and wondered if "those little truck-driver pills"—amphetamines—had anything to do with it.[5] Three years later, when *Rolling Stone*'s Jann Wenner asked if drugs influenced his song-writing, Dylan told him, "No, not the writing of them. But it did keep me up there to pump 'em out."[6]

Henry Strzelecki joined the sessions that day, so it was his first opportunity to get paid to sit around while Dylan wrote songs. The bassist had been busy with other studio work the first two days Dylan was in Nashville, and his presence freed Joe South to focus on guitar.

Al Kooper was enjoying working with the Nashville musicians:

> I loved that they had a piano player, and that I could just concentrate on playing organ. It was the first time I had played outside the New York studio system, and I had played in that system since 1959. And I was amazed at the quality and musicianship of the people I was working with—who seemed to be approximately my age.
>
> I mean they played so magnificently, and perfectly. I'd just never been on sessions like that before in my life—and I had done a lot of sessions. And you know, I had never worked with these people before, . . . but they made me feel totally comfortable.[7]

Kooper, who had just turned twenty-two, was correct in thinking the Nashville musicians were around his age. Charlie McCoy was twenty-four, the same age as Dylan; Jerry Kennedy was twenty-five, South was twenty-six, and Strzelecki was twenty-seven. Moss and "Pig" Robbins were the old-timers in the group at twenty-eight, and amazingly, Kenneth Buttrey was only twenty years old.

———

The song Dylan was working on that evening was another piece that would top the seven-minute mark, "Stuck Inside of Mobile with the Memphis Blues Again." A manuscript from that period—part typed, part handwritten—contained the seeds of the song. The typewritten part at the top of the page apparently was the product of some free-association at the typewriter and was simply a number of words and phrases that would make it into the song in revised form: "mama–memphis blues," "people just get uglier," "honky tonk," "black lagoon," "waltz," "neath the panamanium [sic] moon," "over sexed Boston debutantes," "neon," "white medicine," and "20 pounds of headlines laying on his . . ." At the end of the last phrase, Dylan wrote by hand the word "chest." Below the typed section, he had begun to develop the "mama–memphis blues" idea, writing:

> Oh MAMA you have
> IN MOBILE ALABAMA with the Memphis blues again
> Oh MAMA / I'm stuck without a friend
> These Memphis blues are bound to drive me mad

From his initial burst of inspiration for the chorus that was preserved on the manuscript, it was only a short leap to the finished refrain:

> Oh, Mama, can this really be the end
> To be stuck inside of Mobile
> With the Memphis blues again

As he had on "Visions of Johanna," Dylan was exploring feelings of alienation on "Stuck Inside of Mobile with the Memphis Blues Again." Describing the song in *No Direction Home*, Shelton wrote, "If 'Desolation Row' has become Main Street, the 'Memphis Blues' has become the national condition of a mobile, lonely, and lost society."[8]

While the chorus addressed a traditional blues theme, that of longing for another place, often specifically longing for home, the song's nine eight-line verses were like nothing the blues had ever seen, like the blues on a bad trip, harkening back to the more esoteric material populated with fantastic characters found on *Highway 61 Revisited*, songs like "Tombstone Blues," "Desolation Row," and the album's title track.

The first verse seems to draw inspiration from Joseph Conrad's novel *Secret Agent*. One of the main characters in the novel is mute and continuously draws circles, not unlike the ragman in the first verse:

> Oh, the ragman draws circles
> Up and down the block
> I'd ask him what the matter was
> But I know that he don't talk

Dylan concluded the verse with an expression of futility: "But deep inside my heart, I know I can't escape."

Like the first, the remaining verses featured a cast of absurdly colorful characters: Shakespeare "with his pointed shoes and his bells," Mona who warned "to stay away from the train line," Grandpa who "built a fire on Main Street" and "shot it full of holes," the senator who was "handing out free tickets to the wedding of his son," the preacher "with twenty pounds of headlines stapled to his chest," the rainman who gave him "Texas medicine" and "railroad gin," Ruthie who says "your debutante just knows what you need, but I know what you want," and neon madmen who climb only to fall "so perfectly." Dylan concluded the final verse with a defeated, but hopeful twist:

> An' I sit so patiently
> Waiting to find out what price
> You have to pay to get out of
> Going through all these things twice[9]

As the hours passed, Dylan sat at a table at the rear of the studio, working diligently on the song. Mid-evening, he got up and went over to the control room at the front of the room. "He was out in the studio writing, by himself," Swan recalls. "I was in the control room, nobody else was there. He came in and said somebody was looking through the door and it was bothering him. So I went out to check and it was somebody I knew. So I walked down and said, 'Hey, it's kind of bothering him, you know, you looking through the window.' And he said, 'Oh, no problem,' then he left."[10]

Just like the night before, the musicians finally got the call to come up to the studio at around 4:00 AM. Besides Dylan on acoustic guitar and harmonica, the lineup was McCoy on acoustic guitar, Moss and South on electric guitars, Robbins on piano, Kooper on organ, Strzelecki on bass, and Buttrey on drums. Over the next three hours, engineer Tom Sparkman logged seventeen takes of "Stuck Inside of Mobile with the Memphis Blues Again," the first two being rehearsal takes not officially slated.

Dylan ran down the song's chords on his Gibson acoustic for them, singing the melody, "Doo, doo, doo, doo-doo, doo-doo-doo." As they got ready to rehearse the song, McCoy, who initially was going to play harmonica, asked Buttrey if he would count off the song. "You wanna count it?" he said. "I've got a mouthful of harp over here."

Dylan may have still had that religious feeling from the night before, because the first take had a bit of a slow, gospel feel to it, especially Robbins's piano part. When Dylan got to the first chorus, he gave a little nod to the local musicians, singing, "Oh, Mama, this might be the end / I'm stuck inside of Mobile / with the Nashville blues again."

They worked on the arrangement during a couple of rehearsal takes. On the first rehearsal take, McCoy played harmonica, but as they were preparing for the second rehearsal take, Dylan subtly let the Nashville harp ace know he intended to play harmonica on the song. "Aren't you going to play the guitar, Charlie?"

"Well," McCoy said, pausing to think. "Yeah."

They ran through the first verse and chorus, then Dylan took a harmonica solo. Satisfied with the arrangement and tempo, Dylan stopped the music as the band transitioned into the verse, and asked Johnston in the control room, "Ready? Ready?"

"Yeah," the producer told him.

McCoy had noticed it was going to be tight for Dylan to get out of the solo and into the second verse, so he said to Dylan, "You might add an extra bar."

"Oh, yeah, yeah," Dylan said. "It's gonna be hard for me to come back because I'll be playing the harp so it will be an extra . . ."

"Okay, let's add a bar," McCoy said. "Let's add a bar."

Dylan was still making some last-minute refinements to the lyrics as he went along. For example, on the first official take, he tried a new second line for the chorus, singing "down in Mobile," as opposed to "stuck inside of Mobile." A little more than a minute into the take, Dylan realized there was a problem with the arrangement and stopped the musicians. "Wait, no," he said to McCoy. "Hey, it's gonna be very hard for me to do this on the harmonica."

"It's fast—is it too fast?" McCoy asked.

"No, it's not too fast," Dylan told him. "It's gonna be kinda hard for me to get the harmonica in there."

"Yeah," McCoy agreed.

"'Cause we're gonna have to have a whole beat, and then the drum will be accented after that. If we can remember all the time. It'll sound kinda corny with the drum accent and then nothing."

"Yeah," McCoy said.

From the control room, Johnston added, "Kenny, don't forget those pickup notes when he says, 'Down in Mobile with the Memphis blues again.' On Memphis, you're coming out of the pickup."

"We can do it, if we're gonna do it all the time now," Dylan continued, then blew the harmonica line. "We should tone it down there, too, you know."

Take two broke down immediately after the intro because Strzelecki was uncertain about the bass turnaround leading into the verse. After they got that straightened out, work on the song continued. Take five, which would be released in 2005 on *The Bootleg Series, Vol. 7,* was the first complete take, but the tempo was a little too fast for the words in places.

Before take six, Dylan said to Johnston, "Are we rolling, Bob?"

"Yeah, we're rollin' on six. Let's get it," the producer said.

Dylan counted off, "One, two, three," then went right into playing and singing the song, but Buttrey wasn't ready, and asked McCoy, "Is he gonna start like the other one?"

"He's not," McCoy said. "He's just gonna count it in."

From the control room, Johnston added, "Yeah, and everybody hit a groove this time. Seven."

Takes seven through twelve all broke down within the first minutes of the take. On the eleventh take, Dylan almost sang "Nashville blues" again, which distracted him, then stumbled through the first few lines of the second verse, before stopping the music and saying apologetically, "I'm sorry, I'm sorry. I, uh, I am kind of jumpy." He paused, then added, "It should be just, uh, a little slower." He strummed the opening chords, then said to Johnston, "All right."

The producer slated the take number: "Twelve."

McCoy asked Johnston, "Did that sound all right, Bob?"

"Yeah."

Still thinking about the arrangement, Dylan said, "Let's play soft on the 'Oh, Mama,' part."

"Yeah, everybody, more dynamics," McCoy instructed.

"Except the organ, man," Dylan said to Kooper. "The organ part there, a very high, soft organ—you know."

Johnston cautioned Strzelecki, "Only put that run where it's supposed to come, Henry."

When McCoy let Johnston know they were ready to record, the producer said, "On twelve. Take it easy."

Take twelve quickly broke down, but they took Johnston's advice to heart on a slower, softer thirteenth take, and it worked; although the take broke down when Dylan either accidentally or experimentally sang, "Oh, Mama, I just need a friend," as the opening line of the seventh chorus. He finished singing the chorus, but then stopped the music and said, "Oh, wait a second. I'm sorry. Let's try it again, let's start from the beginning."

They took take fourteen at a faster rock tempo, and everything clicked over Buttrey's unwavering 4/4 beat. It took them one more take to totally lock in on their new approach, and that take was deemed the master take, despite Dylan stumbling in the fourth verse about Grandpa, singing at the beginning of the fifth line, "When I . . . "—before quickly correcting himself—" . . . he built a fire on Main Street." Considering the flubbed line, it's unclear why Dylan didn't ask to do another take or why Johnston didn't insist on one. It may have been that they simply ran out of time, since according to session records, it was 7:00 AM when they finished take fifteen. Some of the musicians would have had morning sessions to attend, and there may well have been a session booked that morning in Columbia Studio A.

While once again Buttrey's dynamic drumming set the tone, the keeper take featured some inspired exchanges between Kooper and South, who was playing a customized Gretsch "Country Gentleman" guitar with a distinctive sound. "That's Joe South playing guitar on 'Memphis Blues Again,'" Kooper recalled to Andy Gill. "He was fantastic; he has that sort of hammering-on style that Curtis Mayfield and Reggie Young have.

"I was very happy with the organ on that, too," he continued. "It has a lot of spontaneity. I think there's lovely interplay between us. . . . That's where the organ and guitar are most perfectly matched."[11]

With the master take of "Stuck Inside of Mobile with the Memphis Blues Again" in the can, Dylan's first Nashville sessions came to a close, and he was feeling good about his decision to record there. He had recorded five songs, including what would be the three longest tracks on the album—more than half an hour of music altogether. On the next leg of his tour, he added "Fourth Time Around" to the acoustic portion of his concerts and "Leopard-Skin Pill-Box Hat" to the electric set.

As the Nashville musicians headed to their cars a half hour after sunrise on that cold morning, the main thing they were feeling was tired. With the exception of Strzelecki, they had just spent three and a half bizarre and exhausting days recording a handful of songs in the dead of night when they were usually asleep. But sleep was not on their schedules. They barely would have time to rush home, eat breakfast, and clean up before returning to Music Row for 10:00 AM sessions with producers who didn't believe in paying musicians to sit around drinking coffee.

While Dylan was pleased with his sessions at Columbia's Nashville facilities, some of the staff there were not so thrilled. After Dylan left town, Johnston, who was still in Nashville, received a letter from Columbia's staff engineers there, who were all members of the International Union of Electrical Workers. The letter was in reaction to not only whatever alterations Johnston had made in Studio A, but also several other breaches of union protocol, such as moving the tape machine into the control room—it was in a small room adjacent to the control room—and making them work all night. They weren't too happy with Johnston's dictatorial ways either. "They sent me a letter, and said in the future, I would not touch anything, and they would move the machines, they would leave for lunch or dinner, and I wouldn't have anything to say about it, and we could wait—they went through that routine," the producer told me.

The engineers also planned to send the letter to Bill Gallagher, vice president of the Columbia label, in charge of all label activities, including artists and repertoire. "So, I called Gallagher and asked him to please come down," Johnston continued. "And he came down, and I told him what the story was."

That one of Columbia's top executives in New York considered the matter important enough to fly to Nashville speaks to Dylan's stature within the company. Upon his arrival, Gallagher and Johnston went to see the engineers and the producer recalled what happened at that meeting: "They read the letter to him, and he said, 'I understand how you feel, Johnston's a hard nut; but I've only got one thing to say: If I were you—just giving you a piece of advice—if I were you and he asks for a microphone on the ceiling, I'd get the tallest goddamn ladder I could find and I'd start climbing, or I'll shut this motherfucker down.'"[12]

9

ABSOLUTELY SWEET MUSIC

THE PLAN WAS FOR DYLAN to return to Nashville for more sessions beginning Monday, March 7. At 8:00 AM on the morning of Thursday, March 3, prior to flying to Miami for a show that evening, he had another photo shoot with Jerry Schatzberg, this one for the cover of the *Saturday Evening Post*.

Once again, Schatzberg shot him outdoors, this time at a location on Jacob Street below the Brooklyn Bridge, according to PopSpots' Bob Egan.[1] Dylan was wearing a white scarf with a dark suit, and he was smoking a cigarette in the shot used on the cover of the July 30 issue of the magazine, which featured a cover story by Jules Siegel titled, "Bob Dylan: 'Well, What Have We Here?'" On the magazine's cover, the photograph was flopped, Dylan looking left to right, rather than right to left, as he does in the original photo.

After the shoot, Dylan flew to Florida for a performance that night at the Convention Hall in Miami. Two days later on Saturday, March 5, he played a show at the Jacksonville Coliseum. From Jacksonville, he went on to Nashville to resume work on the album. His wife, Sara, his infant son, Jesse, Albert Grossman, and Robbie Robertson all accompanied him. Traveling separately as he had in February, Al Kooper met Dylan and his party in Nashville for the sessions scheduled to resume at six o'clock that Monday evening.

"[Dylan] had gone to Nashville and he had recorded four of the songs for *Blonde on Blonde*," Robertson recalled during an interview with Michael Gray and Pete Finney, cocurators of the *Dylan, Cash, and the Nashville Cats: A New Music City* exhibit at the Country Music Hall of Fame and Museum. "When Bob came back, and he played me some of the things he had recorded there, he was really impressed by the Nashville [musicians]. He said, 'I just went in there—these guys didn't know me, they didn't know this music—I went in there, and they just all get in a huddle, and they figure it out so quickly and come up with an arrangement, a whole idea for the song.'"

Dylan went on to tell Robertson he planned to return to Nashville for additional sessions. "He said, 'I'm going to go back and record some more, and I would like you to come with me and have you play on some of the things.'"

What Dylan didn't know was Robertson had been to Nashville five years earlier for a Ronnie Hawkins session at Bradley studios and had not found it quite so welcoming. "Ronnie Hawkins—it was like 1961, I think—he decided he wanted to make an album of folk music and wanted to do it in Nashville," Robertson explained.

Hawkins planned to use only two of his band members on the Nashville sessions, Levon Helm and Robertson, otherwise he would be backed by some of the city's leading session cats. "So we went there," Robertson continued, "and we found out in a very mysterious way that they conveyed to you, 'We don't do that. We work with our own people because we have a thing, and we have a rapport with one another, and we can get it done. When somebody else comes into that, it makes it not work so well, so we don't encourage that.'

"And what was really interesting to me for that record was that Grady Martin and Hank Garland played guitar, and they were both like maestros on the guitar. They played so beautiful, and everybody in the studio played so beautiful, I was happy just to witness it. And how smooth everything went—they did have their own [thing]—everybody there, they could just look at one another and pass signals around. It was something that I absorbed, and I appreciated that they had this beautiful formula with one another."

It just so happened that while Hawkins, Helm, and Robertson were at Bradley studios, a monster R&B hit was being cut in the Quonset hut. "To top it all off, after this recording session, we went down into another studio and Bobby Blue Bland and his band—'cause we just thought it was country music everywhere you went—and Bobby Blue Bland and his band were in another studio recording 'Turn on Your Love Light,'" Robertson recalled. "So anyway, my first impression of Nashville was large."

So, Robertson told Dylan that when he had been to Nashville before he hadn't actually been welcomed. "I said, 'You know they don't much like outsiders.' When I first said that, he said, 'What do you mean? They're like great guys, and they just like to play music.'

"And I told my whole thing with Ronnie Hawkins, and he said, 'Really? Well, I don't think that's going to be a problem. They seem like the door's wide open.'"

Although not necessarily in the way Dylan meant, Robertson knew "there was a door that you needed to go through to get into that world."[2]

When Dylan and his party reached Nashville, he, his family, and Grossman checked into the Ramada Inn on James Robertson Parkway, while Robertson and Kooper had rooms at Roger Miller's King of the Road Motor Inn, located further downtown on the east bank of the Cumberland River.[3]

Since Dylan had Sara and Jesse with him, Johnston had hired Lamar Fyke, who was part of Elvis Presley's Memphis Mafia, to act as a driver/bodyguard for the artist and his party while they were in Nashville that week. As the producer describes him, Fyke was a large, loud, gregarious man. "I hired him because he had a black Cadillac and people would shy away from him," Johnston said.[4]

Dylan arrived at the rear entrance to Columbia's Nashville facilities on that clear, cold Monday evening accompanied not only by Robertson, Kooper, and Grossman, but also by Sara and the baby. Once in the studio, Dylan told Johnston he needed to do some more work on the song he wanted to record that evening, so the Nashville musicians who were on hand—Charlie McCoy, Kenneth Buttrey, Wayne Moss, Joe South, Hargus Robbins, Henry Strzelecki, and Mac Gayden—headed down to the musicians lounge for more waiting, this time seven hours.

Dylan was delighted with the situation, as he told Stan Rofe during an interview the following month on Radio 3UZ in Melbourne, Australia. "In Nashville, people sit around if they want to," he said. "If they want to make good records, they sit around all night 'til you're ready. But they won't do that in New York; they get bored and talk and bring you down some kind of way."[5]

Dylan may have thought that's how things were done in Nashville, but it actually was the opposite of how things usually worked there. And even though they were getting paid, for some of the Nashville cats, Dylan's approach to recording was getting a little old.

"It was to the point of ridiculous," says Moss, who by then was way over the novelty of being paid to do nothing and starting to resent all the downtime.[6] The musicians couldn't do their best work under those conditions.

McCoy acknowledges it was frustrating for the musicians and dampened their enthusiasm. "Well, it's hard to be upbeat," he says, "especially when you feel like, 'Man, I really need a nap, but I'm afraid to take one,' because just any second he may say, 'Let's go.' But there were a few naps along the way, I can tell you that."[7]

Gayden, who was one of the guitarists on that night's session, remembers that as the time dragged on, he took a nap on the floor in the back of the studio while Dylan worked on the lyrics at the piano and his wife nursed the baby in the corner. "That was so cool," Gayden says. "I had never been on a session where a wife was breastfeeding. It was so bohemian."

To Gayden, Dylan was "otherworldly." "Dylan had a mystique and he brought it into the studio," says the guitarist, who also recalls there being a white Bible on a music stand nearby.[8]

Not yet a successful songwriter, Kris Kristofferson recently had started working at Columbia as an engineer's assistant, taking over the position formerly held by Billy Swan. "I saw Dylan sitting out in the studio at the piano, writing all night long by himself, dark glasses on," he recalled to David Bowman in a 1999 interview for *Salon*. When Bowman asked if he spoke to Dylan, Kristofferson said, "No! The closest I got was Al Grossman. Even to his wife and his son Jesse. I wouldn't have *dared* talk to him. I'd have been fired."[9]

Around 9:30 or 10:00, Dylan realized his harmonicas didn't make it to Nashville with him, so Johnston dispatched Kristofferson to borrow some harps from singer-songwriter Chris Gantry, who lived not far from the studio in the West End area of the city.

Gantry, whose song "Dreams of the Everyday Housewife" would become a Top 5 pop hit for Glen Campbell two years later, will always remember that late-night visit in March of '66. "Kristofferson knocked on my door at about ten o'clock or ten thirty," Gantry recalls. "He took all my harmonicas and gave them to Bob to use on the session—I had a slew of them. I never got them back, but that was cool." After all, it *was* Bob Dylan.[10]

Even after Kristofferson returned to the studio with Gantry's harps, Dylan kept the musicians waiting for another two hours or so. It was around 1:00 AM when the Nashville cats finally were called up from the lounge two levels below, and when they got there, Kooper and Robertson were already in the studio. Dylan introduced Robertson and told McCoy he wanted the guitarist to play on the song. Robertson vividly recalled that moment. "These guys looked at me like, 'Oh, Jesus, here we go again,'" he said. "You know, another guy that we're going to have to teach how to do this.

"No one was being necessarily cold or anything; they just wanted to do their thing," he continued. "They just wanted to get the job done in the way they knew how to do it. And it was no different than when I went down there before and it was Grady Martin and Hank Garland and all these guys; they just wanted to get the job done. Somebody else comes in, it just makes the whole thing feel unbalanced."[11] Gayden also remembers that moment and says he could tell Robertson also was "checking us out," meaning the Nashville players.[12]

Dylan ran down the song for everyone, and they quickly worked out the basic arrangement. From the first run-through, the song captured the thin, wild mercury sound Dylan was in search of—an electrifying and transcendent blend of guitar, organ, and harmonica.

Before the first slated take, Johnston asked through the talk-back mic, "What's the name of this, Bob?"

"'Where Are You Tonight, Sweet Marie,'" Dylan said of the song that eventually would be released as "Absolutely Sweet Marie."

Dylan may have gotten the name from an old Irish folk song by Percy French called "Sweet Marie," a song he would have been familiar with through his friends the Clancy Brothers and Tommy Makem, both of whom had the song in their repertoires during Dylan's days as part of the Greenwich Village folk scene. But the only thing the two songs had in common was the name. In French's composition, Sweet Marie was a racehorse who lost the big race and cost the owner, who had wagered on the mare, a considerable sum.

During the rehearsal, they had played the song in the key of C, but on the first official take, Dylan changed it to D, and that's where it remained. They got a complete take, but Dylan wasn't completely satisfied with the lyrics yet. After he made a few more tweaks, they tried another take.

They were only ten seconds or so into the second take when Johnston heard something he didn't like and interrupted the musicians from the control room. "Hold it, Bob," he drawled over the talk-back mic. "Do it one more time just in case you get it—and everybody, on the intro, the organ was late then and a couple of other things."

A slightly more uptempo take three was the keeper, an exhilarating romp powered by Buttrey's thrilling drum work. Using mostly bass drum and snare, he laid down an insistent, up-tempo beat and punctuated it with timely crash cymbal accents and dazzling tom and snare rolls as the song built toward its climax. "The real unsung hero on that track is the drummer, Kenny Buttrey," Kooper told Andy Gill. "The beat is amazing, and that's what makes the track work."[13]

Kooper shined, too, delivering another unforgettable organ riff that enhanced the beat and gave the song its primary melodic hook. Bassist Strzelecki, pianist Robbins, and guitarists McCoy, South, and Gayden reinforced Buttrey's rollicking rhythm. McCoy played an acoustic rhythm part that ultimately got buried in the mix, and Gayden contributed a locked-in, tic tac guitar part, a technique unique to Nashville that added a high-end, percussive complement to the bass. South added some R&B

flavored electric rhythm, often working the low strings of his custom Gretsch to echo what Robbins was playing.

During the spaces in the verses, Moss and Robertson engaged in a duel of Fenders, with Moss serving up some tight, twangy licks on his Jazzmaster, while Robertson made his Telecaster ring out with a harder blues edge.

South may have had "Absolutely Sweet Marie" in mind when he told Dutch journalist Jan Donkers in 1988 what he remembered about the *Blonde on Blonde* sessions was "trying to get a lick in."[14] One of the earmarks of the Nashville sessions was that many of the tracks featured four and five guitarists, and not just any guitarists, guitarists who would rank among the most celebrated guitar players in the history of popular music.

On top of the cacophony of sound created by the other nine musicians, Dylan delivered a clear, confident vocal performance, and during both the instrumental break after the fourth verse and the song's outro, he blew some unhinged harmonica lines that underscored the song's urgency.

"Absolutely Sweet Marie" is a tale of unrequited sexual longing that prominently features two of the album's prevailing lyrical themes, waiting and gates, in this case, a railroad gate. There was a one-page, handwritten manuscript for "Absolutely Sweet Marie," a single sheet from a legal pad, one of several lyric sheets saved from the March sessions by engineer Charlie Bragg. Historian and collector Jeff Gold owns two of those manuscripts, including the one for "Absolutely Sweet Marie," a piece he describes as "halfway there," obtained from a private collector.[15]

Unlike the four songs Dylan recorded during the February sessions in Nashville, "Absolutely Sweet Marie" included a bridge or middle eight—two of them, in fact—but on the manuscript, there is only the beginnings of one line from the first bridge and nothing from the second. There also is no sign of the chorus ("But where are you tonight, sweet Marie?") on the manuscript, suggesting that was already set in his mind. So, on the handwritten sheet, he was focusing on the five verses.

The first was the least-developed verse on the manuscript. Dylan had scratched out the first line and added, "your [sic] now the eagle." The second line begins with the word "Your," but the rest of the line had been marked through, and the words "eagle teeth" written above it. There are two more lines that contain elements of the final version of the verse: "Yes, I can see you ve [*sic*] left him for me" and "the promises you left gave to me."[16]

By the time they got around to recording a rehearsal take, Dylan had tightened up the first verse some, but he still didn't have a complete first line, half humming, half mumbling the beginning of it. During the rehearsal, Dylan sang the verse as follows:

> [Hum/mumble] don't understand me
> Sometimes it's so hard for me to see
> And the eagle's teeth down above the train line
> And the promises that you left for me

By the first slated take, Dylan had introduced the railroad gate metaphor and "promises" had become "memories," making the first verse:

> Well, the railroad gate, I just can't jump it
> Sometimes it gets so hard for me, you see
> And the captain, there beating on his trumpet
> He's now got the memories you left for me

By the third and master take, Dylan had reworked the first verse further, deciding he preferred "promises" to "memories," and revising the second and third lines into the now-famous ones laden with more overt sexual innuendo:

> Well, your railroad gate, you know I just can't jump it
> Sometimes it gets so hard, you see
> I'm just sitting here beating on my trumpet
> With all these promises you left for me

The "Absolutely Sweet Marie" manuscript shows Dylan was pretty far along with the other four verses, although on some lines there were missing words denoted by long dashes, words he either didn't need to write down in order to remember them or needed to still write. For example, the second verse appeared on the lyric sheet as follows:

Well, I waited for you——half sick
I waited for——hated me
I waited for——frozen traffic
Now tho I had some other place to be

He filled in the blanks on the rehearsal take, with a slight tweak at the beginning of the fourth line:

Well, I waited for you when I was half sick
Yes, I waited for you when you hated me
Well, I waited for you inside of the frozen traffic
Even though I had some other place to be

Dylan revised the beginning of the fourth line again on the master take, making it clear who had inconvenienced whom: "When *you knew* I had some other place to be."

The first bridge followed the second verse, and on the manuscript Dylan had just the beginnings of the idea for the couplet that would become one of his most vicious put-downs, a string of words that hinted at where he was headed, including: "but then again / not many / perhaps not any."

He had the basic lines by the rehearsal take and continued to refine the brutal smackdown on the fly until the third and final take: "Well, anybody can be just like me, obviously / But then, now again, not too many can be like you, fortunately."

The third verse began with one of Sweet Marie's promises, "six white horses."[17] In some circles that imagery has been interpreted as code for heroin. But more notably, the third verse contains what may be Dylan's most-quoted line: "To live outside the law, you must be honest." In a major essay for *Harper's* in 2007 on the subject of artistic appropriation, Jonathan Lethem suggested the line was inspired by a 1958 noir film in which a psychopathic killer named Julian said something nearly identical. In the piece, Lethem wrote:

"When you live outside the law, you have to eliminate dishonesty." The line comes from Don Siegel's 1958 film noir, *The Lineup*, written by Stirling Silliphant. The film still haunts revival houses, likely thanks to Eli Wallach's blazing portrayal of a sociopathic hit man and to Siegel's long, sturdy auteurist career. Yet what were those words worth—to Siegel, or Silliphant, or their audience—in 1958? And again: what was the line worth when Bob Dylan heard it (presumably in some Greenwich Village repertory cinema), cleaned it up a little, and inserted it into "Absolutely Sweet Marie"? What are they worth now, to the culture at large?[18]

If Dylan did see the film, whatever specific value the line had before he heard it, it was unquestionably worth more after he "cleaned it up a little," considering it's his more artful expression, not Silliphant's original dialogue, that is so often quoted.

The third verse was followed by the second bridge, this one four lines long. There was no hint of it on the manuscript retrieved from the session, and Dylan still was figuring it out on the rehearsal take, but by the first official take, he had the lyrics for the bridge together. In the quatrain, the singer announced he wasn't the only one who was "gonna have to wait," that other than the riverboat captain, everyone else including Sweet Marie would have to wait to know his fate.

On the manuscript, the fourth verse looked a lot like the second, mostly complete, but with some words missing from each line and indicated by long dashes.

> I got fever—in my pocket
> While the——follows me
> I can take——I can't un
> You see——your key

By the first take, he had filled in all the blanks:

> Well, I got the fever down in my pockets
> The Persian drunkard, he follows me

Yes, I can take him to your house, but I can't unlock it
You see you forgot to leave me with the key[19]

Aside from making another overt reference to unfulfilled physical yearning—"the fever down in my pockets"—Dylan introduced the person following him, "the Persian drunkard," considered by some to be a reference to the eleventh-century Persian scholar, teacher, and poet Omar Khayyam, who so loved wine he believed it provided a path to the divine. One of Khayyam's quatrains or rubaiyats in particular may have informed the fourth verse:

There was a door to which I found no key;
There was a veil past which I could not see:
Some little talk awhile of me and thee
There seemed—and then no more of thee and me[20]

On the manuscript, Dylan had the first two lines of the fifth and final verse nailed down, and part of another, but there was no mention of a "yellow railroad."

I been jail——mail showed
That a man can't give his address to bad company
Standing in the ruins of your balcony
Wondering where you are

The rehearsal take didn't make it to the final verse, but Dylan had introduced the yellow railroad by the first official take:

Well, I been in jail, but all the mail showed
That a man can't give his address out to bad company
And now I stand here looking at your yellow railroad
Standing in the ruins of your balcony[21]

By the final take, he had decided he didn't want to use a variation of the word "stand" in consecutive lines, so he trimmed the last line to simply, "In the ruins of your balcony."

In a rare instance in which Dylan was willing to speak to specific lines in his songs, he talked about the "yellow railroad" when asked by Paul Zollo about it in a 1991 interview for *SongTalk* magazine. "That's as complete as you can be," he said. "Every single letter in that line. It's all true. On a literal and on an escapist level—'yellow railroad' could have been a blinding day when the sun was so bright on a railroad someplace and it stayed on my mind. These aren't contrived images. These are images which are just in there and have got to come out. You know, if it's in there, it's got to come out."[22]

In the early 1980s, a pioneering cowpunk outfit called Jason and the Scorchers jumpstarted the alternative rock scene in Nashville, drawing major-label interest in the process. They inked a deal with EMI Records and their first release was the EP *Fervor*. *Fervor* included an amped-up cover of "Absolutely Sweet Marie," which became the band's first single for the label. A music video for the song landed Jason and the Scorchers on MTV.

"I was listening to *Blonde on Blonde* ceaselessly in those days, especially the first side," lead singer Jason Ringenberg recalls. "I had an instinct that our band could do a good version of 'Absolutely Sweet Marie,' so I simply played it for them on my guitar and off it went. It was magic the first time we played it."[23]

Warner Hodges, Scorchers lead guitarist who supplied the unforgettable solos on their recording, confesses, "You see it was a weird thing, when we recorded that song, I did not know it was a Dylan tune. I thought it was the best song Jason had ever written."

Hodges didn't learn it had been written by Dylan until the mixing stage. "We recorded that with [producer] Terry Manning, and I remember coming in one day, and he started talking about the Dylan tune. And I was like, 'The Dylan tune. What Dylan tune?' And he said '"Absolutely Sweet Marie."' And I said, 'No, no, no, no, no—that's the best song Jason's ever wrote.' And he kind of laughed at my young, punk rock ass, and said, 'No, I'm sorry, you're wrong. Mr. Bob Dylan wrote that.'

"I think part of our take on the tune, the reason the tune came out the way it did—I don't know about anybody else in the band, but I had never heard the original," Hodges continues. "I approached it as if it was one of our songs, you know. But after the fact for me, that record [*Blonde on Blonde*] had a huge bearing on what Jason and the Scorchers were."[24]

Aside from a faster tempo, the Scorchers' version has the distinction of repeating the first half of the chorus twice—"Where are you tonight, where are you tonight, sweet Marie"—and even three times at the end. "As soon as we worked up our version of it, we played it almost every show," Ringenberg says. "To this day, it is a mainstay of our set. I never tire of singing it.

"Even as a teenager I was aware and amazed that *Blonde on Blonde* was recorded in Nashville," he continues. "As I got older and more in tune to the whole Nashville cats history, I grew to believe that only Nashville in the mid-'60s could have produced that record. Those musicians were so intuitive, and Dylan needed that for those sessions."

Jason and the Scorchers wound up touring with Dylan at the end of the decade. "He was very friendly and generous of spirit when we toured with him in 1989," Ringenberg says.[25]

Hodges says the song wasn't initially in the band's setlist. "The first couple of nights, we weren't doing the song, because it was his song and we were opening for him," Hodges explains. "He finally came up to me and said, 'Hey, man, why ain't you guys doing "Sweet Marie"?' 'Well, sir, it's your song.' 'Yeah, but your version's better than mine.' So, we started doing the tune."[26]

10

QUARTERS IN THE CEILING

DYLAN AND THE MUSICIANS RECONVENED at the studio at 2:00 PM, and, not surprisingly, the players immediately were told to take a break. In the alternate reality of recording with Dylan, this was becoming their routine, their new normal.

Singer-songwriter Chris Gantry stopped by the sessions twice that day, in the afternoon and in the evening. "I knew Bob Johnston really well—he and I had dealings over the years," Gantry explains of his access to the Dylan sessions. "Bob Johnston was always the same—hyper, moving fast, talking real fast, talking big, big stuff."

Gantry confirmed not much was happening when he stopped by Columbia that afternoon. "Everybody was just sitting around," he recalls. "Dylan was in the studio writing whatever song he was about to record."[1]

The number he was about to record was "Just Like a Woman," an extremely sophisticated piece of pop rock that Dylan began writing in Kansas City on Thanksgiving Day.[2] An intentionally sexist kiss-off/put-down, it was another song thought to be inspired in part by Edie Sedgwick. It also has been speculated the song was about Joan Baez, primarily because of the third and final verse, which includes an apparent reference to when Dylan was an unknown folk singer whom the already established Baez took under her wing and championed: "When we meet again /

Introduced as friends / Please don't let on that you knew me when / I was hungry and it was your world." It seems likely the song drew from his experiences with both women.

Once Dylan had a full set of lyrics, the musicians returned to the studio, and he ran down the song for them. The lineup that afternoon was Dylan on vocals and harmonica, Charlie McCoy on acoustic guitar, Joe South on electric guitar, Pig Robbins on piano, Al Kooper on organ, Henry Strzelecki on bass, and Kenneth Buttrey on drums. Although he was at the studio, Robbie Robertson remained in the control room, probably because Dylan was hearing a softer sound on the song. When they were ready to record a take, Johnston asked from the control room, "What's the name of it, Bob?"

"Like a Woman," Dylan replied. He hadn't added the word "just" to the title yet.

At first, Dylan had all the choruses in second person; you, not she, was like a woman:

> And you shake like a woman
> And you fake just like a woman
> And you ache just like a woman
> But you break just like a little girl

They recorded four complete takes of the song that afternoon, and Dylan was refining the verses as he went along. For example, on take one, the opening line of the first verse was, "I can't complain," and in the fourth line, it was "Honey," not "Baby," who had new clothes, but the rest of the verse was close to its final version.

The second verse was a little less together: It was "Annie," not yet "Queen Mary," who was his friend. And he had yet to add "fog" and "amphetamine" to the "pearls," initially ending the verse with the line, "But I gave you those pearls."

The first part of the third verse was basically there on the first take, but the rest was in flux, including the apparent reference to Baez, which was absent. He was still working out those lines. Instead he sang, "Don't let me down like you did before / I must go out into the world."

The bridge was mostly undeveloped on the first take, bearing little resemblance to the final version, although he did have the one phrase, "pain in there." But by the second take, the bridge was starting to take shape, with the last half of it complete, and the fourth line was near-complete:

Time waits
When you go back
It's raining in here
A long-curse hurts,
But what's worse
Is this pain in here
I can't stay in here
Ain't it clear that—

Dylan was committed to the rain imagery in the bridge, so he continued to try different variations. On the third take, he had revised the first three lines of the bridge to:

Now don't you ask
Where's my mask
When there's rain in here[3]

But other than the rain element, he had abandoned the rest of that idea by the fourth take, which was still not it, although he did briefly change "long-time curse" to " dead man's curse."

From the beginning, the final arrangement was more or less together, so most of the time was spent trying to find the right tempo for the song. The first three takes featured that arrangement, but on the fourth take, they tried a decidedly different musical approach, with Robertson joining the others in the studio for a surprising up-tempo, Bo Diddley–influenced arrangement of the song. That take broke down as the musicians were vamping out at the end, when Dylan went back to the chorus on harmonica and everyone else kept vamping. When it happened, Dylan laughed and said, "We lost, man," then laughed again.

Johnston liked the faster tempo, prompting him to enthuse from the control room, "That's one helluva beat!"

Recognizing that he still had work to do on the lyrics of "Like a Woman," Dylan decided to table it for a while and move on to another song. But before they did that, the musicians took their dinner break.

As Strzelecki recalled to me, Robbins's wife stopped by the studio during the break. "Pig's wife brought in a Ouija board," he said. "We played with the Ouija board for I don't know how many hours. You know, we were having fun while Bob was finishing writing one of the songs.

"When we were fooling around with the Ouija board, I said, 'You know, this is going to be either the biggest album in the world, or it ain't gonna do nothin'.'"[4]

It was during the dinner break that Gantry returned to the studio. He was accompanied by two members of Bill Monroe's Bluegrass Boys: Peter Rowan and Richard Greene. "You know, we all lived together—me and Peter and Richard Greene and all of Bill Monroe's boys," Gantry says, explaining how they happened to be with him. "We all lived over on West End, and we all lived in the same proximity, so we were around each other all the time."[5]

Dylan was taking a break when the three of them arrived. "It was a very relaxed atmosphere," Rowan told author Neil Rosenberg a few months later. "No one seemed to be working very hard, although the money that—you know, that's a very expensive session."

Dylan was sitting on a stool in the studio, reading a movie magazine, as Rowan remembered it. "He would just do things like read off the names, like 'Melina Mercouri' or 'Anthony Quinn,' then he'd say, 'Right?' And all his crew would go, 'Right,'" Rowan said. "Or he'd laugh, and then Albert Grossman would stand up and wheel his huge body around and throw another quarter into the ceiling. . . . Yeah, in the control room. There were fifteen or twenty quarters stuck up in the ceiling.

"I think they were all stoned," he added.[6]

Gantry puts it more bluntly: "Everybody was whacked! So that had a lot to do with it."

But that's not to suggest the three visitors saw anyone actually smoking marijuana. As Gantry explains, back then, people smoked pot much more on the sly. "In those days, you could go to jail for that shit," he says, referring to simple possession.[7]

Regarding the quarters in the ceiling, Johnston told me it all started when Grossman accidentally flipped a coin in the air, and it stuck in one of the ceiling tiles. "So everybody started throwing coins up there, and three or four days later, the whole ceiling was full of quarters."[8]

In his memoir, Kooper also recalled it starting with Grossman, but that soon others were doing it, too, including himself and Johnston. "I just knew when we left town some enterprising engineer was gonna turn up a bass track to full volume and all them quarters were gonna rain down on the control room like a Las Vegas jackpot," he wrote.[9] The keyboardist later told the *Nashville Scene*, "I'm sure there was about $50 up there."[10]

The quarters did disappear, but Johnston thought the culprit was the musicians, not the engineers. When he realized they were gone, he joked to the engineers, "'I can't get any goddamn sound, I wonder why?' And somebody said, 'There's no quarters up there.'"[11]

Moss, who says he had nothing to do with the missing coins, remembers Grossman saying of the ceiling tiles, "If I tear some of them up, just send Columbia the bill, they've got lots of money."[12]

Grossman's point of view didn't surprise Gantry. "The attitude of the people around Dylan was they were in rarified air," he says. "It had a sense of self-entitlement about it. It was like they were living in the jet stream of someone who was above the clouds."[13]

Whatever Grossman's attitude was, Johnston didn't have a problem with it. And while he didn't want any of the label "suits" at the sessions, he didn't mind Grossman being there. "Grossman was a good guy to me," the producer said. "Never had a bad word with him. He never said, 'Change this, or change that.' Or 'Why don't you do this or why don't you do that?' He was just there as a booster. I liked him."[14]

It wasn't the attitude of Dylan and the people who came from New York with him, but rather their look that caught the attention of Rowan and Greene, just as it had initially with the Nashville musicians. Rowan remembered Grossman as looking "like George Washington" with long, silver hair and "old-timey" glasses; Kooper stood out to Greene because he was wearing a "blue-and-white polka dot shirt" and "looking very." Rowan agreed: "Looking very!"

After the break, the musicians reconvened in the studio. When Johnston asked Dylan the song's name for slating purposes, he replied, "What Can You Do for My Wigwam?" According to Rowan, after hearing the title, Grossman threw another quarter in the ceiling. "Sort of an exclamation point," he said.[15]

"What Can You Do for My Wigwam?" was the working title for "Pledging My Time," and during the first run-through, Dylan sang an extra verse he eventually discarded that referenced a wigwam: "Well, I'm gonna play a wigwam / I'm gonna tell you now / If you don't know how to play it / You better find out how." Four years later, he would record an unrelated song called simply, "Wigwam."

The song's hook line and eventual title probably was a riff off the title of the number-one R&B smash hit by Johnny Ace, "Pledging My Love," which ironically does not include the actual words "pledging my love" anywhere in its lyrics. But beyond sharing the word "pledging," the two songs were dissimilar. Released in 1954, Ace's song, written by Ferdinand Washington and Don Robey, was a much slower R&B ballad.

According to Clinton Heylin, the line "PLEDGING MY TIME If nothing comes outa this, you'll soon know," appeared on one of Dylan's typescripts from this era, "one of the single-line 'song ideas' on the 'You Can't Get Your Way' sheet."[16]

Initially, the lyrics consisted of six four-line verses and a two-line chorus: "I'm pledging my time to you / Hopin' you'll come through, too."

The first verse was still not in its final form when Dylan ran down the song for the musicians. On the first take, he sang the first verse as:

> Baby got jealous
> She took five
> Trips with the hobo
> And left me here alive

That remained the first verse until take three, the master take, on which he sang a new opening verse:

> Well, early in the mornin'
> 'Til late at night
> I got a poison headache
> But I feel all right

Except for a few inconsequential words, the remaining verses were essentially finished on the first take. The opening two lines of the second verse that Dylan sang on the master take differ, however, from the official published lyrics for the song. The official lyrics have the first two lines as, "Well, the hobo jumped up / He came down natur'lly," while Dylan actually sang, "Well, the hobo got too high / He came to me natur'lly."[17]

The picture he painted in the song was neither pretty, nor uncommon, as Robyn Hitchcock notes. "Dylan has always been a visual writer, but I really can see the scene," Hitchcock says of "Pledging My Time." "The late night and the party and the smoke and the windows not opening and somebody chatting somebody else up, not knowing if it's going to work or not. And, you know, Dylan being so gloriously kind of seductive, but also double-edged; you know, he's not really promising them anything. [Laughs] He's not making himself to be a particularly good deal, but at the same time, he is very insistent, you know. He's not very gallant. It's almost like being, I would imagine, like being wooed by Groucho Marx or somebody."[18]

"Pledging My Time" undeniably includes a healthy helping of comic cynicism, exemplified by lines like, "And if it don't work out / You'll be the first to know," and "Ev'rbody's gone, but me and you / And I can't be the last to leave." Even the chorus only offers a pledge of time, not love.

Two of the lines—one in the second verse and one in the fifth—seem to be derived from a couplet that appears in "Come on in My Kitchen" by Robert Johnson. On that song, Johnson sang, "Ah, the woman I love, took from my best friend / Some joker got lucky, stole her back again."

In the second verse, Dylan sang about the hobo, "After he stole my baby / Then he wanted to steal me." In the fifth verse, he sang, "Somebody got lucky / But it was an accident."[19]

Musically, too, the song was influenced by "Come on in My Kitchen," but also by the blues standard "It Hurts Me Too," specifically Elmore James's 1957 cover of the song. Dylan himself would cover "It Hurts Me Too" a few years later during sessions in Nashville for his album *Self Portrait*.

The first take featured an up-tempo blues shuffle approach, almost as if the musicians were just continuing with the same approach they had tried on take four of "Just Like a Woman." The uptempo approach worked, but by the second take, they had abandoned it, settling into a slower blues groove after some instruction from Dylan. "It's got to have a very strong beat," he told Buttrey following the initial attempt. Hearing that, Robbins began to play a slow, eight-bar blues riff on the piano, and Dylan and the rest of the musicians joined in. Still not satisfied with what Buttrey was playing, Dylan stopped the music after ten or so bars. "No, no, no, no, don't . . . let me play it, I'll show you," he said and went over to the drum kit to show Buttrey what he wanted, taking one of the drumsticks and tapping out the rhythm he wanted on Buttrey's snare drum.

In the control room, Greene and Rowan were unimpressed with what they were hearing, not surprising considering they were bluegrass musicians, who are known to often have a superior attitude toward other kinds of music. Greene called the song "abominable. I was really surprised by the low quality of the music. . . . I mean it was just, it was amateurish."

"There's so much that can be done," Rowan added. "I don't know why [Dylan] keeps using those same old chord changes and melodies, you know, old rock and roll things over and over again."

"It was definitely uninteresting," Greene said. So uninteresting that he and Rowan left before Dylan and the musicians got the master take, leaving not long after the uptempo first take.[20]

Shortly after the departure of the two Bluegrass Boys, Dylan and the musicians put down the keeper take. After a quick rehearsal of the slower groove and a false start, they got it on what was slated officially as take three.

Buttrey had gotten Dylan's message. He kicked off the take with a short, snappy snare roll that led into a heavy-swinging, downtempo groove the rhythm musicians locked in on: Strzelecki with some deep, rumbling bass, McCoy with an acoustic part, and South with some funky swamp boogie riffing. When he wasn't fattening the rhythm even further, Robbins delivered some of the track's tastiest moments, most notably at the end of the choruses, where he set up the upcoming verses with a cascade of descending notes; but he also threw in some flashy trills, particularly near the end of the song.

During the verses, Robertson played some biting solo bits, while Dylan stepped into the spotlight during the instrumental breaks after the third and fifth verses, blowing some dexterous and dynamic harp lines that at times were transcendent.

After hearing Robertson's stinging guitar parts on the song—which are most prominent on the choruses, but can be heard throughout, snaking around Dylan's harmonica lines—the Nashville musicians began to understand why he had been invited to the party; the eight-bar blues was right in his wheelhouse. "I did something that they didn't do, I wasn't taking anybody's seat at the table," Robertson explained in his interview with the Country Music Hall of Fame and Museum. "And the way that I played, none of those guys played that way."[21]

To say the Nashville players were impressed with Robertson's playing would be an understatement. In an article published under his byline in *Hit Parader* magazine six months later, McCoy called him "one of the best blues guitar players I've ever heard in my life."[22]

After "Pledging My Time," Robertson began to feel more accepted by the Nashville cats. "I remember those guys giving me some good back-slapping, you know, for that," he said. After that, the Nashville musicians were the ones saying "Robbie should play on this one, too."

During some of the downtime that day, Robertson got to know a little bit about the Nashville musicians. "I remember these guys saying that they were a band," Robertson said of learning about Charlie McCoy and the Escorts. "And at that point, things changed for me in the back of my mind. That's when I really embraced everything that they did. And it didn't matter if it got down and dirty, it didn't matter whether it just had to float like a bird in the sky, they were right there to just go with it, you know, and I so respected that.

"That's why they were so good because they were a band," he continued. "I remember them saying that they played in a joint there, you know, in town; that they played together. I had a bit of a thing . . . I really approved of bands that played together, but I was suspicious of studio musicians that just had a formula."[23]

With a master take of "Pledging My Time" in the can, Dylan turned his attention back to "Just Like a Woman." By the time they resumed recording, the lyrics were mostly complete: he had replaced "Honey" with "Baby," "Annie" with "Queen Mary," switched the chorus from second person to third, and changed the line "But I gave you those pearls" to "With her fog, her amphetamine and her pearls," further stoking the flames of speculation the song was about Sedgwick. He also had completed the first half of the bridge:

> It was raining from the first
> And I was dying there of thirst
> So I came in here
> And your long-time curse hurts[24]

Thirteen more takes of the song were slated that evening, but only three were complete takes. As far as the arrangement was concerned, Dylan had decided to ditch the up-tempo approach they had tried on take four and stick with the original arrangement, so Robertson remained on the sideline. But on what was slated as take five, after the intro, Buttrey dropped out on the first verse, and Dylan noticed immediately, stopping the music at the end of the first line.

"No, no, no, no, no, no," he said.

"Hold it," Johnston said from the control room.

"There's no drums," Dylan said, then had a discussion with Buttrey about why they weren't using the same approach as earlier, a discussion that ended with Dylan saying, "I think the drums should be there. I can't sense it without the drums."

Gantry, who decided to stick around when his friends left, remembers Dylan trying the song at several different speeds. "He went through about four different tempo changes on that song before he got the one that he wanted," Gantry recalls. "That was the big question. He could not figure out the tempo to do that lyric to."[25]

The first complete take they got was take seven, which was mislabeled as take eight, but it was deemed too slow. The take slated as ten was promising, but the music broke down when there was some confusion coming out of the bridge. "How are we doing it, Charlie?" Dylan asked McCoy. After some discussion about it, they were ready to continue with take eleven. Before they did, Dylan brought up the tempo again, said he thought it was still too slow, and began strumming the chords, searching for the right feel. He soon found it, saying, "There it is. OK?"

"Rolling on eleven," Johnston said, but when the music started, he quickly stopped them, not liking how the take began. "One more time. Kenny lead in clear. Rolling on twelve."

Take twelve was a false start, but they almost got a complete take on the thirteenth, making it all the way to the outro before breaking down. Buttrey had been using a handkerchief to muffle his snare, but decided to remove it between the fourteenth and fifteenth takes, both of which were false starts.

Johnston interrupted take fifteen because he heard a problem with the intro. "That's too good a feel, Bob," he said. "Go ahead and get the intro, the intro was off, but that's a perfect feel."

Take sixteen was another complete take, but apparently to Dylan's ears, the tempo was still a little slow, so they moved on to a slightly faster take seventeen, which broke down just under a minute in when South hit a wrong note.

They stuck with the slightly faster tempo on take eighteen and it was the one, absolutely beautiful and destined for greatness. That master take featured exceptional performances all around: Buttrey's lively brush work, Robbins' tasteful piano parts weaving in and around Kooper's organ lines, the delicate interplay of the guitars, especially South's lead parts, and Dylan's soulful harmonica leads.

With two more songs in the can, Dylan called it a day, which surely surprised the musicians, since it was only around midnight. They could actually go home and get a good night's rest for a change. They would need it for the marathon Dylan had in mind for the following evening.

11

SPRINT TO THE FINISH

AL KOOPER HAD RESERVATIONS about going to Nashville for the sessions, as he revealed in *Backstage Passes and Backstabbing Bastards: Memoirs of a Rock 'n' Roll Survivor*: "I had never been down South before and was not particularly looking forward to it based on various accounts I had perused in the papers."

And while Kooper hit it off with the Nashville players, a group of local teens gave him more of the kind of welcome he had feared and expected when he ventured out during some downtime to check out Buckley's Record Shop, which had the widest selection of music in the city: rock, pop, R&B, blues, country, and even classical. "I was very anxious to shop there because I was a big fan—I bought a lot of records," he says. "So I walked over there, and when I was coming back, I got accosted by young, as they were called in those days, juvenile delinquents, about five of them, and they wanted to start some trouble."[1]

The teens apparently took exception to Kooper's mod attire and chased him across the street, where he ducked into a drugstore and into a phone booth. Kooper called Albert Grossman at his hotel room and told him what was going down. Grossman called Lamar Fyke to go to the keyboardist's rescue.

Kooper remained in the phone booth "mock-chatting" for a few minutes, then pretended to be browsing the store's selection of paperback books. "One of the punks entered the shop and was heading right for me," Kooper recalled in his memoir. "I could see it all happening: books flying, jail cells, death notices. Concurrent with the guy entering the shop, Lamar arrived in a fat Caddy, screeching to a halt in front of the store. He jumped out of the car, spotted me through the window, then casually strolled into the store. The kid headed right for me, and my adrenaline was at the bursting point. I grabbed him by his collar and said, 'Look, you motherfucka, you and your friends get the fuck off my back or I'm gonna get MAD!'"[2]

Of course, Fyke came up at that very moment; he collected Kooper and escorted him out to the car. On the way back to the hotel, Fyke joked to the keyboardist, "I can't let you go for five minutes without you getting in another fight with somebody."[3]

Dylan and the musicians returned to Studio A at 6:00 PM on Wednesday, March 9, and didn't leave until after sunup the following morning around 7:00 AM. During those thirteen hours, they recorded six songs—not the three or four per three-hour session the Nashville cats were accustomed to, but still, a little closer to their normal pace. The key musicians on the sessions—Charlie McCoy, Kenny Buttrey, Wayne Moss, Al Kooper, Pig Robbins, Joe South, Robbie Robertson, and Henry Strzelecki—were all present, but they didn't all appear on every song.

The first song on the agenda that evening was "Most Likely You Go Your Way and I'll Go Mine," with Dylan and the players working on the bouncy breakup number between six and nine o'clock. The song is about a man who has had enough of a dishonest and unfaithful woman, who was ready to let her "pass." As good-bye songs go, this is not an especially harsh one, more a case of the man just being completely over the woman, done with her.

Some people have suggested the song was inspired by Edie Sedgwick, and it did have something in common with another song from *Blonde on Blonde* thought to be about Sedgwick, "Leopard-Skin Pill-Box Hat"—the inclusion of another suitor. In "Leopard-Skin Pill-Box Hat," the woman has "a new boyfriend," whereas in "Most Likely You Go Your Way and

I'll Go Mine," the woman has "some other kinda lover." Those inclined
to cast Dylan's friend Bob Neuwirth in the first role might also see him
in the other.

It took Dylan and the musicians six takes to get the master recording,
only two of which made it all the way through the song. As with most
of the material he recorded in Nashville, Dylan was still refining the
lyrics even after they began recording. The first verse and the chorus
were essentially finished on the initial attempt, except the last line of
the chorus was simply, "You go your way and I go mine." By take three,
he had added "when" at the beginning of the line to finalize the chorus:

> I'm gonna let you pass
> And I'll go last
> Then time will tell just who has fell
> And who's been left behind
> When you go your way and I go mine

The second and third verses and the bridge all underwent significant
changes between the first take and the sixth, the only complete takes—
none of the other four made it past the first verse and chorus. Dylan
also made a key lyrical change in the bridge between the first and final
takes, adding "the judge" who "holds a grudge." The introduction of
the judge underscored the reckoning awaiting the woman for what she
had done to the man, when "time will tell just who has fell and who's
been left behind."[4]

The uptempo arrangement (in the key of G) developed fairly
quickly—it was mostly together on the first take. Between the first and
second takes, they settled on the primary melody line, a catchy, bluesy
riff suggested by McCoy that was repeated in unison by a number of
instruments throughout the song.

"There was a little figure after each chorus that he [McCoy] wanted
to put in on trumpet, but Dylan was not fond of overdubbing," Kooper
recalled in his memoir. "It was a nice lick, too. Simple, but nice. Now
Charlie was already playing bass on the tune. So we started recording, and
when that section came up, he picked up a trumpet in his right hand and

played the part while he kept the bass going with his left hand without missing a lick in either hand. Dylan stopped in the middle of the take and just stared at him in awe."[5]

In a 2011 appearance on Chicago Public Radio's *Sound Opinions*, Kooper said after McCoy showed he actually could play both trumpet and bass, Dylan agreed to have him do it as long as McCoy was set up out of his sight line—he apparently didn't trust himself not to laugh or become otherwise distracted if he was watching McCoy do both.[6]

There is no question McCoy *could* play the two instruments at the same time—he did it regularly with the Escorts, teaming with the saxophonists to give the band a horn section. "He would squeeze the bass with his left hand and make the note, and then play trumpet with the right hand, and sing in between," Moss explains.[7]

In multiple interviews for this book, however, McCoy has insisted he didn't play both instruments, that he only played trumpet, and Moss's recollection supports that. "It simply didn't happen," McCoy says, without a trace of doubt. He points out there was no need for him to play both instruments with Strzelecki at the session.[8] But session records show McCoy played bass and trumpet on "Most Likely You Go Your Way and I'll Go Mine," and also seem to indicate Strzelecki didn't arrive until 9:00 PM, after the song was recorded. Still, even if Strzelecki didn't arrive until nine, South was on hand and could have manned the bass, as he had on Dylan's first two days of sessions back in February.

With McCoy playing the riff on trumpet, Dylan decided to join in on harmonica—he hadn't played harp at all on the first take. Before the second take, a rehearsal, Johnston said, "Ever'body together on the intro." After Buttrey gave the count off, they launched into the song, with McCoy on trumpet, Dylan on harmonica, Robertson on electric guitar, and Kooper on organ, all playing the main riff together.

Still working out the arrangement, the third take broke down after the first chorus when the musicians repeated the primary riff as Dylan was going to the beginning of the second verse. "No, uh-uh," Dylan told the musicians.

"I'm sorry, I'm sorry," McCoy said. "Did you want to do it twice there?

"Figure out how many times you are going to do it," Johnston said from the control room, referring to the riff.

"Let's not do it there, it's gonna be kind of hard," Dylan said. "We'll just do it after the break—after the bridge."

"After the bridge?" McCoy confirmed.

"After the bridge, yeah," Dylan replied.

"OK," Johnston said.

Continuing, Dylan said, "Let's do it three times, and then the drums lead in." He paused, then said, "No, let's do it—hey, you do it four times, I'm only gonna do it three."

At the beginning of the fourth take, Dylan instructed the musicians to play the middle eight at a slightly lower volume. "Why don't you play the bridge down?" he said. "Wait a second, play the bridge down," he continued, then strummed the chords on his acoustic guitar to show what he meant. "Just play very lightly," he told them, but take four never made it to the bridge.

Johnston interrupted the fifth take after the first chorus. "OK, hold it a second," he said. "I'm sorry, Bob, you're too close to the mic. You're right on top of it, and we're not picking up your diction good."

The sixth and master take for "Most Likely You Go Your Way and I'll Go Mine" clocked in at just under three-and-a-half minutes, making it the second-shortest track included on the album. Buttrey counted off the take and his drumming propelled the song, punctuating the verses with spirited snare rolls and the choruses with cymbal crashes. Much like they had on "Absolutely Sweet Marie," the rest of the players, which included Robbins on piano and Moss on electric guitar, combined to create a cacophony of sound, especially on the main riff.

———————

Next, Dylan wanted to work on a slow blues he was calling "Like Achilles." With Moss sitting it out and Strzelecki apparently not yet at the studio, the lineup was Buttrey on drums, McCoy on bass, Robbins on piano, Kooper on electric piano, Robertson and South on electric guitars, and Dylan on harmonica and vocals.

The song was a lover's lament built around one of the album's recurring themes: the narrator being blocked in one way or another, resulting in unfulfilled sexual longing. In this case, the woman has him "barred" by Achilles, who is acting as her guard. Achilles, of course, had one vulnerability, his heel, which suggests the man still has a slim chance with the woman.

On "Like Achilles," Dylan finally found a home for the two-line chorus that had been around since the first *Blonde on Blonde* session on October 5 in New York: "Well, I know you want my loving / Mama, but you're so hard." The phrase "honey but it's just too hard" had appeared at the top of the "Stuck Inside of Mobile with the Memphis Blues Again" typescript.

The first take of the song they attempted was a complete take, and on it, Dylan was singing the two lines as, "Well, you I know *I* want *your* loving / But honey, you're so hard." Take two broke down in the first verse, but by take three, he had made the final tweaks to the chorus, singing, "Well, you I know I want your loving / Honey, why are you so hard," after the first two verses, but a different second line—"Honey, but you're so hard"—after the last two verses. The woman is so hard that Dylan wondered in the bridge if her heart was "made out of stone, or is it lime, or is it solid rock."

With the exception of the first verse, the rest of the lyrics were basically intact by the third take, although Achilles was still in the "hallway" instead of the "alleyway." Two of the lines first appeared on a typescript of lyric ideas: "like a rich man's son," which appeared in the second verse as "I'm helpless like a rich man's son" and "like a poor fool in his prime," which became the first line of the bridge. Dylan first used another line from the fourth verse—"he's hungry, like a man in drag"—during his appearance on Bob Fass's radio show back in January, asking a caller, "Tell me, are you hungry as a man in drag?"[9]

After the third take, Dylan finished the lyrics for the first verse, and a slightly faster fourth take was the keeper. The master take was highlighted by Robbins's exquisite piano work, South's guitar trills, and Dylan's mournful harp lines and his plaintive vocals.

Johnston recalled to me how the next song they worked on that evening came together: "Dylan came to the piano and said, 'Listen to this, man,' and he played 'Rainy Day Women.' I said, 'Goddamn, that sounds like a Salvation Army band.' And he said, 'Can we get one?' And I said, 'I don't think so, but I'll try.'"[10]

It was already close to midnight, pretty late to be calling anyone, but Johnston was determined to give Dylan what he wanted, so he turned to McCoy and asked the session leader if there was anyone they could get at that hour. McCoy said he could try Wayne "Doc" Butler, one of his bandmates in the Escorts who played both trombone and saxophone. Butler was already in bed asleep when he got the call from McCoy, but nevertheless, he agreed to come to the studio.

While they waited for Butler to arrive, McCoy wrote out horn parts for the song. He planned to play trumpet and have Butler play trombone to simulate a basic Salvation Army brass lineup. The simple arrangement Dylan had played for them on the piano included a phrase derived from the instrumental intro to "The Rheumatism Blues" by Gene Autry. McCoy's horn arrangement was built on that phrase, although McCoy himself was not familiar with the Autry recording.

Songwriter Chris Gantry had stopped by the studio again that evening and was there while they waited for Butler. "McCoy was in the control room working on the horn charts," Gantry recalls. "Dylan was in the studio on a stool working on the lyrics. The rest of the musicians were just milling around."[11]

As Moss remembers it, at some point while they were waiting, Dylan asked him and some of the other musicians, "What do you guys do here?" Moss told him they played golf when they had time. "That's not what I mean," Dylan said. "What do you *do* here?" Moss then realized he meant what did they do to get buzzed, so he told him they sometimes had some beers or mixed drinks. "For sure, he didn't want to cut 'Everybody must get stoned' with a bunch of straight people," Moss explains.[12]

As the story goes, Johnston called someone he knew at a nearby restaurant who was willing to do the producer an illegal favor and prepare some cocktails for pickup at the back door. He dispatched studio maintenance man Ed Grizzard to bring the drinks back to the studio.

Normally Grizzard wouldn't be around in the evenings, but he ran a small beer concession on the side, selling cold ones to session musicians at an inflated price, and he would stick around after hours if he thought he might do a little business.

The restaurant in question, Ireland's, specialized in a widow maker of a drink called the Leprechaun, and Grizzard returned with eighteen milk cartons filled with the lime-green concoction. At least some of the players, including Moss, Strzelecki, and Robbins, proceeded to imbibe. In addition, Strzelecki recalled there were some joints of high-quality marijuana being passed around.

But according to both McCoy and Kooper, none of that happened. "Baloney," Kooper says regarding the drinking, insisting neither Dylan nor Grossman would have allowed it. As for the marijuana, "Well, I didn't know about it," he insists, then adds with a laugh, "They weren't sharing with the Easterners."[13]

"I never saw Dylan smoke, I never saw any of the Nashville people smoke," Johnston says. "I'm not talking about me and Al and Robbie and all of those guys, you know, but nobody else did. . . . I didn't want everybody to be loaded trying to remember their part. 'Cause we didn't have arrangements, and we didn't have charts; Dylan would say this is C, G, D, and off we'd go."[14]

Regarding the Leprechauns, McCoy says that happened at another session a few years later, and one important fact supports the contention it didn't happen the night they recorded "Rainy Day Women." In March 1966, it still was illegal for restaurants in Nashville to sell liquor by the drink—that wouldn't be allowed in the city for another year and a half. But despite it being illegal, some restaurants and nightclubs did sell cocktails, primarily businesses downtown in the entertainment district known as Printer's Alley and clubs located just outside the Nashville city limits who probably paid off someone to get the sheriff's department to look the other way. Ireland's, however, was not a restaurant where you could purchase a drink illegally.

That doesn't necessarily mean Moss, Robbins, and Strzelecki didn't have some cocktails that night; just that they couldn't have been Leprechauns from Ireland's. Grizzard could have been sent to bring back a bottle of whiskey or Scotch. The musicians' lounge was two levels below Studio A, so some of the players could have been drinking down there without either McCoy or Kooper being aware of it. Same with the joints— the lounge was also near the back door, so they could have easily stepped out to the parking lot to smoke without anyone in the studio knowing about it.

But whether they had a drink or two, or shared a joint, they certainly didn't do it to excess; not only did they record "Rainy Day Women," they would record master takes of three more songs after that.

Kooper vividly remembers the arrival of McCoy's bandmate Wayne Butler. "He got there in forty-five minutes," the keyboardist says. "And he was clean-shaven and had a suit on. . . . He played like one or two takes of that song, and then thanked everybody and went back home. It was pretty funny."[15]

While they had waited for Butler, Kooper had been listening to a transistor radio out in the studio. As they prepared to do a quick rehearsal, Johnston joked with him from the control room, "During the take, Al could you keep that radio off?"—which got a laugh from Dylan and some of the other musicians. In response, Kooper turned up the volume on the radio, which happened to be tuned to a Top 40 station spinning Nancy Sinatra's "These Boots Are Made for Walkin'," drawing a laugh from Johnston.

"Hey, what do you think about a little bit of the bass drum, and the drum thing before we start?" McCoy suggested to Dylan and Johnston.

Dylan liked the idea immediately. "Oh, yeah," he said excitedly.

When Buttrey began playing the song's signature snare and bass drum riff, Johnston pushed the talk-back button and enthused, "Yeah, man," then said to McCoy, "Charlie, with the trumpet a little bit."

Robbins joined Buttrey on the piano, but Dylan stopped them, saying, "No, no, no, that's too fast, Charlie."

"Hey, Charlie," Buttrey said.

"Yeah."

"When I do that da-da-da-da, da-da-da-da, da-da-da-da-da-da, crack, you oughta make the trombone, baaa-aaahhhhh—" the drummer suggested.

"What's the name of this, Bob?" Johnston asked.

"—right on that crack," Buttrey said, continuing his suggestion to McCoy.

"A Long-Haired Mule and a Porkepine Here," Dylan told the producer and laughed.

The actual title, which he would settle on later, apparently was a jokey reference to a line from the Bible, Proverbs 27:15: "A continual dropping in a very rainy day and a contentious woman are alike."[16] The eventual title "Rainy Day Women #12 & 35" was a teasing invitation for the listener to infer Dylan has had at least thirty-five contentious women in his life, and that this particular composition is about two of them, the twelfth and the thirty-fifth.

The following month during the European leg of his world tour, Dylan discussed the song with Klas Burling of Swedish Radio 3. "'Rainy Day Women' happens to deal with a minority of, you know, cripples and Orientals, and uh, you know, another sort of North Mexican kind of a thing, uh, very protesty," Dylan jokingly told him, after being asked about his "protest" songs. "Very, very protesty. One of the protestiest of all things I ever protested against in my protest years."

When Burling asked why the title was never mentioned in the song, Dylan told him, "Well, we never mention things that we love. And that's, where I come from that is, that's blasphemy. . . . It has to do with God."[17]

The most famous account of stoning in the Bible appears in the book of Acts, in which a Christian named Stephen was falsely accused of blasphemy and stoned to death by an angry mob. Dylan, who was observed consulting the Bible throughout the sessions in Nashville, easily could have drawn a parallel between the plight of Stephen and his own situation: a righteous revealer of a new truth falsely accused of blasphemy.

As with so many of the songs on the album, there is a duality to "Rainy Day Women." Dylan overtly invoked images of the biblical practice of stoning while laughing out loud literally during the recording of the song at its countercultural inside joke, a reference to being high on marijuana.

After "Rainy Day Women #12 & 35" was released, producer Phil Spector told Robert Shelton he had been with Dylan at Fred C. Hobbs

Coffee Shop during Dylan's visit to Los Angeles the previous December when Ray Charles's recording of "Let's Go Get Stoned" came on the jukebox. Spector said they both were "surprised to hear a song that free, that explicit."[18] In Spector's mind, Dylan was inspired to write "Rainy Day Women" after hearing the Charles hit at the coffee shop that day. But Spector and Dylan could not have heard Charles's recording of "Let's Go Get Stoned" then because it hadn't been released yet, and wouldn't be released for another six months.

That's not to suggest, however, they didn't hear a recording of "Let's Go Get Stoned" on the jukebox that day. Charles's recording of the song written by Nickolas Ashford, Valerie Simpson, and Josephine Armstead was not the first cover of the song to be released—it was the third. The Coasters had the initial release of the song as the flip side of "Money Honey," but that single went nowhere. Charles first heard it on the B-side of a hit by a young Ronnie Milsap, who was signed to Scepter Records at the time as an R&B artist, long before he would move to Nashville and turn his powerful brand of country soul into a string of Top 40 hits. The A-side of the single was another Ashford and Simpson composition, "Never Had It So Good," which was still in the Top 40 of *Billboard*'s Top Selling Rhythm & Blues Singles chart when Dylan and Spector met for coffee in December. So it had to be Milsap's recording of "Let's Go Get Stoned" Dylan and Spector heard that day.

While he knew his recording had inspired Charles to record a version of the song, Milsap had never considered the possibility it may have sparked Dylan to write "Rainy Day Women #12 & 35." He was traveling to Chicago to play a show at the Regal Theater with Maxine Brown, Jerry Butler, and Billy Stewart when he initially heard it. "I was on my way to Chicago when I heard it on the radio. I thought, 'Man, that's cool, what a cool record. And it was.'"

Without realizing there was a direct connection, Milsap knew his recording and Dylan's had one thing in common. "I knew what getting stoned meant," he says with a laugh.[19]

For the Nashville players, the session for "Rainy Day Women" was easily the one they remembered best, in no small part because of the apparent drug reference in the song's chorus. Like Milsap, they knew what getting stoned meant.

To give it a sloppier, Salvation Army kind of feel, some of the players swapped instruments. Moss picked up Strzelecki's bass, and the bass man was on the floor playing the foot pedals of Kooper's organ with his hands, while the organist shook a tambourine. Robbins was on piano and Buttrey was on drums. (Contrary to reports otherwise, Buttrey did not disassemble his drum kit so he could hit the kick drum like the bass drum in a marching band.) McCoy and Butler rounded out the lineup on trumpet and trombone respectively.

"Bob wanted everybody to scream and shout, and so we did that," Kooper recalls. "I remember recording that because it was very funny. And Bob laughed on the record, which is very unusual."[20]

Dylan does indeed laugh on the recording, as he had at the beginning of "Bob Dylan's 115th Dream." In the first verse as he sang the line, "They'll stone you when you're trying to go home," one of the musicians let out a series of hoots, which made him laugh. In the second chorus, just as he was about to sing the hook line, "Everybody must get stoned," the same musician let out a shriek, and Dylan laughed again. Strzelecki can be heard enjoying himself throughout the track.[21]

"I was laying on floor, and I got so tickled during the recording of it on that particular song," Strzelecki recalled to me. "I was down there by the microphone, by the organ pedals—you know, the sound came out from under the organ, under the keyboard there. So I was playing the bass with my hands on the foot pedals—I got tickled and started laughing, and you can actually hear me laugh on that record. Somewhere down in the middle of the song, and they didn't take it out, they left it in there. Kenny Buttrey pointed that out to me. I didn't even know it until he said, 'Hey, man, I heard you laughing on the record.' Then I heard it. I actually heard it on the radio and said, 'That's me laughing.'"[22]

Dylan's admiration for Smokey Robinson has been well documented, so the idea to have a party-type vibe on the track may have been inspired by "Mickey's Monkey," a 1963 hit by Smokey Robinson and the Miracles that opened with a similar feel-good ambience.

After the brief run-through, Dylan and the musicians nailed "Rainy Day Women" in one take. It happened so fast that Robertson, who had gone down to the lounge to buy a pack of cigarettes, missed it entirely.[23]

Back in the studio after his smoke break, Robertson impressed the guys from Guitar Town with his six-string work on the next two songs, "Obviously Five Believers" and the final, master version of "Leopard-Skin Pill-Box Hat."

"Bob wanted to record this song, 'Obviously Five Believers,'" Robertson recalled during his interview with the Country Music Hall of Fame and Museum. "When we recorded that song, it changed everything. . . . After we cut it, these guys came over—Kenny and everyone—came over to me and said, 'That's wicked, that's fantastic,' and they really embraced me into the club.

"And I got it, I understood," he continued. "If I was doing, you know, the same thing as what Joe South could do, or something, then it's like you're stepping on somebody's toes. But I brought a different thing to the table, and they were completely cool with that."[24]

A handwritten manuscript for "Obviously Five Believers," probably one of the lyric sheets saved from the sessions by engineer Charlie Bragg, was auctioned off by Christie's in the early 1990s.[25] The manuscript contained a near-final set of lyrics with six verses—the first verse repeats as the last—and no bridge. "Obviously Five Believers" was another song about longing for an absent lover. As far as the songs on *Blonde on Blonde* go, the lyrics were fairly conventional and straightforward—with the exception of the fifth verse, which provided the song's ultimate title, the verse featuring "fifteen jugglers" and "five believers," dressed like men.

Once they had the basic arrangement down, Johnston announced from the control room, "83277, 'Leopard-Skin Pill-Box Hat,' take one."

"No, no," Dylan told him. "No, this isn't 'Leopard-Skin Pill-Box Hat.' This is, uh, 'Black Dog Blues.'"

"Oh, I'm sorry," the producer said.

Buttrey asked Dylan, "Hey, are you going to start it by yourself?"

Before Dylan could respond, Johnston answered, telling the drummer, "No, man, ever'body's starting together, right on the beat."

"All right," Buttrey said.

"'Black Dog Blues,' take one," the producer said.

McCoy, who was playing harmonica on the song, asked Buttrey, "You want to count it off, Head?" calling him by his nickname in the Escorts.

"Might as well," the drummer told him.

"I've got a mouthful of harpoon," McCoy told him.

As McCoy explained to the *Tennessean* in 2016, he played harmonica on "Obviously Five Believers" instead of Dylan "because it was not in his wheelhouse." He continued, "Also, this riff went on constantly while he was singing, and so there was a problem there—he couldn't sing and play it at the same time. But what he wanted—the riff on it—is not what he does."[26]

"Ever'body together from the top and all the way through, because one take is all we need on this, man," Johnston urged the players as time was running short. "It's there."

It took more than one take—four in fact—but the first two were incomplete. Johnston interrupted take one after only a few seconds to ask McCoy to move closer to the mic. The second take broke down a little more than a minute into the song when one of the players missed his cue, which clearly frustrated Dylan. It was one of the few times he expressed dissatisfaction during the Nashville sessions. "Hey, hey, what the fu—," he said, cutting himself off before he said a word that might offend some of the southern gentlemen he was working with. "This is very easy, man, this is very easy to do."

Robertson, who had probably heard the song in Dylan's hotel room, spoke up at that point and explained where the change was, playing the preceding two bars on his Telecaster to make it totally clear. After that, Dylan said, "OK, let's try it one more time. I don't want to spend no time on this song, man."

They got a complete take on the third try, but some of the lyrics were still in flux, with Dylan seeming to lose focus on what was then the second verse, the "black dog barking." They moved on to take four, and it was the keeper.

Musically, "Obviously Five Believers" was the hardest-rocking song on the album and borrowed heavily from Sonny Boy Williamson's "Good Morning, School Girl," which he released in 1937 on the Bluebird label. That version of the song was not necessarily the one Dylan was most familiar with. Memphis Minnie's 1941 release on Okeh Records, "Me and My Chauffeur Blues," had the same basic melody, but more recently, Muddy Waters had covered the song on his 1964 Chess release, *Folk Singer*, slightly revising the title to "Good Morning Little School Girl." Chuck Berry copped the song's central riff for his song "I Want to Be Your Driver," which appeared on the album *Chuck Berry in London*, released in April 1965 on Chess. Considering Dylan's extensive knowledge of folk and blues recordings, it's possible, if not likely, he was familiar with all those sides.

McCoy, who finally got a chance to show his harmonica wizardry on "Obviously Five Believers," may well have been familiar with all those sides, too. Considering the Hawks' live repertoire, Robertson probably also knew them. The guitarist made himself at home on the song, joining McCoy in the spotlight with some stirring lead guitar fills. They were joined on the song by Buttrey on drums, Robbins on piano, Strzelecki on bass, Kooper on organ, and South on electric guitar. Dylan played his electric guitar, too.

With the musicians thoroughly warmed up from "Obviously Five Believers," Dylan decided to revisit "Leopard-Skin Pill-Box Hat," foregoing the take from his first Nashville date with the car horn and door bell and returning to the Chicago blues approach he had tried twice before. This time they really did nail it in one take.

After Dylan refreshed everyone's memory of the song, Robertson made some suggestions regarding the riff Dylan should play, to which Dylan responded, "Oh," and played the riff. "That?" he asked.

Robertson said, "Right."

Dylan responded, "OK."

"How're you gonna start it?" McCoy asked. "You just wanna vamp on that rhythm?"

Johnston offered an idea from the control room. "Hey, Bob, why don't you start off on your guitar yourself?"

"OK," Dylan said.

"Yeah, play a lead kind of a thing to start it off," the producer added.

Dylan played around with the lick Robertson suggested, then said, "Everyone play with me. OK, start in. Go ahead," he says.

"Everybody together?" McCoy confirmed.

"82378, 'Leopard-Skin,' rolling on one," Johnston announced for the slate.

Dylan counted off the song, "One, two, three," and off they went. Robbins played some swinging, and at times flashy, blues piano that along with Buttrey and Strzelecki carried the rhythm, but the moment belonged to Robertson. The guitarist shined brightest on the song, playing some blistering lead over Moss's boogie groove and South's complementary trills, then he really stepped to the front on the song's long instrumental outro. After they were well past the point the track would have faded out, Johnston came on the talk-back mic and said, "OK," then added, "Next!" As the music stopped, McCoy said to Robertson, "Robbie, the whole world'll marry you on that one."[27]

With dawn approaching, they began work on the final song, "I Want You," for which Kooper had an idea. "When I was running the songs over with Bob, my favorite was 'I Want You,' because I had this whole arrangement in my head," he explains. "And Bob knew it was my favorite, so he didn't do it till the very end—he made me suffer."[28]

Dylan ran the song down for the musicians on his acoustic guitar. It was the most pop of any of the songs included on *Blonde on Blonde*. The chorus was a straightforward expression of desire, bordering on being cliche: "I want you, I want you / I want you so bad / Honey, I want you."[29] But the verses, like so many of the songs on the album, featured an absurd cast of characters: the guilty undertaker, the lonesome organ grinder, the drunken politician, the queen of spades, and a dancing child in a Chinese suit, not to mention weeping mothers and sleeping saviors.

A handwritten manuscript for "I Want You" in author and historian Jeff Gold's collection contains the first, second, and fourth verses, and the bridge; each are pretty far along, but there is no sign of either the chorus or the third verse.

Dylan was backed on the track by Buttrey on drums, Moss on electric guitar, McCoy on acoustic guitar, Robbins on piano, Strzelecki on bass, and Kooper on organ. By the time they were ready to try one, Kooper had already found an orchestral bells sound he wanted to use on the organ riff that would be the song's primary melody line.

"What's the name of this, Bob?" Johnston asked.

"I Want You," Dylan told him.

"Okay, 83279 'I Want You,' take one," the producer announced.

"Wait a minute, hold it," McCoy said. "We haven't decided on the intro, did we?"

Dylan told him, "The intro is just the—," then strummed the chord progression.

After they made it all the way through the song on the first take, there was some further discussion about the arrangement before take two. "You can put four bars at the end of the bridge," McCoy suggested, then played an example on his guitar of what those four bars might sound like.

When they were ready to try another take, Johnston said, "Seventy-nine, rolling on two."

"Let's put it in there for Jackie Fargo or somebody," McCoy joked, naming a professional wrestler of local fame.

The take broke down in the bridge, and they followed that with a false start on take three. Take four was another complete take, and on that take, Moss played a run on his acoustic guitar at the end of one of the choruses that caught Kooper's ear. "Right at that point, Wayne played like a sixteenth-note run, and I had never heard anybody play that fast before," Kooper says. "So I stopped and I said, 'Can you play that each time?' and he said, 'Sure.' I said, 'Boy, that would be great, Wayne.' And

I was just thinking to myself, 'Boy, they can't do this in New York.' I couldn't believe he played that."[30]

Take five allegedly was the keeper take, but there was also a take marked as "5b, insert, guitar overdub" that included Moss's sixteenth-note runs, and that was the only difference between the two takes. Like all the other musicians interviewed for this book, Moss insists there was not any overdubbing on the *Blonde on Blonde* sessions, and that included "I Want You." Overdubbed or not, Moss's virtuosic sixteenth-note runs are one of the highlights of the master take, along with Kooper's organ lines and Dylan's harmonica parts.

It was 7:00 AM, an hour past sunrise, when they packed up their gear to head home. That brought the total number of hours Dylan and the musicians were on the clock in Nashville to nearly seventy.

"For the way we recorded in Nashville, the time spent on *Blonde on Blonde* was for us like an eternity," McCoy told the *Tennessean*. "Most Nashville artists at the time would record a whole album in three [three-hour] sessions. You know, it's just the way it was. For us, this was so unusual."[31]

Dylan left Nashville later that day for a gig in St. Louis the following night. He took with him another thirty-plus minutes of music. Combined with what he already had in the can from February, he had enough material for the first-ever double album in rock history.

PART III

LOS ANGELES
AND BEYOND

12

THREE HITS
AND A DOUBLE

DYLAN LEFT NASHVILLE for a show in St. Louis on Friday, March 11, and there, he added another song from the forthcoming album to his acoustic set, "Just Like a Woman." After a date in Denver, Colorado, two nights later, he returned to New York City for a few days before embarking for the West Coast and shows in Portland, Seattle, and Vancouver, British Columbia. After those dates, he would fly to Honolulu for a concert, then on to Australia to begin the international leg of his tour.

While in New York, Dylan and Robbie Robertson went by Jerry Schatzberg's studio to look at photos. As Robertson recalled in his memoir, Schatzberg projected some slides onto a white wall for them to consider.

"He gave a running commentary with each photo," Robertson wrote. "'Oh, there's a nice one. That's too dark. That's got a nice composition, but it's a bit out of focus.'"

Dylan stopped him. "I like that slightly blurry one," he said.[1]

It was one of the shots Schatzberg had taken on February 8 in the meatpacking district, blurred as a result of the photographer's camera moving in the biting wind and extreme cold they experienced that day.

"When Bob saw them, he chose the [blurry shot], to his credit, because if it was Columbia choosing, I'm sure they would never have chosen something out of focus," Schatzberg says. "So I was quite pleased, and because of that, it stands out that much more."[2]

Dylan took the photos they selected at Schatzberg's to a meeting at Columbia with art director John Berg to finalize the photos for the album. As Dylan was walking down the hall, he was approached by a young photographer named Charlie Steiner, a student at the University of Pennsylvania who had taken some live shots of Dylan when he had performed at the Academy of Music in Philadelphia on February 24.

"I was in touch with the art department at Columbia Records and told them I had some pictures of Dylan," Steiner recalls. "And I brought them over, and I met a young art director, and I left them with her. She called me back a few days later, and she said, 'We really like these pictures, we just don't have any use for them. So, you can come and pick them up.'

"So I went to pick them up, and as I was in her office, Bob Dylan walked by. He was there picking out pictures for the album. I went out in the hallway, and I gathered my composure. Then I found him and said I had some pictures, and I showed him my pictures. He was carrying around Schatzberg's pictures in a box, and he showed them to me—and he looked through mine, and he liked them."

What appealed most to Dylan about Steiner's photos was they showed him with an instrument. "None of the pictures he had picked showed him with a guitar," the photographer explains.

While Dylan was looking over Steiner's photos in the hallway, they were interrupted by some passing people. "At one point when I was with him, some Columbia executives came by that he had to shake hands with—somebody introduced him," Steiner recalls. "It was interesting to see him [in that situation]. He was being real polite and businesslike, and the only thing he had to say was, 'I've got a new single coming out—it's called "I Want You."' He repeated that two or three times."

One of the prints Steiner had with him was an enlargement of the photo Dylan chose. "I had made this extreme blow-up photo that is very high contrast," Steiner says. "Going through my box of photos, when he got to that picture, he said, 'That's weird, man.' For me, that's an honor for one of my photos to be called 'weird' by Dylan."[3]

Because it was a double album, it was necessary to use a gatefold cover. Berg decided to take the blurred shot from the meatpacking district and spread it across both the front and back covers so the album opened to show a three-quarters-length shot of the artist. "That was a big selling point," Berg said in a 2012 interview with the *East Hampton Star*. "Everybody wanted one, because they'd never seen that before."[4]

Another unusual feature of Berg's cover design was the fact neither Dylan's name nor the name of the album appeared anywhere on the front or back cover. That seemingly essential information was printed only on the album's spine.

Dylan selected nine photos for use inside the cover—eight photos by Schatzberg he had brought to Columbia and one of Steiner's concert shots. On the inside left cover, there were four horizontally cropped photos: two shots that ran the full width of the sleeve, and two smaller ones across the bottom. The photo at the top of the inside left sleeve showed Dylan facing the camera and lighting a cigarette. In front and slightly to the left of him is another man whose back is to the camera, and over the years, there has been considerable speculation as to the man's identity. Schatzberg confirms the man is Albert Grossman and that the photo was taken at the first shoot at his studio with Dylan the previous fall.

The photo below that has also been shrouded in mystery over the years. The photo shows Dylan sitting on a sofa and another person sitting in a chair to his left in the shadows. Speculation regarding the other person centered on Grossman, but Schatzberg says it was a woman named Lady Sandra Suffolk. As the photographer recalled in his book, *Thin Wild Mercury: Touching Dylan's Edge*, Lady Suffolk had called him and said the publisher of the British magazine *Queen* wanted him to photograph her for the magazine, so he invited her to his studio to discuss it. Once she arrived, Schatzberg quickly realized what she really wanted was for him to arrange an interview for her with Dylan. Dylan agreed, as long as the photographer would accompany him. Their meeting took place on the afternoon of February 26 at the Dakota, where she was staying in a friend's apartment. Schatzberg took several photos during the interview, including the one selected for the album.[5]

There were a pair of photos across the bottom of the inside left sleeve: on the left Steiner's concert shot and on the right, a shot Schatzberg took of Dylan while riding in the car with him.

On the right inside sleeve, there were five vertically cropped photos—one that ran the inner third of the sleeve, and four other smaller shots that were stacked in two columns in the outer two-thirds of the sleeve. Two of the smaller photos featured a pair of people whose identities also were a mystery.

The photo in the upper right corner featured a woman wearing a headband who was leaning over, saying something into Dylan's ear, her face partially obscured by Dylan's hair, and was taken by Schatzberg on October 5 at Ondine.[6] Dylan was in the studio that night with the Hawks, and, according to label records, they took a break between 10:00 and 11:30 PM. Ondine was on East Fifty-Ninth Street, less than two miles from the Columbia studios, so it seems they spent their break at the discotheque.

There was speculation that the woman in the photo was Edie Sedgwick, but Sedgwick was a blonde at the time, and the woman in the photo was a brunette. Also, Schatzberg says he didn't know the woman, and he knew Sedgwick, had in fact photographed her. According to the Dylan rarities website *Searching for a Gem*, a more likely candidate may be the daughter of harmonica virtuoso Larry Adler, Carole Adler, a brunette who was moving in Dylan's circle during that time period. Ironically, Larry Adler, who called the instrument a "mouth organ," is on the record as hating Dylan's harmonica playing.

To the left of that photo there was a photo of Dylan holding a framed painting and a pair of pliers which, like the one of Dylan and Grossman, was taken during his first shoot at Schatzberg's studio. "When he trusts you, he is a fantastic subject," the photographer says. "Almost anything you ask—you give him a prop, he starts to work with it."[7]

In the lower right-hand corner there was a photo Schatzberg took of Dylan on Jacob Street on the morning of March 3, the same day as the cover photo for the *Saturday Evening Post*. In the shot used in the album, Dylan has turned to face the camera as he crosses the street, walking right to left.

To the left of that was the other mystery photo, a shot of a man who looked dark and mysterious, like he might be the intense leading man in a Tennessee Williams drama. Schatzberg had no problem identifying that subject. It was a photographic self-portrait taken in Trinidad in 1964. "When the album came out, I was really flattered, because that was probably hanging somewhere in my studio. I was flattered by that, but I kept looking for my credit, and then I realized that was my credit," he says with a laugh.

The photo that occupied the inner third of the right sleeve was a shot of Italian film star Claudia Cardinale, another shot Dylan saw at Schatzberg's studio. "He saw it—because I would have things lying around the studio—he saw it and said, 'Oh, we'll put that on the inside.'"

As it would turn out, that decision resulted in a redesign of the right inside sleeve for the second pressing of *Blonde on Blonde*. "When it was published, they [Cardinale's representatives] knew nothing about it because we didn't even think of notifying them," Schatzberg explains. "Her people objected to it, and Columbia worked out something with them that was agreeable." Part of that agreement entailed removing the photo of Cardinale from future pressings of the album.[8]

In the redesign for the album's second pressing, the shot of Cardinale was not the only photo Berg removed; he also took out the photo of Dylan and the mystery woman speaking into his ear. He then enlarged the photo of Dylan from Jacob Street to occupy the inner two-thirds of the righthand sleeve, with the photo of Dylan holding the painting and the pliers in the upper right corner and the self-portrait of Schatzberg in the lower right corner.

After the final session in Nashville, Johnston worked up mixes for the thirteen songs recorded there. Then on March 26, Grossman delivered acetates of Johnston's mixes to Dylan at his hotel in Vancouver where he would play the final North American date of the tour.[9]

After that show, Dylan met Johnston in L.A. for further work on the mixes; Al Kooper and Robertson were on hand, as well.

During that time, Dylan stayed at a mansion in the Los Feliz hills known as the Castle. The house was owned by brothers John Phillip Law and Tom Law and their friend and real estate investor Jack Simons. Tom Law was the road manager for Peter, Paul and Mary, who like Dylan were managed by Albert Grossman, and it was Grossman who had arranged for Dylan and road manager Victor Maymudes, who had taken over for Bob Neuwirth, to stay there while they were in Southern California.

Photographer Lisa Bachelis, who is best known as Lisa Law, was living at the Castle with her future husband, Tom Law, and during those days in early April, she took some of the most iconic photos of Dylan from that time period: shots of him in the mansion's solarium, in the dining room, and on the grounds, as well as shots of his room showing his typewriter on a writing desk.

For a year or so, the Castle was ground zero for beat and hippie culture in L.A., in no small part because Dylan stayed there. The month after Dylan's visit, Andy Warhol, along with the Velvet Underground and Nico, would stay at the mansion during the band's residency at The Trip on the Sunset Strip.

According to Kooper, several of the song titles were decided during the mixing, including "Rainy Day Women #12 & 35," which had been slated at the session as "A Long Haired Mule and a Porkepine"; "Pledging My Time," which had been "What Can You Do For My Wigwam?"; and "Obviously Five Believers," which had been labeled "Black Dog Blues." In addition, Dylan tweaked the titles of a few other songs, including "Like a Woman," which became "Just Like a Woman"; "Where Are You Tonight, Sweet Marie?," which became "Absolutely Sweet Marie"; and "Like Achilles," which became "Temporary Like Achilles."

The album title was decided at that time as well. Over the years, as with the individual songs, there has been a lot of speculation about the meaning of the album's title. The most popular theories have centered on the idea that *Blonde on Blonde* was a reference to one of his former girlfriends. High school sweetheart Echo Helstrom thought it may have referred to her white hair and pale skin, but most of the speculation has centered around Edie Sedgwick, who dyed her hair platinum blonde. In a poem written for Sedgwick after her death, Patty Smith included the line, "Everyone knew she was the real heroine of *Blonde on Blonde*." A less likely theory suggested the title referred to Dylan's pal Brian Jones of the Rolling Stones, and his girlfriend, Anita Pallenberg, both blondes. Finally, there is also the fact that taken as an acronym, the title spells BOB.

Dylan told *Rolling Stone* three years later he couldn't recall whose idea it was to call the album *Blonde on Blonde*, but insisted it wasn't him. That seems unlikely considering his dissatisfaction with Tom Wilson naming *Another Side of Bob Dylan*. Kooper remembered the title as coming from an off-the-cuff remark by Dylan. He may have been riffing off the title of George Tabori's *Brecht on Brecht*, a production of which his former girlfriend Suze Rotolo had appeared in.

In 2010, Johnston told reissue producer Steve Berkowitz, "We mixed that mono probably for three or four days, then I said, 'Oh shit, man, we gotta do stereo.' So me and a coupla guys put our hands on the board, we mixed that son of a bitch in about four hours! . . . So my point is, it took a long time to do the mono, and then it was, 'Oh, yeah, we gotta do stereo.'"[10] As unbelievable as that may sound half a century later, in 1966, before the spread of stereo radio via FM stations, the primary mixes were mono.

According to the April 8 edition of the *Honolulu Advertiser*, Dylan and his band had not left L.A. on April 7 for a concert in Hawaii on April 9 as originally planned. They delayed their departure by a day "to do extra work on a long-playing album."[11]

On the evening of April 7, after they had put the finishing touches on the mixes, Dylan, along with Robertson, Maymudes, and some others, went to the Whisky a Go Go to catch a set by Otis Redding. Redding was doing the first of four nights at the Whisky, of which the following three nights would be recorded for a live album.

As Robertson recalled in his memoir, Dylan had an acetate for "Just Like a Woman" with him for the purpose of playing it for Redding. Robertson had suggested the soul singer as someone "who could sing the hell out of [the song]," and Dylan had agreed. Backstage after the set, Dylan played the recording for the singer and his manager, Phil Walden, and they both loved it. According to Robertson, Redding quietly sang along with the record, and afterward, he laughed and told Dylan, "Man, I dig that song."[12]

But during a tour of the United Kingdom five months later, Redding spoke to *Melody Maker* about the song, after calling Dylan "his favorite singer now." "He gave me 'Just Like a Woman' to make as a record, y'know," he said of Dylan. "But I didn't do it because I just didn't feel it. Mind you, I dig his work like mad."[13]

Robertson later heard from Walden that Redding had gone into the studio and attempted the song but had a problem singing the line, "With her fog, her amphetamine and her pearls." During an appearance on the *BluesMobile* radio show in 2011, Robertson recalled how the manager explained Redding's issue to him: "[Walden] said he couldn't get those words to come out of his mouth in a truthful way. He didn't know how to do it. The rest of the song, no problem."[14]

———————

The final sequence of the double album's fourteen songs went as follows:

Record 1, Side 1
1. "Rainy Day Women #12 & 35"
2. "Pledging My Time"
3. "Visions of Johanna"
4. "One Of Us Must Know (Sooner or Later)"
Record 1, Side 2
1. "I Want You"
2. "Stuck Inside of Mobile with the Memphis Blues Again"
3. "Leopard-Skin Pill-Box Hat"
4. "Just Like a Woman"
Record 2, Side 1
1. "Most Likely You Go Your Way and I'll Go Mine"
2. "Temporary Like Achilles"
3. "Absolutely Sweet Marie"
4. "Fourth Time Around"
5. "Obviously Five Believers"
Record 2, Side 2
1. "Sad Eyed Lady of the Lowlands"

After hearing the sequenced double album, Robert Shelton wrote: "*Blonde* begins with a joke and ends with a hymn; in between, wit alternates with a dominant theme of entrapment—by circumstance, love, society, illusions, and unrealized hopes."[15]

By placing "Sad Eyed Lady of the Lowlands" at the end of the sequence and dedicating an entire side of the double album to it, Dylan not only concluded *Blonde on Blonde* with what he considered at the time to be the best song he had ever written, he tied together several of the themes that run throughout *Blonde on Blonde*, most notably in the final couplet of the chorus, which includes a gate and waiting: "Should I leave them by your gate / Or, sad-eyed lady should I wait?"

In addition, by giving the song he acknowledged was written about her a side unto itself, he underscored his wife Sara's place in the pantheon of women who provided inspiration for the album.

"Rainy Day Women #12 & 35" backed by "Pledging My Time" was released as a single on March 22. Both sides, which featured Johnston's original mixes, were edited for radio. The third and fifth verses were removed from "Rainy Day Women" to cut it down to 2:26, while the second and fifth verses were cut from "Pledging My Time" to make it 2:06. The single entered the *Billboard* Top 40 on April 23 and made it all the way to number two during a nine-week stay. It entered the UK Top 40 on May 12 and peaked at number seven during an eight-week run.

There are some people who think "Rainy Day Women" is another of Dylan's recordings that influenced the Beatles. In *Revolution in the Head: The Beatles' Records and the Sixties*, Ian MacDonald suggested "Yellow Submarine" may have been "a musical spinoff from Bob Dylan's march-tempo 'Rainy Day Women Nos. 12 and 35.'"[16]

Robyn Hitchcock had a similar thought about "Yellow Submarine" because "they both had those voices" in the background. "It's funny, it's a weird coincidence because it was around the same time the Beatles did 'Yellow Submarine,'" Hitchcock notes.[17]

Dylan may have played *Blonde on Blonde* acetates for them himself during the three weeks his 1966 tour was in the United Kingdom, but even if he didn't, it would have been hard for the Beatles not to have heard "Rainy Day Women" before they recorded "Yellow Submarine." It entered the UK Top 40 on May 12 at number thirty-two, then jumped into the Top 10 the following week, where it would remain for a month. So the single was in heavy rotation on British radio during the two recording dates for "Yellow Submarine"—May 26, when they cut the basic tracks, and June 1, when friends and guests, including Mick Jagger, Brian Jones, Marianne Faithfull, and Pattie Boyd, recorded the background voices and special effects. This isn't to suggest "Rainy Day Women" was an influence on the song itself but rather on the way the Beatles approached its production: the background voices, party atmosphere, and Salvation Army–style brass band.

In addition to "Yellow Submarine," one also has to wonder if the ambience on "Rainy Day Women" also may have inspired George Harrison's count off to "Taxman," which includes one of the other Beatles coughing in the background during it. That spoken intro was added to *Revolver*'s opening number on May 16, more than three weeks after the song originally was tracked.

Blonde on Blonde yielded two more Top 40 hits for Dylan: "I Want You," which was backed by "Just Like Tom Thumb Blues," and "Just Like a Woman," which was backed by "Obviously Five Believers." "I Want You" was released on June 10 and reached number twenty on the *Billboard* singles chart. The version of "Tom Thumb Blues" on the B-side was recorded live in concert on May 14, 1966, at the Odeon Theatre in Liverpool, England, backed by the Hawks (with Mickey Jones on drums), and it was the first live recording Dylan had ever released. Renowned music critic, author, and historian Dave Marsh considers it one of the most important B-sides in the history of singles "because it offers something that wasn't legally available until the early '70s: a recorded glimpse of Dylan's onstage prowess."[18] "Just Like a Woman" dropped in early August and went to number thirty-three, making *Blonde on Blonde* Dylan's only album to yield more than a single Top 40 hit.

"I Want You" would become one of Dylan's most covered songs, and a lot of prominent recording artists would cover "Just Like a Woman," too, including a number of women, like Nina Simone, who changed the final chorus to first person on her 1971 recording of the song. That same year, however, "Just Like a Woman" would come under fire as being misogynistic, a charge that has persisted to this day. In an article titled "Does Rock Degrade Women?" in the *New York Times*, Marion Meade wrote, "There's no more complete catalogue of sexist slurs than Dylan's 'Just Like a Woman,' in which he defines woman's natural traits as greed, hypocrisy, whining, and hysteria. But isn't that cute, he concludes, because it's 'just like a woman.' For a finale he throws in the patronizing observation that adult women have a way of breaking 'just like a little girl.'"[19]

One more single was released from *Blonde on Blonde*: "Leopard-Skin Pill-Box Hat" backed by "Most Likely You Go Your Way and I'll Go Mine" in March 1967. It broke into the *Billboard* Hot 100, but failed to crack the Top 40, peaking at number eighty-one.

As late as 2010 and the release of *The Original Mono Recordings*, Columbia listed the official release date for *Blonde on Blonde* as May 16, 1966. (It should be noted the label considered the release date to be the date a record was shipped to distributors from their pressing plants, not the date it would be on sale in stores, which was usually about a week later.) But compelling circumstantial evidence pointed to a later date, including when the label launched its advertising campaign for the album (late June) and when the first press coverage for it appeared (July).

By 2013 and the release of *The Complete Album Collection Vol. One*, Columbia had revised *Blonde on Blonde*'s release date to mid-July. When the label released *The Bootleg Series Vol. 12: The Cutting Edge 1965–1966* two years later, they had the release date as June 20 and the booklet accompanying the *Collector's Edition* included a copy of Dylan's artist card showing that date.

The *Collector's Edition* booklet also included a copy of the album's yet-to-be amended release card from 1966 that showed May 16 as the ship date. The label clearly had planned to ship the album on May 16, but its release was delayed for more than a month for additional work on the album. Although Johnston had already done an admittedly hurried stereo mix of the album in April, according to Robertson's memoir, Columbia wanted an improved stereo mix, and he was enlisted to oversee it in early June. There was also a one-hour overdub session in Nashville on June 16 for "Fourth Time Around" at which Kooper's organ part was erased. The new stereo mix apparently was completed before the overdub session as evidenced by the inclusion of the version of "Fourth Time Around" with Kooper's organ part on the original stereo release of the album.

At some point after the mixing sessions in L.A., probably after returning from the international leg of his tour, Dylan had decided he didn't like the organ part on "Fourth Time Around." Because *Blonde on Blonde* was recorded on a four-track machine, multiple instruments were recorded on each track. Kooper's organ was on the same track as Kenneth Buttrey's drums, so Buttrey was brought in on June 16 to redo his drum part. Also according to label records, a harpsichord was booked for the session, and Charlie McCoy was called in to play it. As the final version of the song shows, at some point during the session it was decided the harpsichord was not going to work as a replacement for the organ, so Buttrey just redid his part.

The fact there was an overdub session on June 16 calls into question whether Columbia could have met a ship date of June 20. It could have been done, but it probably would have required the label's pressing plants to work on the weekend. June 27 seems to be the more likely ship date. *Blonde on Blonde*'s release date matters because it has long been considered the first double album of studio material aimed at the teen market, beating out the Mothers of Invention's double album, *Freak Out!*, for that distinction. But that was based on the May 16 date, so it now appears *Freak Out!* probably was released before *Blonde on Blonde* by a week or two.

Whatever its release date, *Blonde on Blonde* spent thirty-four weeks on the *Billboard* album chart, peaking at number nine, and was certified gold the following year for one million dollars in retail sales. But those numbers only speak to the album's immediate commercial success, which pales in comparison to its lasting impact.

13

NASHVILLE AD (AFTER DYLAN)

UPON ITS RELEASE, the impact of *Blonde on Blonde* reverberated across the globe, but nowhere was it felt more strongly than in Nashville. The album's effect on the city was nothing short of transformative, elevating it as a recording center on par with New York and Los Angeles. After *Blonde on Blonde*, the secret was out about Music City.

"That's when the floodgates opened," Charlie McCoy says. "Nashville had a reputation of [being] just a country music center, although they had been cutting pop records in Nashville since they started cutting records here. Still, in the folk-rock world, I don't think anyone ever considered Nashville. A lot of those people thought: 'Oh, you know, it's a formula down there. It's a formula—four songs a session, bang, bang, bang.' Maybe because the music was simple, the people could sing, and the songs were great, yeah, you could do three and four songs a session and do great work, you know," he explains. "And the idea of spending two days on a song, that wasn't on anybody's radar back then.

"But the fact that Dylan came here, I think it sent a message around the folk-rock world that, 'Hey, it's OK to go there. These guys can do this.' And it was after he came, that all the others came. Dylan let everyone know Nashville was cool."[1]

If there was ever any question regarding the magnitude of *Blonde on Blonde*'s impact on Nashville, it was answered when the Country Music Hall of Fame and Museum debuted a new exhibit in March 2015 titled *Dylan, Cash, and the Nashville Cats: A New Music City.*

Chronologically, the exhibit covered the period from 1966, when Dylan first came to the city to record *Blonde on Blonde*, through the summer of 1974, when Paul McCartney spent time in Nashville rehearsing his band Wings and recording a pair of hits. But make no mistake about it: Dylan's *Blonde on Blonde* sessions were the wellspring for the exhibit. It all flowed downhill from there.

The seventeen "Nashville cats" featured in the exhibit included five of the musicians who accompanied Dylan on *Blonde on Blonde*: Charlie McCoy, Kenneth Buttrey, Wayne Moss, Hargus "Pig" Robbins, and Mac Gayden. It also included three other session players who backed Dylan on subsequent albums he recorded in Nashville: Fred Carter Jr., Charlie Daniels, and Pete Drake.

"When Bob Dylan first came to Nashville in '66 to record *Blonde on Blonde*, he was as central and influential to the emerging youth culture as any single figure," Michael Gray, co-curator of the exhibit, says. "And his decision to record with Nashville musicians was a key factor in bringing so many seemingly unlikely people to record in Middle Tennessee. He prompted other rock and folk acts to follow his example, because in the politically charged '60s, Nashville was thought of as this small, backwater, conservative town. When Dylan came here to make *Blonde on Blonde*, he changed people's perceptions of the city. The fact he had made one of the benchmark albums of American popular music in Nashville really turned people's heads."[2]

McCoy was correct when he said pop records had been cut in Nashville from the city's earliest days as a recording center. Composer/band leader Francis Craig scored the city's first million seller in 1947 with his song, "Near You," which went on to become a pop standard after spending seventeen weeks at number one on the *Billboard* singles chart, a feat no artist since has been able to match. Some of the most influential and successful early rockers recorded in Nashville in the mid-to-late 1950s and early '60s, including Elvis Presley, Buddy Holly, Gene Vincent, Johnny Carroll, the Rock 'n Roll Trio, the Everly Brothers, Roy Orbison, Brenda Lee, and even the Beach Boys. In addition to Nashville being home to several R&B labels, most notably Excello Records, as well as a thriving live blues and R&B scene, blues and R&B legends like Wynonie Harris, Fats Domino, Bobby "Blue" Bland, Etta James, Slim Harpo, and Brook Benton traveled to the city to record during the same time period. Well-known pop artists like Pat Boone, Perry Como, Nancy Sinatra, Patti Page, and Bobby Vinton also made records in Nashville in the 1950s and early '60s.

The fact all those rock, pop, and R&B artists were recording there, however, was not generally known. Back in those days, recording credits were not usually included on album jackets, and there wasn't a media industry built around Nashville music, as there would be later, to get that kind of information out to the public.

But as he had done on *Highway 61 Revisited*, Dylan included the musician credits on *Blonde on Blonde* (across the bottom of the inside gatefold), so other artists saw who backed him on the album. Moss, for one, appreciated the recognition. "Before he got here, nobody ever gave anybody album credits," the guitarist says. "They might say something was cut at RCA Studio, or something like that; or maybe the engineer or the producer, but never who the guitar player was, steel player, drummer, nobody. But after *Blonde on Blonde*, they kind of got shamed into doing it and started giving musicians credit."[3]

In the decade after Dylan's first visit to the city, all kinds of folk and rock artists were not only considering Nashville, but making pilgrimages of their own to the emerging music mecca to record with the cats who played on *Blonde on Blonde*, and others. "If you look at the number of artists from outside the world of country music that came to Nashville in Dylan's wake in a period of just a few years, it's really staggering," Gray says. "And as we dug deeper and deeper into the story, we kept finding that Dylan's influence was everywhere, his fingerprints were everywhere. There was hardly one-to-two degrees of separation from all those artists, all those outside folk and rock artists who came to Nashville during that period seemed to all be connected to Dylan in one way or another."[4]

The first big wave to hit Nashville was a mix of artists with a direct connection of some kind to Dylan and acts signed to Columbia working with Johnston. Despite his original uncertainty about Dylan recording there, manager Albert Grossman was thrilled with the results of the *Blonde on Blonde* sessions. Soon a number of Grossman's other clients made their way to the city to record.

Peter, Paul and Mary was the first of his acts to follow Dylan to Nashville. They recorded tracks for *The Peter, Paul and Mary Album* there in 1966, working with McCoy, Buttrey, Moss, and Robbins. Peter Yarrow returned again in 1968 to do some recording for the group's album *Late Again*.

Grossman's company also managed the popular Canadian folk duo Ian and Sylvia, who made a trio of records in Nashville beginning with *Lovin' Sound* in 1967.[5] They recorded two albums there in 1968, cutting one of the first country rock albums in February, *Nashville*. Elliot Mazer produced the other album they recorded in Nashville that year, *Full Circle*, which was recorded at Bradley's Barn, the studio Owen Bradley opened in Mt. Juliet, Tennessee, in 1967.

Canadian singer-songwriter Gordon Lightfoot was the next of Grossman's clients to make the trek to Music City, recording *The Way I Feel* there in 1967 and *Back on Earth* in 1968. *Back on Earth* was recorded with Mazer at the helm in September of that year at Bradley's Barn. Lightfoot also did some recording there in 1969 while he was in town for a television appearance on *The Johnny Cash Show*.

Dylan himself returned to Nashville in October of 1967 for sessions that would yield the album *John Wesley Harding*. After the dense sound of *Blonde on Blonde* that sometimes featured as many as four and five guitars on a single track, Dylan went in the opposite direction on *John Wesley Harding*, choosing to pursue a sparse sound, backed only by McCoy on bass and Buttrey on drums on ten of the tracks, with Pete Drake adding pedal steel to that lineup on two others. When Dylan went back to Music City in February of 1969 to record *Nashville Skyline*, Buttrey, McCoy, and Drake all got the call, as did Fred Carter Jr. and Charlie Daniels. Those five musicians also were on hand when Dylan returned a couple of months later for three dates at the end of April and the beginning of

May, during which he recorded material that would be released on *Self Portrait*.

"You know, the steel wasn't accepted in pop music until I had cut with people like Elvis Presley," Drake told *Guitar Player* in 1973. "But the kids, themselves, didn't accept it until I cut with Bob Dylan. After that, I guess they figured steel was all right. I did the *John Wesley Harding* album, then *Nashville Skyline*, and *Self Portrait*.

"Bob Dylan really helped me an awful lot," Drake continued. "I mean, by having me play on those records, he just opened the door for the pedal steel guitar, because then everybody wanted to use one. I was getting calls from all over the world. One day my secretary buzzed me and said, 'George Harrison wants you on the phone.' And I said, 'Well, where's he from?' She said, 'London.' And I said, 'Well, what company's he with?' She said, 'The Beatles.' The name, you know, just didn't ring any bells—well, I'm just a hillbilly, you know [laughs]. Anyway, I ended up going to London for a week where we did the album *All Things Must Pass*."[6]

Not surprisingly, Joan Baez followed Dylan to Nashville and made a number of records for Vanguard there, as well as two for A&M. She first came to the city in September 1968 to record a pair of albums at Columbia Studio A: *Any Day Now*, a collection of Dylan covers that included one song from *Blonde on Blonde* ("Sad Eyed Lady of the Low-lands"), and *David's Album*, a selection of country material dedicated to her husband, David Harris, who was about to go to prison for draft evasion. Baez mostly worked with the older A-team of Nashville musicians on those two records, although Buttrey got the call on drums. Norbert Putnam, who had relocated to Nashville from Muscle Shoals a few years earlier and worked a lot of sessions with the cats who backed Dylan, got the call to play bass on some of those sessions.

Baez returned in October 1969 to record *One Day at a Time* at Bradley's Barn. Although she again worked mostly with the A-team musicians on those sessions, Buttrey was once more the drummer and Putnam was one of the bassists. David Briggs, a buddy of Putnam's who also had moved from Muscle Shoals to Nashville, played piano and harpsichord on that album.

Baez was back in Music City in January 1971 to record her next album, *Blessed Are . . .*, with Putnam sliding into the producer's chair behind the console at Quadrafonic Sound Studio, the studio he and Briggs had opened the previous year. *Blessed Are . . .* included Baez's cover of Robbie Robertson's "The Night They Drove Old Dixie Down," which would become the biggest hit of her career, climbing all the way to number three on the *Billboard* Hot 100 during a thirteen-week stay in the Top 40. Baez recorded two more records at Quadrafonic with Putnam at the helm: 1972's *Come from the Shadows* and 1973's *Where Are You Now, My Son?*

By 1968, after cofounding, then departing from Blood, Sweat and Tears, Al Kooper had his own recording contract with Columbia. Kooper had enjoyed working in Nashville so much, he returned to the city that year to record tracks for his first solo album, *I Stand Alone*, at the label's facilities there, working with McCoy, Buttrey, Moss, and Jerry Kennedy. "Hell, yeah, I wanted more of that," Kooper says with a laugh.[7] He came back again in 1970 to record a track for his third solo release, the double album *Easy Does It*, and once again worked with McCoy, Buttrey, and Moss. When Kooper moved into record production, he helmed several albums for other artists in Nashville. The rock legend moved to the city in 1989 and lived and worked there through most of the 1990s.

In addition to Kooper, a number of other folk and rock artists signed to Columbia went to Nashville to record, most notably Simon and Garfunkel, the Byrds, Johnny Winter, and Leonard Cohen, who moved to the Nashville area in 1968 and remained there until late 1972. Johnston was the producer on the Simon and Garfunkel and Cohen recordings made there.

It wasn't only artists one degree removed from Dylan going to the city to record. Other major labels with Nashville footprints, as well as producers who liked to work there, were also fueling the city's increase in recording activity. In the decade following the release of *Blonde on Blonde*, an array of artists would record there, including the Monkees' Michael Nesmith, Country Joe McDonald, Eric Anderson, Ramblin' Jack Elliott, John Stewart, Jerry Jeff Walker, Linda Ronstadt, the Steve Miller Band, Neil Young, David Bowie, Steve Goodman, Leo Kottke, Dan Fogelberg,

Grand Funk Railroad, Ringo Starr, John Prine, Dobie Gray, Loudon Wainwright III, Bob Seger, Donovan, and McCartney.

With so many noncountry artists making their way to Nashville to record, the demand for studio time quickly exceeded the capacities of the label-owned facilities, and a number of important independent studios opened to fill the need, including Bradley's Barn in 1967, Woodland Sound Studios in 1968, Sound Shop and Jack Clement Recording Studios in 1969, and Quadrafonic Sound and Creative Workshop in 1970. In addition, two other studios operating in Nashville since the early 1960s underwent upgrades to help meet the demand: Scotty Moore's Music City Recorders underwent an expansion to eight-track recording in 1968, while Wayne Moss's Cinderella Sound made the move to eight tracks in 1969.

The lives of the Nashville session cats who appeared on *Blonde on Blonde* were forever changed after the album's release. Johnston knew that would happen. "I told them on *Blonde on Blonde*, before they went in to cut the first thing, if this works out, your lives are made; you'll be the talk of the world before it's all over—and they were," he recalled.[8]

The Lovin' Spoonful's John Sebastian quickly picked up on the direction of those musical currents and penned a tribute to the musicians in the city called "Nashville Cats." The band scored a Top 10 hit at the beginning of 1967 with the song, which included some outrageously hilarious lines like: "Nashville cats, been playin' since they's babies / Nashville cats, get work before they're two."[9] The bandleader and songwriter told CBS News in 2015 the song was inspired by what musicians were talking about: "'Man, did you hear these Nashville cats play this thing?'"[10]

"The reason I believed what John Sebastian was saying when he sang that song was because of *Blonde on Blonde*," critic and author Dave Marsh says of "Nashville Cats." "I knew it was true. I didn't have to guess, 'Well, maybe he's right or maybe he's wrong.' It was like, 'Oh, yeah, that makes sense.'"[11]

The majority of the musicians who appeared on *Blonde on Blonde* not only were getting calls to play on the growing number of folk rock and R&B sessions in Nashville, but also went on to have their own recording careers.

Joe South, who moved back to his hometown of Atlanta, scored pop hits as a solo artist with a pair of his own compositions, "Games People Play" in 1969 and "Walk a Mile in My Shoes" in 1970, both of which reached number twelve on the *Billboard* Hot 100. He won the Song of the Year Grammy in 1969 for "Games People Play."

Charlie McCoy was already releasing his own records backed by the Escorts when Dylan came to town, but two years after *Blonde on Blonde*, he transitioned into a solo recording career as an instrumental artist, releasing fourteen albums on Monument Records between 1968 and 1979. He won a Grammy award in the Best Country Instrumental Performance category for his 1972 album, *The Real McCoy*, and reached number one on the *Billboard* country chart the following year with his album *Good Time Charlie*. Between 1972 and 1988, he won nine Instrumentalist of the Year awards from the Country Music Association and the Academy of Country Music. He has been inducted into the Country Music Hall of Fame, the International Musicians Hall of Fame, and the West Virginia Music Hall of Fame.

McCoy was also a member of the pioneering nine-piece instrumental group Area Code 615, which included Buttrey, Moss, and Gayden, as well as Putnam, Briggs, and three others: violinist Buddy Spicher, pedal steel player Weldon Myrick, and banjo/guitar player Bobby Thompson. The group recorded two albums at Cinderella for the Polydor label—1969's *Area Code 615*, which included a cover of "Just Like a Woman," and 1970's *A Trip in the Country*—that influenced the growing subgenres of country rock and southern rock. *A Trip in the Country* was nominated for a Grammy award in the Best Contemporary Instrumental Performance category. Their composition "Stone Fox Chase" from that album, which featured some dazzling harmonica work by McCoy over layers of percussion by Buttrey, was used as the theme music for the BBC's long-running rock music TV program *Old Grey Whistle Test*.

After Area Code 615 performed four dates in February 1970 at the Fillmore West in San Francisco, opening for Country Joe and the Fish, and made an appearance on *The Johnny Cash Show* that same year, the band broke up because most of the members were too busy with their session work to devote time to the group. The inevitability of the breakup was hinted at in a postscript at the end of the track listing for *A Trip in the Country* that read, "Ding Dong the Code Is Dead?" That reinforced a snippet of the melody to "Ding Dong! The Witch Is Dead" from *The Wizard of Oz* that they added onto the end of the album's final track.

After the Code disbanded, Buttrey, Gayden, and Moss joined with keyboardist John Harris to form the seminal southern rock outfit Barefoot Jerry, which was among the bands name-checked in the Charlie Daniels Band's 1975 paean to rockers from below the Mason-Dixon line, "The South's Gonna Do It." Barefoot Jerry's 1971 debut album, *Southern Delight*, was a bold and sweeping expression of both the musical and lyrical possibilities of the emerging subgenre of rock; an uplifting and expansive record that traveled from the mountaintop to the church, from acoustic simplicity to majestic rock sophistication, with a nod to Motown, jazz, and classical along the way. Buttrey and Gayden departed after the group's first album, but Moss kept the outfit going for five more full-length records.

With Bob Johnston producing and Buttrey on drums, Gayden recorded a solo album at Ray Stevens's Sound Lab for EMI, *McGavock Gayden*, which included many of the songs he had intended for the second Barefoot Jerry record. By the mid-'70s, he had moved to ABC-Dunhill and released two albums of cosmic, R&B–inflected rock for the label.

As for percussion phenom Buttrey, he continued to be an in-demand studio drummer, working with a wide array of rock and folk artists who made the journey to Nashville to record, including Bob Seger, the Manhattan Transfer, the Pointer Sisters, Buffy Sainte-Marie, the Sir Douglas Quintet, Willis Alan Ramsey, John Hammond Jr., and Jesse Winchester; but he was probably most identified with Neil Young and Jimmy Buffett, going so far as to even spend time on the road with them as a member of Young's Stray Gators outfit and Buffett's Coral Reefer Band.

Musicians weren't the only group of people in Nashville whose lives were changed dramatically by *Blonde on Blonde*: the city's community of songwriters were affected as well. "Nashville songwriters like John Hartford and Kris Kristofferson and Mickey Newbury and Chris Gantry were approaching their craft in new ways," Michael Gray notes. "They were influenced by Dylan's writing, and then they were kind of changing the way songs were being written in Nashville from then on."[12]

Dylan's old running buddy Bob Neuwirth echoed that point during an appearance in Nashville in 2016. "He inspired a lot of people, he inspired a lot of people that could write better, you know," Neuwirth told the audience. "He inspired a lot of Nashville songwriters."[13]

With their long hair and beards, Kristofferson, Newbury, Hartford, and Gantry were more bohemian than traditional Nashville songsmiths, part of a new guard in the city of hippie songwriters. "We were all starting to listen to Bob Dylan and looking into that outside folk-music influence," Hartford, who is best known as the writer of "Gentle on My Mind," told the *Los Angeles Times* in 1986.[14] He told the *Fretboard Journal* in 2006 that RCA signed him because "they thought I could be their Bob Dylan."[15]

Kris Kristofferson, who was present at the second set of *Blonde on Blonde* sessions, told Karla DeVito, host of the 1984 television series *Rock Influence*, "Dylan opened up all the new doors for a different kind of songwriting than what was going on in the '50s and early '60s. All of a sudden you could write like a poet, and you could have strange imagery; personal, private imagery that wasn't usually found in the old songs by the Clovers, and the Coasters, and the Leiber and Stoller songs. . . .

"Bob Dylan continued to inspire throughout the five years that I was going to school there in Nashville; when I was just paying my dues more or less, and trying to figure out how to do what it was I wanted to do. Bob Dylan was a man that continually, every record, we waited for it, you know, to come out and find out how he was doing it now."[16]

Dylan's magnum opus unquestionably inspired singer-songwriter Chris Gantry, who had a ringside seat for some of the sessions. "*Blonde on Blonde* was such an important album for the times," Gantry says. "It was such a freeing agent to writers to be able to hear something that was expressed in abstracts, and in ways nobody ever heard before."[17]

Mac Gayden, who would pen the pop and soul standard "Everlasting Love" the following year while living in a duplex next door to Kristofferson, talked with the *Nashville Scene* in 1996 about how working on *Blonde on Blonde* affected his own songwriting. "Dylan broke all the rules, lyrically and musically," he said, then added that after working with him up close, "I just kind of threw all the formula songwriting totally out the window."[18]

Gayden picked up on that theme two decades later. "Dylan affected all of us [songwriters]," he says. "He expanded the boundaries for what was acceptable in popular songwriting and gave us all room to be more creative with our songs."[19]

Nashville became a place to live for this new breed of folk and rock singer-songwriters, attracting now-legendary writers like Townes Van Zandt, J. J. Cale, Jimmy Buffett, John Hiatt, Steve Young, Dave Loggins, Guy Clark, Rodney Crowell, Steve Earle, and John Prine, all of whom count Dylan among their primary influences.

Hiatt spoke with *Rolling Stone* in 1995 about Dylan's impact on his writing. "My early writer influences were pretty much songwriters—Bob Dylan and Leonard Cohen were my two favorites initially," he said. "I locked myself in my room for a year and listened to 'Visions of Johanna' over and over. My sisters told me later they were quite concerned about my mental health. Something about the feeling of it just nailed me. That's where I started picking it up."[20]

Earle, who was a protege of Van Zandt and Clark, talked about Dylan's influence in a 2007 interview with *Pitchfork*. "I am who I am as much because of Bob Dylan as anybody," he said. "Just like what we had talked about Townes [Van Zandt]. Townes was fully aware that Bob Dylan invented his job. Make no mistake about that. I am, too."[21]

Today, Dylan's influence on Nashville still can be heard in listening rooms and nightclubs across the City of Song, where on any given night, some of the greatest singer-songwriters on the planet are singing their songs. Kristofferson has no doubt regarding the extent of Dylan's impact on the city: "He was kind of a savior for Nashville," he told the *Nashville Musician* in 2013. "I don't know how much he was aware of it then—how much good he was doing or not."[22]

Johnston took his assessment of Dylan's effect even further in an interview with *On the Tracks*. "It seems like anybody that you ask will say that Nashville began when Dylan came down here," he said. "That's the way I feel about it, too. I think Nashville was a different place before that."[23]

14

A LASTING LEGACY

WHILE *BLONDE ON BLONDE*'s effect on Nashville was great, its impact on the rest of the world was even greater. Looking back on the album forty-five years after its making in 2011, Bob Johnston says, "It was the beginning of everything, I think."

Continuing, Johnston adds, "I think Dylan changed the world. I think he changed writing, I think he changed music. I think he changed the world—and I think he changed it for the better."[1]

The Swedish Academy seemed to express its agreement with that sentiment when it surprisingly—even shockingly to some—named Dylan the 2016 Nobel Prize in Literature recipient. In an interview following the announcement of the award, Sara Danius, a literary scholar and the academy's permanent secretary, was asked by a Swedish journalist how someone should explore Dylan's work. "I think if you want to start listening or reading, you may start with *Blonde on Blonde*, the album from 1966," she said. "You've got many classics, and it's an extraordinary example of his brilliant way of rhyming and putting together refrains, and his pictorial thinking."[2]

Johnston had a strong hunch Dylan could create something truly special with the young musicians the producer had been working with in Nashville, and history has borne that out: *Blonde on Blonde* not only is widely regarded as one of Dylan's three best albums (along with *Highway*

61 Revisited and *Blood on the Tracks*), but was rock's first double album and is regularly listed among the greatest rock albums ever recorded.

While Johnny Cash first suggested to Dylan that he record in Nashville, it was undeniably Johnston who envisioned putting Dylan with Charlie McCoy and the other young Nashville cats. "The Nashville musicians came through for themselves and Nashville and me and the future," the producer says. "I would have looked pretty dumb if they hadn't been worth a shit. Dylan would have gone, 'Goddamn, what I am I down here for?'"[3]

"This was all Bob Johnston's idea, and [Dylan] trusted Bob Johnston's idea," Al Kooper says. "It was a great idea."[4]

Looking back on the results of that idea fifty years later, critic Dave Marsh says, "It was so unprecedented—I mean, it was like, 'Okay I knew he could do things, but I didn't know he could do these things, and do them so comprehensively.' Bob was not trying to take two things and put them together, he was trying to take about fifteen things and put them together. He's got country, he's got blues, he's got R&B, he's even got soul music in there.

"And then it turns out the way you do those things, as you begin to look at the credits and stuff, is that rather than retreating from the music industry, you go right into the commercial maelstrom, and that's where you nail it—that's where you nail it!"[5]

Speaking in Nashville in the summer of 2017, Princeton professor of history and official Bob Dylan historian Sean Wilentz addressed the album's impact. "Both Dylan and Nashville were kind of on a cusp, something was going to change," Wilentz said. "It was 1966: Musically, culturally, and in all sorts of ways, the country was going through all sorts of changes, and in effect, the explosion that happened here with these sessions was kind of inevitable almost. We didn't know where the cusp, how it was gonna work out, but it worked how it did, in part, because of what happened here."[6]

Without question, the album itself represented a tipping point in popular music, redefining the possibilities of rock and roll and more. It changed the way artists approached the genre, as well as the way fans listened to it. With his fusion of poetry and rock in its broadest sense,

Dylan liberated other artists, giving them license to express their inner poet through their music. The record also accelerated the shift of focus in popular music from singles to albums, and in the process, elevated the long-playing record as an art form.

"It's the culmination of something," Marsh says.

> To me, from *Bringing It All Back Home* through *Blonde on Blonde*, that's a trilogy. And you really can't have one without the others. The whole premise of those Dylan records—none more than *Blonde on Blonde*—is that nothing is predictable and controllable. And that the gods laugh at you, the world laughs at you, and you yourself have to laugh at yourself, and be ashamed of yourself even sometimes, if you presume otherwise.
>
> It's a much more realistic record than *Highway 61*—a lot more realistic, if you know what I mean by realistic. You weren't going to run into anybody from "Tom Thumb Blues" on the street corner. You were definitely going to run into "Just Like a Woman" on the street corner.
>
> People talk about the run from *Rubber Soul* to *Sgt. Pepper's*. To me, I would apply all of that to those three Dylan albums. And I would particularly say that if you compared *Sgt. Pepper's* to *Blonde on Blonde*, one of them has more to do with the future than the other, and I don't think it's *Sgt. Pepper's*.

For Marsh, it's easy to connect the dots from *Blonde on Blonde* to some of the music that followed. "I would think its greatest impact, on a lyrical level, was with the singer-songwriter groups," he says. "That whole thing that happened in the early '70s around singer-songwriters starts with Dylan, and more with *Blonde on Blonde* because *Blonde on Blonde* got away from the blues a little bit, and explored some other kinds of sounds."[7]

Blonde on Blonde unquestionably had an impact on singer-songwriter Chris Gantry. "I remember the flurry around that album, and the flurry of the people during that time, how everybody was in hyper awareness to Dylan—what was he going to do next, what was he going to do next, what was he going to do next?" Gantry recalls. "It was a great amazing time, and that album was one of the pinnacles of those times.

"It's interesting what time does to art—it capsulizes it; and that's what makes it so important," he continues. "*Blonde on Blonde* was such an important album for the times—it was such a freeing agent to writers to be able to hear something that was expressed in abstracts, and in ways nobody ever heard before."[8]

While the record undeniably influenced the emerging class of folk-influenced singer-songwriters, to Marsh, *Blonde on Blonde* had the greatest influence on rock singer-songwriters. "In my mind, that is a much more important group of people," he says. "Here's who it influenced most: Tom Petty, Bruce Springsteen, John Mellencamp—there're a lot more, but those are just the three that come to mind first. You know the guys who are not singer-songwriters really because they rock too hard, but they aren't hard rockers because they don't obliterate thought with volume. They're not busy trying to have people avoid listening to their lyrics because their lyrics are so bad; which is a phenomenon. But I think it's that group of people, who are much more important."[9]

Petty acknowledged the album's influence. "We hadn't heard Dylan [growing up in Florida] until 'Like a Rolling Stone' came out as a single," he recalled in a 2012 interview with Paul Zollo for *American Songwriter*. "And we loved that right away. We learned that, did it in the show. We learned all his singles. We didn't have Dylan albums until *Blonde on Blonde*. I had heard *Highway 61 Revisited*. A friend of mine had that. But I actually bought *Blonde on Blonde*. That's where I really got into Bob. And I started to really dig his thing.

"He influenced my songwriting, of course," he continued. "He influenced everybody's songwriting. There's no way around it. No one had ever really left the love song before, lyrically. So in that respect, I think he influenced everybody, because you suddenly realized you could write about other things."[10]

To Mellencamp, Dylan is the best songwriter ever. "Bob Dylan was always the ultimate songwriter, and nobody could ever write a song as good as him, and nobody has ever written a song as good as him.

"With Bob, it's from God's mind to Bob's fingers," Mellencamp told Zollo.[11]

Although he is a little older than the rock singer-songwriters Marsh noted, Neil Young also was influenced by Dylan, telling *Time* magazine in 2005, "He's the one I look to . . . . He's the master. If I'd like to be anyone, it's him. And he's a great writer, true to his music and done what he feels is the right thing to do for years and years and years. He's great. . . . The guy has written some of the greatest poetry and put it to music in a way that it touched me."[12]

Robyn Hitchcock, who emerged in the late 1970s as the leader of British quartet the Soft Boys, was another rock singer-songwriter influenced by *Blonde on Blonde*—it was the album that inspired him to pick up a guitar and start writing songs. "Hearing Bob Dylan when I was twelve, just turning thirteen, just completely reoriented me," Hitchcock told Jeremy Dylan, host of the podcast *My Favorite Album*. "And by the end of the year [1966] when I had marinated myself in *Blonde on Blonde*, I knew instinctively what I was going to be, even if I had no idea how I was going to be it."

But for Hitchcock, *Blonde on Blonde* is so much more than just his favorite album. As he told Jeremy Dylan, it is "the alpha and omega of rock records."[13]

Picking up on that theme later, he says, "It's a grail, really.

"It's a world, you know, and you're in it, and you listen to it," Hitchcock continues.

> People kind of speak it. There's a way of seeing, there's a way of feeling which is all *Blonde on Blonde*. You know if you listen to it for ten minutes, everything starts to kind of develop. A *Blonde on Blonde* kind of tone, a *Blonde on Blonde* color, a *Blonde on Blonde* feel. . . . It's like a frozen moment, only it's a bunch of them. It's a bunch of frozen moments.
>
> I suppose *Blonde on Blonde*, because it was a double album and it had a sort of double title, it really implied that it was a double world. It sort of has a unified sound, and it almost doesn't begin and end. I mean, it obviously ends with "Sad Eyed Lady," but you could simply kind of go round and round inside it. It's almost like a—it's a point of view, I suppose, [laughs] really; I mean, perhaps more than any other record.

As far as the album's influence half a century later goes, Hitchcock expresses the feelings of so many Dylan fans. "What did you mean?" he says. "We still want to know fifty years later, what did you really mean?"[14]

APPENDIX
Blonde on Blonde Credits

Producer: Bob Johnston
Engineers: Roy Halee, Tom Sparkman, Charlie Bragg, Mort Thomasson, Shelby Coffen
Assistant engineers: Pete Dauria, Larry Keyes, Ed Hudson, Jim Williamson

"Rainy Day Women #12 & 35"
Bob Dylan: vocals, harmonica
Charlie McCoy: trumpet
Wayne Moss: electric bass
Henry Strzelecki: organ
Hargus "Pig" Robbins: piano
Al Kooper: tambourine
Kenneth Buttrey: drums
Wayne Butler: trombone

"Pledging My Time"
Bob Dylan: vocals, harmonica
Charlie McCoy: acoustic guitar
Robbie Robertson: electric guitar
Joe South: electric guitar
Al Kooper: organ
Hargus "Pig" Robbins: piano
Henry Strzelecki: electric bass

Kenneth Buttrey: drums

"Visions of Johanna"
Bob Dylan: vocals, acoustic guitar, harmonica
Charlie McCoy: acoustic guitar
Jerry Kennedy: electric guitar
Wayne Moss: electric guitar
Al Kooper: organ
Joe South: electric bass
Kenneth Buttrey: drums

"One of Us Must Know (Sooner or Later)"
Bob Dylan: vocals, electric guitar, harmonica
Robbie Robertson: electric guitar
Al Kooper: organ
Paul Griffin: piano
Rick Danko: electric bass
Bobby Gregg: drums

"I Want You"
Bob Dylan: vocals, acoustic guitar, harmonica
Charlie McCoy: acoustic guitar
Wayne Moss: electric guitar
Al Kooper: organ
Hargus "Pig" Robbins: piano
Henry Strzelecki or Joe South: electric bass
Kenneth Buttrey: drums

"Stuck Inside of Mobile with the Memphis Blues Again"
Bob Dylan: vocals, acoustic guitar
Charlie McCoy: acoustic guitar
Wayne Moss: electric guitar
Joe South: electric guitar
Al Kooper: organ
Hargus "Pig" Robbins: piano
Henry Strzelecki: electric bass

Kenneth Buttrey: drums

"Leopard-Skin Pill-Box Hat"
Bob Dylan: vocals, electric guitar, harmonica
Charlie McCoy: acoustic guitar
Robbie Robertson: electric guitar
Wayne Moss: electric guitar
Joe South: electric guitar
Al Kooper: organ
Hargus "Pig" Robbins: piano
Henry Strzelecki: electric bass
Kenneth Buttrey: drums

"Just Like a Woman"
Bob Dylan: vocals, acoustic guitar, harmonica
Charlie McCoy: acoustic guitar
Joe South: acoustic guitar
Al Kooper: organ
Hargus "Pig" Robbins: piano
Henry Strzelecki: electric bass
Kenneth Buttrey: drums

"Most Likely You Go Your Way and I'll Go Mine"
Bob Dylan: vocals, harmonica
Robbie Robertson: electric guitar
Wayne Moss: electric guitar
Al Kooper: organ
Hargus "Pig" Robbins: piano
Charlie McCoy: trumpet
Joe South or Charlie McCoy: electric bass
Kenneth Buttrey: drums

"Temporary Like Achilles"
Bob Dylan: vocals, harmonica
Robbie Robertson: electric guitar

Joe South: electric guitar
Hargus "Pig" Robbins: piano
Al Kooper: electric piano
Charlie McCoy: electric bass
Kenneth Buttrey: drums

"Absolutely Sweet Marie"
Bob Dylan: vocals, harmonica
Charlie McCoy: acoustic guitar
Robbie Robertson: electric guitar
Wayne Moss: electric guitar
Joe South: electric guitar
Mac Gayden: electric guitar
Al Kooper: organ
Hargus "Pig" Robbins: piano
Henry Strzelecki: electric bass
Kenneth Buttrey: drums

"Fourth Time Around"
Bob Dylan: vocals, acoustic guitar, harmonica
Charlie McCoy: acoustic guitar
Wayne Moss: acoustic guitar
Al Kooper: organ*
Joe South: electric bass
Kenneth Buttrey: drums

---

* A version of "Fourth Time Around" with Al Kooper's organ part was included on the mono editions of *Blonde on Blonde* released in Canada and France, and on all initial stereo releases of the album. The version of "Fourth Time Around" included on later stereo editions did not include Kooper's organ part.

"Obviously Five Believers"
Bob Dylan: vocals, guitar
Charlie McCoy: harmonica
Robbie Robertson: electric guitar
Wayne Moss: electric guitar
Al Kooper: organ
Hargus "Pig" Robbins: piano
Henry Strzelecki: electric bass
Kenneth Buttrey: drums

"Sad Eyed Lady of the Lowlands"
Bob Dylan: vocals, acoustic guitar, harmonica (takes 3–4)
Charlie McCoy: acoustic guitar
Wayne Moss: acoustic guitar
Al Kooper: organ
Hargus "Pig" Robbins: piano
Joe South: electric bass
Kenneth Buttrey: drums

ACKNOWLEDGMENTS

I WANT TO THANK the following people, who helped make this book possible:

My editor, Yuval Taylor, who believed in this book and who, with saintly patience, helped me make it better all along the way.

My agent, Janet Rosen, who got my vision for the book from the start and found a home for it with Mr. Taylor.

Chicago Review Press managing editor, Michelle Williams, and her team of editors for their help in bringing the book to print.

Jeff Rosen and Callie Gladman with Bob Dylan Music Company for their help in securing permissions.

Producer Bob Johnston and the *Blonde on Blonde* musicians—Charlie McCoy, Al Kooper, Wayne Moss, Pig Robbins, Jerry Kennedy, Henry Strzelecki, Mac Gayden, and Bill Aikins—who gave many, many hours of their time to interviews with me about the making of the album.

All the other interview subjects who also contributed their time, thoughts, and memories to the book: Billy Swan, Chris Gantry, Jerry Schatzberg, Charlie Steiner, Dave Marsh, Robyn Hitchcock, Jeff Gold, Michael Gray (Museum Editor, Country Music Hall of Fame and Museum), Norbert Putnam, Elliot Mazer, Harold Bradley, Ronnie Milsap, Harold Hitt, Jason Ringenberg, Warner Hodges, Jimmy Miller, David Briggs, George Schowerer, Lou Bradley, Lisa Law, Bob Tubert, Todd Snider, Delores Buttrey Rhoten, and Cheri Buttrey-Jenkins.

Richard Johnston, who first encouraged me to write this book and introduced me to Ms. Rosen. Paul Kingsbury, who also encouraged me early on and gave me guidance during the process of writing a proposal for the book. David Daniel, who not only gave me early encouragement, but who also gave me counsel during the entire process of writing the book. Warren Denney (Senior Creative Director, Country Music Hall of Fame and Museum), who also gave me important counsel and assistance throughout the entire process.

All the people who helped with the book's research: Tom Cording (Sony Legacy), Lynsey McDonald, Travis Stock, Tia Dunn, Ron Wynn, Drew Mahan (Archivist, Metro Nashville Archives), Bob Egan (PopSpot), Michael McCall (Museum Editor, Country Music Hall of Fame and Museum), Kathleen Campbell (Print Collections Librarian, Country Music Hall of Fame and Museum), Bryan Jones (Still Image Librarian and Editor, Country Music Hall of Fame and Museum), Dave Booth (Showtime Music Archives), Karin Johnson (Bill Lowery Music), Roger Ford, Peter Coulthard, H.R., and Briagha McTavish (TAXI).

And the following people who offered assistance to me along the way on this journey: Skip Bayless, Jason Pierce, Dean Hitt, Holly Gleason, Burt Stein, Carl Thomason, Dave Pomeroy, Ray Hair, Courtney Haley, Jody Lentz, Randy Horick, Greg Hallmark, Doug Chavis, Hadley Moore, Mike Simmons, Michael Lydon, Debbie McClanahan, and Lewis Allen.

SOURCES

Bronson, Fred. *The Billboard Book of Number One Hits*. New York: Billboard Publications, 1985.

Cash, Johnny, and Patrick Carr. *Cash: The Autobiography*. San Francisco: Harper San Francisco, 1997.

Cott, Jonathan, ed. *Bob Dylan: The Essential Interviews*. New York: Wenner Books, 2006.

Dylan, Bob. *Chronicles: Volume One*. New York: Simon & Schuster, 2004.

Dylan, Bob. *The Cutting Edge 1965–1966: The Bootleg Series, Vol. 12*. Sony Legacy, 2015.

Every Mind Polluting Word: Assorted Bob Dylan Utterances. Artur, ed. http://dvdylanjim50reviews.yolasite.com/resources/Reference%20(1).pdf.

Ford, Roger. *Electric Dylan*, http://www.electricdylan.net, 2000-2020.

Gill, Andy. *Don't Think Twice, It's All Right—Bob Dylan, the Early Years: The Stories Behind Every Song*. New York: Thunder Mouth Press, 1998.

Helm, Levon, and Stephen Davis. *This Wheel's on Fire: Levon Helm and the Story of the Band*. Chicago: Chicago Review Press, 2013.

Heylin, Clinton. *Bob Dylan Behind the Shades: A Biography*. New York: Summit Books, 1991.

Heylin, Clinton. *Bob Dylan: Behind the Shades Revisited*. New York: Harper Collins, 2003.

Heylin, Clinton. *Bob Dylan: The Recording Sessions (1960–1994)*. New York: St. Martin's Griffin, 1995.

Heylin, Clinton. *Judas!: From Forest Hills to the Free Trade Hall, a Historical View of the Big Boo*. New York: Route Publishing, 2016.

Heylin, Clinton. *Revolution in the Air: The Songs of Bob Dylan, 1957–1973*. Chicago: Chicago Review Press, 2009.

Hoskyns, Barney. *Across the Great Divide: The Band in America*. Milwaukee, WI: Hal Leonard, 2006.

Kooper, Al. *Backstage Passes and Backstabbing Bastards: Memoirs of a Rock 'n' Roll Survivor*. Milwaukee, WI: Hal Leonard, 2008.

Krogsgaard, Michael. "Bob Dylan Sessionography." *Telegraph*, Issue 52 (Autumn 1995), Issue 53 (Winter 1995).

Marcus, Greil. *Like a Rolling Stone: Bob Dylan at the Crossroads*. New York: PublicAffairs, 2005.

Robertson, Robbie. *Testimony*. New York: Crown Archetype, 2016.

Scaduto, Anthony. *Bob Dylan: An Intimate Biography*. New York: Castle Books, 1971.

Shelton, Robert. *No Directon Home: The Life and Music of Bob Dylan*. New York: William Morrow and Company, 1986.

Sloman, Larry "Ratso." *On the Road with Bob Dylan*. New York: Three Rivers Press, Revised Edition, 2002.

Sounes, Howard. *Down the Highway: The Life of Bob Dylan*. New York: Grove Press, 2001.

Spitz, Bob. *Dylan: A Biography*. New York: W. W. Norton & Company, 1991.

Whitburn, Joel. *The Billboard Book of Top 40 Hits, Seventh Edition*. New York: Billboard Books, 2000.

Wilentz, Sean. *Bob Dylan in America*. New York: Doubleday, 2010.

NOTES

Unless otherwise noted herein, all studio dialogue was taken from *The Cutting Edge 1965–1966: The Bootleg Series Vol. 12* (limited edition 18-CD set). All chart information comes from *Billboard* unless otherwise noted in the text.

Prologue

1. Ron Rosenbaum, "Bob Dylan Interview," *Playboy*, March 1978.
2. Bob Dylan interview with Cameron Crowe for the liner notes accompanying the Dylan box set, *Biograph*.
3. Bob Dylan, *Chronicles: Volume One* (New York, Simon & Schuster, 2004), 95.
4. Bob Dylan interview, *The Les Crane Show*, WABC-TV, February 17, 1965.
5. Bob Dylan, *Chronicles: Volume One* (New York, Simon & Schuster, 2004), 96.
6. Richard Harrington, "The Gospel According to Mavis," *Washington Post*, October 31, 2004.
7. Bob Dylan acceptance speech, Rock & Roll Hall of Fame Induction, January 20, 1988, New York, New York.
8. Interview with LeRoy Hoikkala, *On the Tracks* 18, July 2, 1999.
9. Matt Diehl, "Remembering Johnny," *Rolling Stone*, October 16, 2003.
10. Cash and Carr, *Cash*, 197.
11. Heylin, *Judas*.
12. Ron Rosenbaum, "Bob Dylan Interview," *Playboy*, March 1978.

1. "I'm Bob, Too"

1. *Billboard*, July 24, 1965.

2. Kooper, *Backstage Passes.*

3. Michael Watts, "The Man Who Put Electricity into Dylan," *Melody Maker*, January 31, 1976.

4. Marcus, *Like a Rolling Stone.*

5. Watts, "The Man Who."

6. Jann Wenner, "The *Rolling Stone* Interview: Bob Dylan," *Rolling Stone*, November 29, 1969.

7. Wenner, "The *Rolling Stone* Interview."

8. Marcus, *Like a Rolling Stone.*

9. Spitz, *Dylan*, 335.

10. Author interview with Norbert Putnam, April 17, 2014.

11. Johnny Cash interview, *The Other Side of Nashville* documentary (MGM/UA Home Video, 1983).

12. Author interview with Mac Gayden, April 2, 2014.

13. Richard Buskin, "Classic Tracks: Paul Simon 'You Can Call Me Al,'" *Sound On Sound*, September 2008.

14. Heylin, *Bob Dylan: Behind the Shades Revisited*, 219.

15. Heylin, *Bob Dylan: Behind the Shades Revisited*, 217.

16. Richard Younger, "An Exclusive Interview with Bob Johnston," *On the Tracks* 20.

17. Younger, "Interview with Bob Johnson."

18. Dan Daley, "Bob Johnston," *Mix*, January 1, 2003.

19. Bronson, *Billboard Book of Number One Hits*, 178.

20. Whitburn, *The Billboard Book of Top 40 Hits*, 99.

21. "Bob Johnston, Part 1," *In Search of a Song*, PRX network radio series, October 13, 2012.

22. "Bob Johnston, Part 1," *In Search of a Song.*

23. Mercury single 70991X45 ("Born to Love One Woman" / "How Many").

24. Algonquin single AR-717; Chic single 1014 ("Whistle Bait" / "The Whipmaster").

25. Dot single 45-15812 ("Luigi Pasquale" / "I'm Hypnotized").

26. Younger, "Interview with Bob Johnston."

27. Irwin Stambler and Grelun Landon, *Country Music: The Encyclopedia* (New York: St. Martin's Griffin), 118.

28. Epic single 5-9308 ("Jaguar" / "Roundabout"), Epic single 5-9325 ("Drive In" / "Exit 6").

29. "Nashville," *Billboard*, October 3, 1960, 43.

30. "Paul Cohen Heads New Kapp C&W Record Division," *Billboard*, October 23, 1961, 2.

31. Columbia single 42157 ("Operation Heartbreak" / "Rock-a-Bye Your Baby with a Dixie Melody"); "Bob Johnston, Part 1," *In Search of a Song.*

32. Kapp single K-465X ("How Could You" / "I'm Always Dreaming").

33. Liberty single 55469 ("What's a Matter Baby (Is It Hurting You?)" / "Thirteenth Hour").

34. Author interviews with Bob Tubert, May 21, 2014, and Charlie McCoy, January 13, 2015.

35. Shawna Ortega, "Charlie Daniels," songfacts.com, March 30, 2007.

36. "Bob Johnston, Part 1," *In Search of a Song.*

37. Capitol single 15383 ("My Heart Would Know" / "Hush . . . Hush, Sweet Charlotte").

38. "Bob Johnston, Part 1," *In Search of a Song.*

39. "Bob Johnston, Part 1," *In Search of a Song.*

40. Author interview with Bob Johnston, June 3, 2011.

41. Author interview with Jerry Schatzberg, June 27, 2016.

42. Jim Walrod and Marc Santo, "Jerry Schatzberg: Filmmaker & Photographer," Revel in New York, www.revelinnewyork.com/interviews/jerry-schatzberg.

43. Author interview with Jerry Schatzberg, June 27, 2016.

44. Daley, "Bob Johnston."

45. Author interview with Bob Johnston, June 3, 2011.

46. Author interview with Charlie McCoy, 2003.

47. Bob Neuwirth interview with Michael Gray, Country Music Hall of Fame and Museum, May 7, 2016.

48. Monument single 45-870 ("HarpoonMan"/"I'm Ready").

49. Author interview with Charlie McCoy, 2003.

50. Author interview with Bob Johnston, June 3, 2011.

2. Airborne with the Hawks

1. Wenner, "The *Rolling Stone* Interview."

2. Author interview with James Burton, October 14, 2015.

3. "Joe Osborn: A Few (Hundred) Hits," *Vintage Guitar*, October 1998.

4. Kooper, *Backstage Passes.*

5. Sloman, *On the Road with Bob Dylan*, 421–422.

6. Hoskyns, *Across the Great Divide*, 76.

7. Jay Orr, "Mary Martin Interview," November 17, 2009, Louise Scruggs Memorial Forum, Country Music Hall of Fame and Museum archives.

8. Jason Schneider, *Whispering Pines: The Northern Roots of American Music from Hank Snow to the Band* (Toronto, ECW Press, 2010).

9. Orr, "Mary Martin Interview."

10. Hoskyns, *Across the Great Divide*, 84.

11. John Hammond Jr. interview, *The Band*, documentary film (TH Entertainment, 1995).

12. Sounes, *Down the Highway*, 188.

13. Robertson, *Testimony*, 160–161.

14. Tammy La Gorce, "For a Legendary Blues Man, Life Hardly Mirrors His Art," *New York Times*, August 5, 2007.

15. Schneider, *Whispering Pines.*

16. Orr, "Mary Martin Interview."

17. Wenner, "The *Rolling Stone* Interview."

18. Hoskyns, *Across the Great Divide*, 94.

19. Robertson, *Testimony*, 167.

20. Hoskyns, *Across the Great Divide*, 95.

21. Robertson, *Testimony*, 168.

22. Robertson, *Testimony*, 169.

23. Helm and Davis, *This Wheel's on Fire*, 131–132.

24. Kooper, *Backstage Passes*.

25. Robertson, *Testimony*, 170.

26. Helm with Davis, *This Wheel's on Fire*, 132.

27. Robertson, *Testimony*, 171.

28. Shelton, *No Direction Home*, 307.

29. Kooper, *Backstage Passes*.

30. Kooper, *Backstage Passes*.

31. Robertson, *Testimony*, 173–175.

32. Hoskyns, *Across the Great Divide*, 99.

33. Robertson, *Testimony*, 179.

34. Helm and Davis, *This Wheel's on Fire*, 137.

35. Helm and Davis, *This Wheel's on Fire*, 136.

36. John Goddard, "When Dylan Got Rocked," *Toronto Star*, November 18, 2000.

37. Michael Corcoran, "Didja know? Dylan and the Band debuted in Austin 9/24/65," *Austin American Statesman*, September 2005, michaelcorcoran. net, October 2, 2011.

38. Kevin Curtin, "Playback: Dylan Goes Electric—Again," *Austin Chronicle*, September 25, 2015.

39. Sounes, *Down the Highway*, 101.

40. Curtin, "Playback: Dylan Goes Electric."

41. Curtin, "Playback: Dylan Goes Electric."

42. Corcoran, "Didja know?"

43. Helm and Davis, *This Wheel's on Fire*, 137.

44. Corcoran, "Didja know?"

45. Don Safra, "Bob Dylan Scores Here in First Dallas Concert," *Dallas Times Herald*, November 27, 1965.

46. Francis Raffetto, "After Dark: Dylan Captures SMU Audience," *Dallas Morning News*, November 27, 1965.

47. Helm and Davis, *This Wheel's on Fire*, 137.

48. Hoskyns, *Across the Great Divide*, 96.

49. Heylin, *Judas!*

50. Jonathan Cott, "Mick Jagger: The *Rolling Stone* Interview," *Rolling Stone*, October 12, 1968.

51. Robertson, *Testimony*, 190.

3. Meet the New Drummer, Same as the Old Drummer

1. "Setlists 1965," www.bobdylan.com, accessed April 9, 2018.

2. Hoskyns, *Across the Great Divide*, 104.

3. Majorie Kaufman, "Rick Danko interview," *On the Tracks* 10 (Spring 1997).

4. Interview with Robbie Robertson by TAXI founder Michael Laskow, onstage at TAXI's Road Rally, November 10, 2006.

5. Dylan interview, *No Direction Home* documentary (Paramount, 2005).

6. Interview with Robbie Robertson by TAXI founder Michael Laskow, onstage at TAXI's Road Rally, November 10, 2006.

7. Jonathan Valania, "A Mellowed Rick Danko Strikes Up the Band," *Morning Call* (Allentown, PA), February 28, 1993.

8. Helm and Davis, *This Wheel's on Fire*, 139.

9. Helm and Davis, *This Wheel's on Fire*, 139.

10. Helm and Davis, *This Wheel's on Fire*, 139–140.

11. Helm and Davis, *This Wheel's on Fire*, 140.

12. Greil Marcus, "Bob Dylan's Dream," *Guardian*, June 21, 2008.

13. Ron Rosenbaum, "*Playboy* Interview: Bob Dylan," *Playboy*, March 1978.

14. Bob Brown interview with Bob Dylan, *20/20*, ABC TV, September 19, 1985.

15. Author interview with David Daniel, December 28, 207.

16. Scaduto, *Bob Dylan*, 201–202.

17. Joan Baez, "Winds of the Old Days," © 1975, Chandos Music (ASCAP).

18. Author interview with Jeff Gold, May 30, 2017.

19. Marcus, "Bob Dylan's Dream."

20. "Visions Of Johanna" lyrics, Copyright © 1966 by Dwarf Music; renewed 1994 by Dwarf Music. All rights reserved. International copyright secured. Reprinted by permission.

21. Author interview with Robyn Hitchcock, January 27, 2017.

22. Paul McHugh, "Long-lost photos capture a young Bob Dylan rubbing elbows in North Beach with Beat poets," *San Francisco Chronicle*, April 4, 2006.

23. Robertson, *Testimony*, 201.

24. *Billboard*, December 25, 1965, 5.

25. Author interview with Jerry Schatzberg, June 27, 2016.

26. Scaduto, *Bob Dylan*, 229.

27. Author interview with Jerry Schatzberg, June 27, 2016.

4. "It Was the Band"

1. Robertson, *Testimony*, 207.

2. Jill Stein with George Plimpton, ed., *Edie: American Girl* (New York, Grove Press, 1982), 349.

3. Wenner, "The *Rolling Stone* Interview."

4. Robert Christgau interview, *Bob Dylan and The Band: Down in the Flood* (Prism Films, Chrome Dreams Media, 2012).

5. Alan Govenar, *Lightnin' Hopkins: His Life and Blues* (Chicago, Chicago Review Press, 2010), 246.

6. Lightnin' Hopkins, "Automobile Blues," © 1961, Prestige Music (BMI).

7. "Leopard-Skin Pill-Box Hat" lyrics, Copyright © 1966 by Dwarf Music; renewed 1994 by Dwarf Music. All rights reserved. International copyright secured. Reprinted by permission.

8. Author interview with Al Kooper, January 21, 2011.

9. Wilentz, *Bob Dylan in America*, 113.

10. "One of Us Must Know (Sooner or Later)" lyrics, Copyright © 1966 by Dwarf Music; renewed 1994 by Dwarf Music. All rights reserved. International copyright secured. Reprinted by permission.

11. Gill, *Don't Think Twice*, 99.

12. Shelton, *No Direction Home*, 322.

13. Wilentz, *Bob Dylan in America*, 114.

14. Author interview with Al Kooper, January 21, 2011; Gill, *Don't Think Twice*, 99.

15. Marc Fisher, "Voice of the Cabal: Bob Fass and the Slow Fade of Countercultural Radio," *New Yorker*, December 4, 2006.

16. Wenner, "The *Rolling Stone* Interview."

17. Mick Houghton, *Becoming Elektra: The True Story of Jac Holtzman's Visionary Record Label* (London: Jawbone Press, 2010), 95; Bob Dylan interview for *The Bootleg Series, Vol. 1–3* liner notes.

18. Richard Witts, *Nico: The Life and Lies of an Icon* (London: Virgin, 1995).

19. Shelton, *No Direction Home*, 336.

20. Heylin, *Revolution in the Air*, 203.

21. "Leopard-Skin Pill-Box Hat" lyrics, Copyright © 1966 by Dwarf Music; renewed 1994 by Dwarf Music. All rights reserved. International copyright secured. Reprinted by permission.

22. Shelton, *No Direction Home*, 361.

5. The Nashville Cats

1. Phil Sullivan and Jack Hurst, "Columbia Buys Bradley Studio," *Tennessean*, January 16, 1962.

2. Jessi Maness, "The History of Music Row: 60 Years of Greatness," *Sports & Entertainment Nashville*, Fourth Quarter, 2015.

3. "Nash. Columbia Will Host Guest of WSM 'Opry' Fete," *Billboard*, October 16, 1965, 3.

4. "Nash. Columbia Will Host," *Billboard*, 56.

5. Author interview with Harold Hitt, May 17, 2011.

6. Michael Kosser, *How Nashville Became Music City USA: 50 Years of Music Row* (New York: Hal Leonard, 2006), 150.

7. Author interview with Bob Johnston, June 3, 2011.

8. Author interview with Norbert Putnam, April 17, 2014.

9. Norbert Putnam, "The King at B: Top Musicians Remember Elvis," panel discussion, Historic RCA Studio B, August 31, 2017.

10. Author interview with Charlie McCoy, January 13, 2015.

11. Bill Williams, "Charlie McCoy: His Monumental Years," *Billboard*, December 21, 1974, 39.

12. Author interview with Charlie McCoy, January 21, 2011.

13. Author interview with Bill Aikins, January 12, 2011.

14. Author interview with Charlie McCoy, January 21, 2011.

15. Author interview with Bill Aikins, January 9, 2015.

16. Author interview with Jimmy Miller, January 15, 2015.

17. Author interview with Mac Gayden, August 3, 2017.

18. Author interview with Elliot Mazer, April 10, 2015.

19. Author interview with Mac Gayen, August 3, 2017.

20. Author interview with Elliot Mazer, April 10, 2015.

21. Author interview with Charlie McCoy, January 13, 2015.

22. Author interview with Jerry Kennedy, January 19, 2011.

23. Author interview with Charlie McCoy, October 16, 2015.

24. Michael McCall, "Nashville Cats: Salute to Wayne Moss," Country Music Hall of Fame and Museum, www.countrymusichalloffame.org, May 2, 2009.

25. Author interview with Mac Gayden, January 15, 2015.

26. Author interview with Harold Bradley, August 22, 2016.

27. Author interview with Harold Bradley, August 22, 2016.

28. Author interview with Jerry Kennedy, January 19, 2011.

29. Author interview with Charlie McCoy, October 16, 2015.

30. Author interview with Hargus "Pig" Robbins, January 13, 2011.

31. Author interview with Henry Strzelecki, January 12, 2011.

32. Jan Donkers interview with Joe South for VPRO radio, www.youtube.com /watch?v=bHfmrQ2epw0.

33. Author interview with Norbert Putnam, July 23, 2015.

34. Michael Shelley interview with Joe South, WFMU FM, Jersey City, New Jersey, April 17, 2010.

35. Author interview with Jerry Schatzberg, June 27, 2016.

36. Tim White interview, "The Blonde On Blonde Missing Pictures," searching foragem.com.

37. Bob Egan, "Bob Dylan's BLONDE ON BLONDE (1966)," PopSpots, www .popspotsnyc.com/blonde_on_blonde.

38. Bob Egan, "Bob Dylan's BLONDE ON BLONDE (1966)," PopSpots, www .popspotsnyc.com/blonde_on_blonde.

6. Hurry Up and Wait

1. Kooper, *Backstage Passes*.

2. Author interview with Bill Aikins, January 12, 2011.

3. Author interview with Bill Aikins, December 6, 2015.

4. Author interview with Bill Aikins, June 18, 2015.

5. Author interview with Charlie McCoy, October 16, 2015.

6. Author interview with Bill Aikins, January 12, 2011.

7. Charlie McCoy interview, *The Band* documentary film (TH Entertainment, 1995).

8. Wilentz, *Bob Dylan in America*, 118.

9. Gill, *Don't Think Twice*, 105.

10. Jean-Michel Guesdon and Philippe Margotin, *All the Songs: The Story Behind Every Beatles Release* (New York: Black Dog & Leventhal Publishers, 2013), 278; John Stevens, *The Songs of John Lennon: The Beatles Years* (Boston: Berklee Press, 2002).

11. David Sheff, "*Playboy* Interview with John Lennon and Yoko Ono," *Playboy*, January 1980.

12. Jonathan Cott, "John Lennon: The *Rolling Stone* Interview," *Rolling Stone*, November 23, 1968.

13. "Fourth Time Around" lyrics, Copyright © 1966 by Dwarf Music; renewed 1994 by Dwarf Music. All rights reserved. International copyright secured. Reprinted by permission.

14. Vic Garbarini, "George Harrison looks back on his days when he played lead guitar for the Beatles, the greatest rock and roll band the world has ever known," *Guitar World*, January 2001.

15. The twentieth take was mistakenly marked as 19.

16. Author interview with Billy Swan, October 30, 2015.

17. "Visions of Johanna" lyrics, Copyright © 1966 by Dwarf Music; renewed 1994 by Dwarf Music. All rights reserved. International copyright secured. Reprinted by permission.

18. Author interview with Bill Aikins, January 9, 2011.

19. Author interview with Charlie McCoy, January 21, 2011.

20. Author interview with Robyn Hitchcock, January 27, 2017.

21. Vanessa Thorpe, "Laureate gives laurels to Dylan," *Guardian*, October 2, 1999.

22. Gill, *Don't Think Twice*, 99.

23. Author interview with Charlie McCoy, October 16, 2015.

24. Author interview with Bob Johnston, June 3, 2011.

25. Author interview with Charlie McCoy, October 16, 2015.

26. Author interview with Al Kooper, January 21, 2011.

7. An All-Nighter with the Sad-Eyed Lady

1. Author interview with Al Kooper, January 21, 2011.

2. Author interview with Wayne Moss, January 17, 2011.

3. Author interview with Al Kooper, January 21, 2011.

4. Author interview with Hargus "Pig" Robbins, January 13, 2011.

5. Author interview with Al Kooper, January 21, 2011.

6. Juli Thanki, "How Bob Dylan Threw Open the Doors to Music City," *Tennessean* (podcast), May 1, 2016.

7. Author interview with Billy Swan, October 30, 2015.

8. Robert Shelton, *No Direction Home*, 325.

9. Paul Nelson, "Bob Dylan Approximately," *Blonde on Blonde Songbook* (London: Big Ben Music Ltd., 1966), 9.

10. Richard Goldstein, *The Poetry of Rock* (New York, Bantam Books, 1969), 76.

11. Robert Hilburn, "The Impact of Dylan's Music 'Widened the Scope of Possibilities,'" *Los Angeles Times*, May 19, 1991.

12. Heylin, *Revolution in the Air*, 296.

13. Jann Wenner, "The *Rolling Stone* Interview: Bob Dylan," *Rolling Stone*, November 29, 1969.

14. Howard Stern interview with Roger Waters, *The Howard Stern Show*, January 18, 2012.

15. Author interview with Robyn Hitchcock, January 27, 2017.

16. Lester Bangs, "Love or Confusion?," in *Studio A: The Bob Dylan Reader*, ed. Benjamin Hedin (New York: W. W. Norton, 2005), 156.

17. Tony Beck, *Understanding Bob Dylan: Making Sense of the Songs That Changed Modern Music* (CreateSpace, 2011), 41.

18. Stephen Scobie, *Alias Bob Dylan: Revisited* (Markham, Ontario: Red Deer, 2003).

19. Robert Shelton, *No Direction Home*, 99–100.

20. Neil Hickey, "Bob Dylan Today: A Rare Interview," *TV Guide*, September 11, 1976.

21. Dylan, *Chronicles*, 288.

22. Antoine De Caunes, "Bob Dylan Interview," June 17, 1984 for the TV series *Les Enfants du rock* (broadcast on Antenne 2, June 30, 1984).

23. "Sad Eyed Lady of the Lowlands" lyrics, Copyright © 1966 by Dwarf Music; renewed 1994 by Dwarf Music. All rights reserved. International copyright secured. Reprinted by permission.

24. Bob Johnson as told to Louis Black, *Is It Rolling, Bob?*, www.bobjohnstonbook.com, 2015.

25. Bob Spitz, *Dylan: A Biography* (New York, W.W. Norton & Company, 1989), 337.

26. Heylin, *Bob Dylan: Behind the Shades Revisited*, 241.

27. Sounes, *Down the Highway*, 202.

28. Author interview with Charlie McCoy, January 21, 2011.

29. Richie Unterberger, "Charlie McCoy," www.richieunterberger.com/mccoy.html.

30. Richard Buskin, "Classic Track: Bob Dylan's 'Sad Eyed Lady of the Lowlands,'" *Sound On Sound*, May 2010.

31. Al Kooper, "100 Greatest Dylan Songs: 'Sad Eyed Lady of the Lowlands,'" *Mojo*, September 2005.

32. Author interview with Wayne Moss, January 17, 2011.

8. Nashville Blues Again

1. Author interview with Wayne Moss, January 17, 2011.

2. Author interview with Billy Swan, October 30, 2015.

3. Daniel Cooper, "Music City Gets Stoned: Dylan's Impact on Nashville's Music," *Nashville Scene*, March 7, 1996.

4. Shelton, *No Direction Home*, 341.

5. Robertson, *Testimony*, 191.

6. Jann Wenner, "The *Rolling Stone* Interview: Bob Dylan," *Rolling Stone*, November 29, 1969.

7. Author interview with Al Kooper, January 21, 2011.

8. Shelton, *No Direction Home*, 323.

9. "Stuck Inside of Mobile with the Memphis Blues Again" lyrics, Copyright © 1966 by Dwarf Music; renewed 1994 by Dwarf Music. All rights reserved. International copyright secured. Reprinted by permission.

10. Author interview with Billy Swan, October 30, 2015.

11. Gill, *Don't Think Twice*, 101.

12. Author interview with Bob Johnston, June 3, 2011.

9. Absolutely Sweet Music

1. Bob Egan, "Dylan on Jacob Street," PopSpots, www.popspotsnyc.com/PIP _Bob_Dylan_on_Jacob_Street/index.html.

2. Robbie Robertson interview with Michael Gray and Peter Finney, Country Music Hall of Fame and Museum archives, April 2014.

3. Author interview with Bob Johnston, June 3, 2011.

4. Author interview with Al Kooper, January 21, 2011.

5. Stan Rofe interview with Bob Dylan, Radio 3UZ, Melbourne, Australia, April 1966.

6. Author interview with Wayne Moss, January 17, 2011.

7. Author interview with Charlie McCoy, October 16, 2015.

8. Author interview with Mac Gayden, April 4, 2014.

9. David Bowman, "Kris Kristofferson," *Salon*, September 24, 1999.

10. Author interview with Chris Gantry, October 22, 2015.

11. Robbie Robertson interview with Michael Gray and Peter Finney, Country Music Hall of Fame and Museum archives, April 2014.

12. Author interview with Mac Gayden, April 4, 2014.

13. Gill, *Don't Think Twice*, 105.

14. Jan Donkers interview with Joe South for VPRO radio, www.youtube.com /watch?v=bHfmrQ2epw0.

15. Author interview with Jeff Gold, May 30, 2017.

16. "Absolutely Sweet Marie" manuscript, Jeff Gold Collection.

17. "Absolutely Sweet Marie" lyrics, Copyright © 1966 by Dwarf Music; renewed 1994 by Dwarf Music. All rights reserved. International copyright secured. Reprinted by permission.

18. Jonathan Lethem, "The Ecstasy of Influence: A Plagiarism," *Harper's*, February 2007.

19. "Absolutely Sweet Marie" lyrics, Copyright © 1966 by Dwarf Music; renewed 1994 by Dwarf Music. All rights reserved. International copyright secured. Reprinted by permission.

20. Omar Khayyam, "Quatrain XXXII," in *The Rubaiyat of Omar Khayyam*, trans. Edward FitzGerald (New York: Dover, 2011).

21. "Absolutely Sweet Marie" lyrics, Copyright © 1966 by Dwarf Music; renewed 1994 by Dwarf Music. All rights reserved. International copyright secured. Reprinted by permission.

22. Paul Zollo, "Bob Dylan: The SongTalk Interview," *SongTalk*, November 1991.

23. Author interview with Jason Ringenberg, October 7, 2015.

24. Author interview with Warner Hodges, August 20, 2016.

25. Author interview with Jason Ringenberg, October 7, 2015.

26. Author interview with Warner Hodges, August 20, 2016.

10. Quarters in the Ceiling

1. Author interview with Chris Gantry, October 22, 2015.

2. Album notes from the box set *Biograph*.

3. "Just Like a Woman" lyrics, Copyright © 1966 by Dwarf Music; renewed 1994 by Dwarf Music. All rights reserved. International copyright secured. Reprinted by permission.

4. Author interview with Henry Strzelecki, February 11, 2011.

5. Author interview with Chris Gantry, October 22, 2015.

6. Neil V. Rosenberg, "Bob Dylan in Nashville: An Eyewitness Account from Richard Greene and Peter Rowan," *Journal of Country Music* 7, no. 3 (December 1978), 63.

7. Author interview with Chris Gantry, October 22, 2015.

8. Author interview with Bob Johnston, June 3, 2011.

9. Kooper, *Backstage Passes*.

10. Daniel Cooper, "Music City Gets Stoned: Dylan's Impact on Nashville's Music," *Nashville Scene*, March 7, 1996.

11. Author interview with Bob Johnston, June 3, 2011.

12. Author interview with Wayne Moss, January 17, 2011.

13. Author interview with Chris Gantry, October 24, 2015.

14. Author interview with Bob Johnston, June 3, 2011.

15. Rosenberg, "Bob Dylan in Nashville," 61.

16. Heylin, *Revolution in the Air*, 306.

17. "Pledging My Time" lyrics, Copyright © 1966 by Dwarf Music; renewed 1994 by Dwarf Music. All rights reserved. International copyright secured. Reprinted by permission.

18. Author interview with Robyn Hitchcock, January 27, 2017.

19. "Pledging My Time" lyrics, Copyright © 1966 by Dwarf Music; renewed 1994 by Dwarf Music. All rights reserved. International copyright secured. Reprinted by permission.

20. Rosenberg, "Bob Dylan in Nashville," 62.

21. Robbie Robertson interview with Michael Gray and Peter Finney, Country Music Hall of Fame and Museum archives, April 2014.

22. Charlie McCoy, "Bob Dylan in Nashville," *Hit Parader*, October 1966.

23. Robbie Robertson interview with Michael Gray and Peter Finney, Country Music Hall of Fame and Museum archives, April 2014.

24. "Just Like a Woman" lyrics, Copyright © 1966 by Dwarf Music; renewed 1994 by Dwarf Music. All rights reserved. International copyright secured. Reprinted by permission.

25. Author interview with Chris Gantry, October 24, 2015.

11. Sprint to the Finish

1. Author interview with Al Kooper, January 21, 2011.

2. Kooper, *Backstage Passes*.

3. Author interview with Al Kooper, January 21, 2011.

4. "Most Likely You Go Your Way and I'll Go Mine" lyrics, Copyright © 1966 by Dwarf Music; renewed 1994 by Dwarf Music. All rights reserved. International copyright secured. Reprinted by permission.

5. Kooper, "1965–1967," in *Backstage Passes*.

6. "Bob Dylan Goes Electric," *Sound Opinions*, WBEZ (Chicago), April 29, 2011.

7. Author interview with Wayne Moss, January 17, 2011.

8. Author interview with Charlie McCoy, October 16, 2015.

9. "Temporary Like Achilles" lyrics, Copyright © 1966 by Dwarf Music; renewed 1994 by Dwarf Music. All rights reserved. International copyright secured. Reprinted by permission.

10. Author interview with Bob Johnston, June 3, 2011.

11. Author interview with Chris Gantry, March 23, 2017.

12. Author interview with Wayne Moss, January 17, 2011.

13. Author interview with Al Kooper, January 21, 2011.

14. Author interview with Bob Johnston, June 3, 2011.

15. Author interview with Al Kooper, January 21, 2011.

16. Proverbs 27:15.

17. Klas Burling, "Bob Dylan interview," Swedish Radio 3, April 28, 1966.

18. Shelton, *No Direction Home*, 322.

19. Author interview with Ronnie Milsap, April 14, 2017.

20. Author interview with Al Kooper, January 21, 2011.

21. "Rainy Day Women #12 & 35" lyrics, Copyright © 1966 by Dwarf Music; renewed 1994 by Dwarf Music. All rights reserved. International copyright secured. Reprinted by permission.

22. Author interview with Henry Strzelecki, February 11, 2011.

23. Jim Irvin, *The Mojo Collection: The Ultimate Music Companion, 4th Edition* (Edinburgh: Canongate, 2000), 69.

24. Robbie Robertson interview with Michael Gray and Peter Finney, Country Music Hall of Fame and Museum archives, April 2014.

25. Heylin, *Revolution in the Air*, 310.

26. Juli Thanki, "How Bob Dylan Threw Open the Doors to Music City," *Tennessean* (podcast), May 1, 2016.

27. Wilentz, *Bob Dylan in America*, 124.

28. Author interview with Al Kooper, January 21, 2011.

29. "I Want You" lyrics, Copyright © 1966 by Dwarf Music; renewed 1994 by Dwarf Music. All rights reserved. International copyright secured. Reprinted by permission.

30. Author interview with Al Kooper, January 26, 2011.

31. Juli Thanki, "How Bob Dylan Threw Open the Doors to Music City," *Tennessean* (podcast), May 1, 2016.

12. Three Hits and a Double

1. Robertson, *Testimony*, 212.

2. Author interview with Jerry Schatzberg, June 26, 2016.

3. Author interview with Charlie Steiner, July 17, 2016.

4. Christopher Walsh, "Album Covers from the Heyday," *East Hampton Star*, November 13, 2012.

5. Jerry Schatzberg, *Thin Wild Mercury: Touching Dylan's Edge* (Guildford, UK: Genesis Publications, 2006).

6. Schatzberg, *Thin Wild Mercury*.

7. Author interview with Jerry Schatzberg, June 26, 2016.

8. Author interview with Jerry Schatzberg, June 26, 2016.

9. Barker, Derek, "A Chat With Jules Siegel," *ISIS*, April-May, 1998, 28.

10. Liner notes for *Bob Dylan: The Original Mono Recordings*.

11. Hoskyns, *Across the Great Divide*, 113.

12. Robertson, *Testimony*, 222–223.

13. "Otis Redding: Mr Cool and the Clique from Memphis," *Melody Maker*, September 17, 1966.

14. "Robbie Robertson Interview," *House of Blues Radio Hour*, June 17, 2011.

15. Shelton, *No Direction Home*, 321.

16. Ian MacDonald, *Revolution in the Head: The Beatles' Records and the Sixties* (Chicago: Chicago Review Press, 2007), 206.

17. Author interview with Robyn Hitchcock, January 27, 2017.

18. Dave Marsh, *The Heart of Rock & Soul: The 1001 Greatest Singles Ever Made* (New York: Plume, 1989), 172.

19. Marion Meade, "Does Rock Degrade Women?," *New York Times*, March 14, 1971.

13. Nashville AD (After Dylan)

1. Author interview with Charlie McCoy, January 21, 2011.

2. Author interview with Michael Gray of the Country Music Hall of Fame and Museum, January 14, 2016.

3. Author interview with Wayne Moss, January 27, 2011.

4. Author interview with Michael Gray of the Country Music Hall of Fame and Museum, January 14, 2016.

5. Ian Tyson, *The Long Trail: My Life in the West* (Toronto: Vintage Canada, 2011), 66.

6. Douglas Green interview with Pete Drake, *Guitar Player*, September 1973.

7. Author interview with Al Kooper, January 21, 2011.

8. Author interview with Bob Johnston, June 3, 2011.

9. John Sebastian, "Nashville Cats," © 1966 Alley Music/Trio Music.

10. "New Look at Nashville Cats, 50 Years Later," CBS News, June 17, 2015.

11. Author interview with Dave Marsh, June 18, 2016.

12. Author interview with Michael Gray of the Country Music Hall of Fame and Museum, January 14, 2016.

13. "Music Masters: A Conversation with Bob Neuwirth," hosted by Michael McCall, Country Music Hall of Fame and Museum.

14. Steve Hockman, "'Boogie'-man Hartford Keeps on Rolling," *Los Angeles Times*, August 22, 1986.

15. Skip Heller, "A Good Act: John Hartford, Hippie, Eclectic Southern Riverboard Intellectual," *Fretboard Journal*, November 2006.

16. "Kris Kristofferson Interview," *Rock Influence*, November 1984.

17. Author interview with Chris Gantry, October 24, 2015.

18. Daniel Cooper, "Music City Gets Stoned," *Nashville Scene*, March 7, 1996.

19. Author interview with Mac Gayden, 2017.

20. Mary Huhn, "John Hiatt Interview," *Rolling Stone*, 1995.

21. Joshua Klein, "Steve Earle," *Pitchfork*, October 8, 2007.

22. Warren Denney, "The Story Is Immortal," *Nashville Musician*, April–June 2013, 16.

23. Author interview with Bob Johnston, June 3, 2011.

14. A Lasting Legacy

1. Author interview with Bob Johnston, 2011.

2. Sven Hugo Persson with Sara Danius, "Interview about the 2016 Nobel Prize in Literature," www.nobelprize.org, October 13, 2016.

3. Author interview with Bob Johnston, June 3, 2011.

4. Author interview with Al Kooper, January 21, 2011.

5. Author interview with Dave Marsh, June 18, 2016.

6. Sean Wilentz opening remarks at the panel discussion: "'Is It Rolling, Bob?': Bob Dylan's Nashville Recordings Revisited," July 15, 2017, Country Music Hall of Fame and Museum.

7. Author interview with Dave Marsh, June 18, 2016.

8. Author interview with Chris Gantry, October 24, 2015.

9. Author interview with Dave Marsh, June 18, 2016.

10. Paul Zollo, "Tom Petty on Bob Dylan," *American Songwriter*, January 24, 2012.

11. Paul Zollo, "John Mellencamp," *American Songwriter*, January 1, 2005.

12. Josh Tyrangiel, "The Resurrection of Neil Young," *Time*, September 26, 2005.

13. My Favorite Album #182 - "Robyn Hitchcock on Bob Dylan 'Blonde on Blonde' (1966)," January 16, 2017 (MrJeremyDylan.com).

14. Author interview with Robyn Hitchcock, January 27, 2017.

INDEX